JAINA RELIGION AND ART

JAINA RELIGION AND ART

Ananda Chandra Sahoo

AGAM KALA PRAKASHAN
DELHI

First Published 1994

ISBN : 81-7320-005-X

Published by
Dr. Agam Prasad, M.A., Ph.D., Diploma in Museology
for Agam Kala Prakashan 34, Central Market, Ashok Vihar
Delhi-110052

Composed by
Ideal Computers Pvt. Ltd.,
2/11, Roop Nagar, Delhi-110007, Ph. 2910909

Printed at
Garg Offset Works
B-76, Nariana Indl. Area
Nariana, Delhi

In the
Sacred memory
of my mother

FOREWORD

The book - *Jaina Religin and Art* is primarily a recast of the author's Ph.D. thesis. The author has viewed the entire problem with historical perspective. Jainism which flourished along with Buddism was but a modified form of the older proto Jainism delineated by the Tīrthaṅkaras particularly by Pārśvanātha, the twenty-third Tīrthaṅkara. Strictly speaking, Jainism is not so much a religion as a monastic organisation. The founder of this order was Vardhamāna popularly known as Mahāvīra or Nigantha Nataputta, an inhabitant of Kuṇḍagrāma in Vaiśālī during c. sixth century B.C. An indeliable contribution of Mahāvīra to Jainism is the construction of an order upon a loose group of ascetics called *acala*.

It is interesting to note that the Jainas unlike the Buddhists share many rituals with the Hindus. They believe in castes and acknowledge the priesthood of the Brāhmaṁas. The Jainas even agree with the Brāhmaśas alone in ascetic self-torture, which Buddhism vehemently opposes. Not only these, the Jainas even observed, of course, in the later period, festivals and fasts which are notionally the festivals of the Hindus, e.g., Ganeśa-caturthī, Anantacaturdaśī, Dipāvalī, Rakshābandhana, etc.

Jainism enjoyed its her-day in Orissa since very early times. Tradition avers that the Tīrthaṅkaras like Aranātha, Pārśvanātha and Mahāvīra visited this region which attained its pinnacle of glory at the time of illustrious king Khāravela of the Mahāmeghavāhana Cedi dynasty. In fact, there had been no significant development of Jainism in Orissa after him till the eighth-ninth centuries A.D.

It is curious that from the earliest time Jainism had a special appeal to the mercantile community, and even today the majority of the followers of this faith are merchants and businessmen chiefly residing in the trade centres of Western India and Rajasthan. During the political hegemony of the Mauryas and the Guptas, Jainism occupied, more or loss, the entire stretch of land from Orissa in the east of Mathura in the west, but its concentration shifted to Gujarat and parts of Rajasthan, in Hyderabad and in Mysore in the mediaeval times. On account of several reasons such as (i) the revival of neo-Brahmanical religion and (ii) the collapse of commercial activities of the trading communities who were its chief patrons on the eastern coast the religion gradually lost its vital support for further growth and development.

Like the Buddhists, the Jainas in the beginning believed in the concept of *Stupa* cult, but in the early centuries of the Christian era, they gave up the cult in favour of temple worship. The Jainas excavated caves, built temples, and carved icons. The most important Jaina sanctuaries of the earlier period hailed from Orissa. But in the subsequent ages Jaina temples, besides Rajasthan are found in Gujarat, Bihar and in Mysore.

Of course, it is needless to say, that there is hardly any distinct peculiarity which can be treated as the salient feature of the Jaina arrt. From the architectural perspectie the temples are not essentially different from the Hindu temple structure. Percy Brown rightly suggested— "The architectural treatment of the Rani Gumpha is characteristic of the Orissan style of rock architecture as a whole and provides the key to the entire movement." This trend continues in the mediaeval period too. The two outstanding temples of Dilwara on the Mount Abu, the Vimala (c. eleventh century A.D.) and the Tejahpala (c. thirteenth century A.D.), for instance, have hardly any architectural feature which is distinctive of Jainism. On the contrary they architecturally belong to the Gujarat tradition of Hindu temple building. These Jaina sanctuaries are aptly described as 'the final baroque culmination of the Gujarat style.' While making an overall observation of these temples, Fergusson also expressed an identical view. The interior of this temple has 'the lace-like delicacy of the fairy forms into which the patient chisel of the Hindu has carved the white marble.'

Dr. Ananda Chandra Sahoo has taken into account all these points in the course of his discussion and he offers an illuminating as well as convincing answers to the readers. It is my conviction that discerning students belonging to the discipline of Indian History and Culture will be benefited by going through the work of Dr. Sahoo

Dr. Pranabananda Jash
Professor and Head of The Department of
Ancient Indian History, Culture and Archaeology,
Visva Bharati, Santiniketan

PREFACE

The present work is a modest attempt to reconstruct the history of Jaina religion and art in ancient Orissa. The primary motive behind this endeavour lies in the fact that a study of this kind has long been overdue. Thus, the attempt here is to offer a diachronic account and analysis of the history of Jaina religion and art from the earliest times to twelfth century A.D.

In the eastern part of the Indian sub-continent Orissa is a potential area for the study of the Jaina religion. In the pan- Indian context attempts have been made to study the history of Jaina religion, its impacts and relevance. Regional studies in this field are limited to the areas such as Gujarat, Rajasthan and Karnataka where Jainism is still a living religon. As far as Orissa is concerned no concentrated effort have so far been made in these directions. Here it may be pointed out that apart from Tamil Nadu, Orissa is the most important region on the eastern sea-board, where Jainism had been a living religion for centuries together. The adherants of the Jaina religion have left for the posterity quite a large number of monumental evidences which speak of the wide prevalence and popularity of Jainism in this region.

The present work substantially represents the author's thesis approved by Visva Bharati for the degree of Doctor of Philosophy in 1987. I would like to take the opportunity to put on record my sincere gratitude to my *guru* Dr. Pranabananda Jash, Professor and Head of the Department of Ancient Indian History, Culture and Archaeology, Visva Bharati. I had the proud privilege to complete my Ph.D. thesis under his affectionate care and supervision. Words really fail to express my experience and gratitude.

I am thankful to Professor Nirmal Chandra Ghosh of the same Department for offering me helpful and constructive suggestions. Dr. Ganapathy Subbiah, my teacher, has always tendered his kind co-operation and incisive comments. I express my deep gratitude and owe a special debt to him. I am also thankful to Dr. Bikash Mukherjee, Curator of the Museum attached to the same Department for his help.

I am extremely thankful to my wife Smt. Gitanjali Sahu for many a reasons. I am also thankful to Dr. Cesare Rizi, formerely Lecturer in Italian Language and Culture, Visva Bharati; Dr. Sri Narayan Ojha, Computer Certre, Visva Bharati and Dr. Narendra Kumar Dash, Research Associate, Department of Sanskrit, Pali and Prakrit, Visva Bharati for their inspiration and timely co- operation.

Finally, I sincerely thank Dr. Agam Prasad, Proprietor, Agam Kala Prakashan, Delhi and other members of his team for timely bringing out the publication.

Ananda Chandra Sahoo

CONTENTS

ABBREVIATIONS

ASI	:	Archaeological Survey of India
ASI, AR	:	Archaeological Survey of India, Annual Report
AV	:	Arhat Vacana (Hindi)
BORI	:	Bhandarkar Oriental Research Institute
BDGP	:	Bihar District Gazetteer, Puri
BODG	:	Bihar and Orissa District Gazettzeer
BUJ	:	Bombay University Journal
BV	:	Bhāratīya Vidyā
CHI	:	Cambridge History of India
CP	:	Copper Plate
CII	:	Corpus Inscriptionum Indicarum
EI	:	Epigraphia Indica
EC	:	Epigraphia Carnatica
Enc. Br.	:	Encyclopaedia of Britannice
ERE	:	Encylopaedia of Religion and Ethics
GIO	:	Gazetteer of India, Orissa
GOS	:	Gaikward Oriental Series
IA	:	Indian Antiquary
IGI	:	Imperial Gazetteer of India
IO	:	Inscriptions of Orissa

IHQ	:	Indian Historical Quarterly
ISBJ	:	International Seminar on Buddhism and Jainism
JAHRS	:	Journal of Andhra Historical Research Society
JAS	:	Journal of the Asiatic Society
JA	:	Jaina Antiquary
JASB	:	Journal of the Asiatic Society of Bengal
JBBRAS	:	Journal of the Bombay Branch of the Royal Asiatic Society
JBORS	:	Journal of Bihar Orissa Research Society
JBRS	:	Journal of the Bihar Research Society
JG	:	Jaina Gazetee
JISOA	:	Journal of Indian Society of Oriental Art
JJ	:	Jaina Journal
JKHRS	:	Journal of Kaliṅga Historical Research Society
JM	:	Jīnamañjarī
JMHS	:	Journal of Mahākośala Historical Society
JNSI	:	Journal of the Numismatic Society of Indian
JOH	:	Journal of Orissan History
JOR	:	Journal of Oriental Research
JRAS	:	Journal of Royal Asiatic Society of Great Britain
JRASB	:	Journal of the Royal Asiatic Society of Bengal

JRASB Lt.	:	Journal of the Royal Asiatic Society of Bengal, Letters
JSB	:	Jaina Siddhāntā Bhāskar (Hindi)
Mbh	:	Mahābhārata
MASI	:	Memoirs of Archaeological Survey of India
NRDCUK	:	Notes on the Remains in Dhauli and in the Caves of Udayagiri and Khaṇḍagiri
NS	:	Nāṇasāyara (Hindi)
JVRI	:	Journal of Vaisali Research Institute
OBI	:	Old Brahmi Inscriptions in the Udayagiri and Khaṇḍagiri Caves
ODG	:	Orissa District Gazetteer
OHRJ	:	Orissa Historical Research Journal
PAIOC	:	Proceedings of All-India Oriental Conference
PHAI	:	Political History of Ancient India
PIHC	:	Proceedings of the Indian History Congress
PTS	:	Pāli Text Series
Pr. TS	:	Prakri Text Series
PV	:	Prākrita Vidyā (Hindi)
RV	:	Ṛg Veda
Sam.	:	Sambodhi
SBB	:	Sacred Book of the Buddhist
SBE	:	Sacred Book of the East

DESCRIPTION OF THE PLATES

Plate I	:	Standing Pārśvanātha from Kosali (stone).
Plate II	:	Ṛṣabhanātha and Mahāvīra on one stele (stone), from Khiching.
Plate III	:	Śāntinātha from Charampa (stone)
Plate IV	:	Standing bronze icon of Candraprabha from Achutrajpur.
Plate V	:	Bāgha-*gumphā*, Udayagiri : the facade.
Plate VI	:	Navagrahārcita Pārśvanātha from Pundal (stone)
Plate VII	:	*Tīrthṅkara* and Śāsnadevīs on the back wall of the Navamuni-*gumphā*, Khaṇḍagiri.
Plate VIII	:	Standing bronze icon of Śṣabhanātha from the district of Puri (Kakatapur ?).
Plate IX	:	*Dhyāni* Pārśvanātha in the temple of *Buḍā* Jagannātha at Baripada (stone).
Plate X	:	Worship of a Jaina symbol, Mañcapuri-*gumphā*, Udayagiri.
Plate XI	:	Mahāvīra from Bhimapur near Balasore (stone).
Plate XII	:	Ṛṣabhanātha from Khiching.

Table showing the names of the twenty-four Tīrthaṅkaras, their respective *Śāsana- devā* and *vāhana* :

I.	Ṛṣabhanātha	Cakreśvari	Bull
II.	Ajitanātha	Rohiṇī	Elephant
III.	Sambhavanātha	Prajñapti	Horse
IV.	Abhinandana	Vajraśṛṅkhalā	Monkey
V.	Sumatinātha	Puruṣadattā	Curlew
VI.	Padmaprabha	Manovegā	Lotus
VII.	Supārśvanātha	Kālī	Svastika
VIII.	Candraprabha	Jvālāmālinī or Jvālinī	Moon
IX.	Suvidhinātha or Puṣpadanta	Mahākālī	Alligator
X.	Śītalanātha	Mānavī	Śrīvatsa
XI.	Śreyāṁśanātha	Gaurī	Rhinoceros
XII.	Vāsupūjya	Gāndhāī	Buffalo
XIII.	Vimalanātha	Vairoṭī	Boar
XIV.	Anantanātha	Anantamatī	Falcon
XV.	Dharmanātha	Mānasī	Thunderbolt
XVI.	Śātinātha	Mahāmānasī	Deer
XVII.	Kunthunātha	Jayā or Vijayā	Goat
XVIII.	Aranātha	Tārā	Nandyāvarta or Fish
XIX.	Mallinātha	Aparājitā	Pitcher
XX.	Munisuvrata	Bahurūpiṇī	Tortoise

XXI.	Naminātha	Cāmuṇḍā	Blue Lotous
XXII.	Neminātha or Ariṣṭanemi	Śmrā	Coṇch- shell
XXIII.	Pārśvanātha	Padmāvatī	Snake
XXIV.	Mahāvīra	Siddhāyikā	Lion

CHAPTER I

Historical Geography

To understand the events of history of a country, a thorough knowledge of geography is essential. Without getting acquainted with the precise location of various places which figure prominently in the texts, it is impossible to follow the course of events in any extent. H.C. Raychaudhuri long ago remarked - "More than the political, social and literary historian, the student of religion and mythology will feel in every step the need of a thorough acquaintance with the divine rivers and mountains which receive to this day the homage of the faithful, and those *Dharma-kshetras* and *Puṇya-sthānas* which even now attract pilgrims from the remotest corners of the country"[1].

Orissa consisted in ancient times, of several *janapadas* and *Mahājanapadas*. The identification of these *janapadas* and *Mahājanapadas* is a pre requisite to study the religious history of this land properly. In course of our study we have made an attempt to delineate the geographical jurisdiction of several *janapadas* that lie within Orissa. The major *janapadas* are Kaliṅga, Toṣala, Utkala, Oḍra, *Dakṣiṇa*-Kośala, and Koṅgoda; and that of the minor are Śvetaka, Khijjiṅga, Khiñjali, Kodālaka, Taitila etc.

Kaliṅga

In the historical geography of ancient Orissa, Kaliṅga was regarded as one of the most important *janapadas*. The geographical boundaries of this *janapada* was never a static one throughout the ancient period.

Pāṇini[2] refers to the Kaliṅga *janapada*, the boundaries of which, according to him, touched that of the Magadha *janapada*. Kauṭilya[3] refers to Kaliṅga where, according to him, the best type of elephants were bred and which produces the best type of touch-stone. Megasthenes[4] mentions Kaliṅga as land of a widely diffused race', who were inhabiting all along the eastern coast up to the delta of the Ganges, but afterwards their kingdom was restricted to southern Orissa. While referring to Kaliṅga, Pliny[5] has suggested the Cape Kaliṅgon, identified with point Godāvarī at the mouth of the same river, as its southern boundary. On this score some scholars[6] have expressed their doubt regarding the extension of Kaliṅga from that of the Gangetic valley up to Godāvarī or even Krisṇā, in the south. The Buddhist literatures refer to Kaliṅgaraṭṭha[7], which was one of the seven political divisions during the time of the mythical king Reṇu; and to Dantapura[8], its capital. The other tradition recorded in the *Buddhavaṁśa*[9] states that after the death of Buddha, one of his tooth relics was carried to, and enshrined in a *caitya* at Dantapura.

The importance and significance of Dantapura requires proper identification. During the pre-Buddhistic period Dantapura appears to have been a geographical unit of considerable importance. Various early texts refer to this place and attach some importance also. It has been referred as Dantakura in the *Mahābhārata*[10]. The *Jātakas*[11] make numerous references to Dantapura as the capital of Kaliṅga. It is further known as Dantapura-nagara[12]. Scholars[13] have identified this geographical unit with the Poloura of Ptolemy, which lies five to six miles to the north of present Ganjam town; bordering the district of Puri[14]. Elsewhere, it has been identified with Dandagulla of Pliny[15]. Other scholars have located it in the neighbourhood of Cicacole and Kalingapatam in present Andhra Pradesh[16]. It has further been maintained that probably the city has been survived by the fort of Dantavaktra near Cicacole[17]. This important township Dantapura of Kaliṅga has been taken to be the same as Poloura in Telegu version[18].

The Buddhist tradition[19] regards Dantapura as the capital of Kaliṅga, where the tooth-relic of Gautama Buddha was deposited within a magnificent *stūpa* by the king Brahmadatta. The *Mahā Govinda Suttanta*[20] mentions Dantapura which is situated in Kaliṅga as one of the six famous cities in ancient India. The Jaina texts[21] refer Dantapura as Dantavakra as the capital city of Kaliṅga. Some other scholars have identified the city of Dantapura with modern Dantan on the bank of river Kasai in the district of Midnapur of West Bengal.[22]

It is difficult to identify the region of Dantapura with a fair degree of certainty. However, keeping in view the evidences at our disposal, it may be suggested that during the early historical period it was located somewhere in the northern portion of Kaliṅga. Further, following its reference in different early texts, it may be pointed out that Dantapura was an important geographical unit of which the city of Dantapura was the main centre.

Reference to Kaliṅga has been made in the *Jātakas*, being ruled by Karaṇḍu[23], a contemporary of Nimi, king of Videha of the Brāhmaṇa period. The *Jātakas* also refer to Dantapuranagara, the capital-city of Kaliṅga, which has been identified by scholars[24] with Dantakura of the *Mahābhārata*[25], and Dantapura of the inscriptions[26]. The *Sarabhaṅga Jātaka*[27] refers to the king of Kaliṅga named Kāliṅga who had acknowledged the supremacy of king Daṇḍakī of Daṇḍaka in the Vindhya region. The *Cullakaliṅga Jātaka*[28] speaks of the defeat of the Kaliṅga king by his contemporary Aruṇa, king of Assaka. Besides this, the *Kaliṅgabodhi Jātaka*[29] also refers to Kaliṅga, elsewhere, the Jātakas[30] mention about Nalikīra, the king of Kaliṅga who brought about destruction to the Kingdom.

In the Jaina literature we see that Aranātha, the eighteenth *Tīrthaṅkara* is said to have received his first alms in the city of Rāyapura[31] (Rājpura), a metropolis in Kaliṅga *janapada*. This Rājpura has found mention as the capital of Kaliṅga in the *Mahābhārata*[32].

Pārśvanātha's (the twenty-third *Tīrthaṅkara*) connection with Kaliṅga has been referred to in the Jaina literature[33] while it narrates the story of the marriage of Prabhāvatī, daughter of king Prasenjit of Kusasthalapura with Pārśvanātha.

The inscriptions of Aśoka[34] remain the first concrete document regarding the antiquity of Kaliṅga. In the said edicts, Toṣali and Samāpā, the two major cities of Kaliṅga have been mentioned. The former has been identified with modern Dhauli[35] in the Puri district, and the latter with modern Jaugaḍa in the district of Ganjam. That the above mentioned cities were the headquarters of Kaliṅga appears to be probable, and during the time of Aśoka, Kaliṅga was roughly extended from the river Gaṅgā as far as the river Godāvarī in the south[36].

The term Kaliṅga has been referred to in the *Mahābhārata* several times, denoting various meanings. In some contexts, the term refers to the people of Kaliṅga[37], and in some other *ślokas* it appears as the name of a race[38]. Still in some other places Kaliṅga itself occurs as a *janapada*.[39] Further the people of Kaliṅga have been depicted as fighting against the Pāṇḍavas[40]. As regards the location of the Kaliṅga *janapada*, the epic says that the river Vaitaraṇī was flowing through the region[41], which was situated in the coastal belt[42].

The *Purāṇa* literature[43] says that the Kaliṅgas were dwelling in the southern region along with the Navarāṣṭras, Mahiṣakas, etc. Elsewhere[44] it has been stated that Kaliṅga was extended as far as up to Amarakaṇṭaka hill in the west, where the river Narmadā drained its western portion.

As regards the evidences drawn out of the epigraphical sources relating to the geographical extent of Kaliṅga, we have referred to that of Aśoka above. Besides that, during the time of Khāravela of the Mahāmeghavāhana dynasty the main centre of activities was near modern Bhubaneswar[45]. Then after a long interval, from the fifth century A.D. onwards, we find that the centres of administration of

Kaliṅga were at the bank of the Godāvarī, the Nāgāvatī, and the Vaṁśadhārā in the districts of east Godavari, Srikakulam and Ganjam respectively[46]. In the above context we may cite the inscriptions of the Māṭhara kings[47] belonging to the fifth century A.D., where it is mentioned that Kaliṅga denoted the territories comprising parts of Godavari, Visakhapatnam, Srikakulam and Ganjam districts. Reference to a number of place names within the jurisdiction of Kaliṅga *janapada*, like Śrīpura[48], Vijayapura[49], Vardhamānapur[50], Sunagarh[51], Sārapalli[52] has been made in inscriptions belonging to the Gupta and post-Gupta period.

The disintegrated Kaliṅga kingdom which was clearly evident during the invasion of *Mahārāja* Samudragupta in or about 350 A.D., when we find several principalities such as Kurāla, Piṣṭapura, Giri-Koṣṭuraka, Eraṇḍapalli, Avamukta, Pālakha, Devarāṣṭra, Kusathalapura etc.[53]; seems to have been integrated during *Mahārāja* Umāvarman of the Māṭhara dynasty, who in turn assumed the title of *Kaliṅgādhipati*[54].

After the Māṭharas, Kaliṅga passed under the subjugation of another family called Śri-Rāma- Kāśyapa[55], who had established their capital at Piṣṭapura near the river Godāvarī[56]. Later on they seemed to have extended their away in the northern portion of Kaliṅga by reaching Birañjā-*nagara*, situated on the bank of the river Vaitaraṇī at Jajpur in the district of Cuttack[57].

The Chinese pilgrim Hiuen-Tsang, who visited Kaliṅga in the first half of the seventh century A.D. has said that it was a little above 500 li in circuit. Further he has also given the position of Kaliṅga while he says that it was bordered by Andhra in the south and by Dhānakaṭaka in the west. He has also made some categorical remarks that its frontiers did not extend beyond the river Godāvarī on the south-west and the Goliya branch of the river Indrāvatī in the north-west[58].

Most of the early Gaṅga rulers of Kaliṅga such as Hastivarman[59], Indravarman[60], Devendravarman[61] issued their grants from the victorious camp (*Vijayavaṭaḥ*) at Kaliṅganagara[62] and described themselves as Lord of Kaliṅga (*Sakala-Kaliṅgādhirājya*). The later Gaṅga rulers also issued their grants from this place in most of the cases[63]. This important capital city has been variously identified by scholars[64]. Besides Kaliṅganagara, another seat of plitical importance, i.e., Śvetaka has also been referred to in the records of the early Gaṅga rulers like Jayavarmadeva and Indravarman[65], and the site has been identified with Chikiti in the Ganjam district.

Another high-sounding title, i.e., *Trikaliṅgādhipati*[61] has been used in some records of the Eastern Gaṅgas, Eastern Chālukyas and the Somavaṁśis. The problem of identification of this Trikaliṅga is manifold[67]. Considering the various theories proposed by different scholars and that of the epigraphical evidences it may be suggested that it was a nomenclature applied to Kaliṅga in its broader conception.

Tosala (Tosali) :

The first epigraphical reference to this geographical unit is made in the Rock Edicts of Aśoka at Dhauli[68], thereby suggesting that the city of Tosali existed around the present Dhauli hill. Commenting on the discovery of the vestiges of a large city not far from the hill, it has been upheld that the Tosali of the Inscription was the capital of the province of Orissa during Aśoka's time[69].

The exclusion of Tosali in the Hāthīgumphā inscription led the scholars[70] to believe that during that period probably it was a division of Kaliṅga, a suggestion that can well be correct. Another epigraphical record[71] of the third century A.D. mentions Tossali as an independent kingdom. Bharata's *Nāṭyaśāstra* also refers to Tosala as a separate kingdom[72]. It has been pointed out that the people living on the banks of the river Veṇā, i.e., around present Cuttack were the inhabitants of Tosala. The *Purāṇas* refer to Tosala as a separate territory[74]. The independence of Toṣala is attested to in the *Kāvya-mīmāṃsā*, from that of Utkala[75], and from the fourth century A.D. two divisions of Toṣala have been traced. The earliest mention of '*Ubhaya* Toṣali' is found in the inscription of Śatrubhañja, which has been assigned to the fourth century A.D.[76]

The division of Toṣala into two parts namely *Uttara* Toṣala[77] and *Dakṣiṇa* Toṣala[78] is recorded. Certain villages of *Uttara* Toṣala are found to be located in the present Balasore district[79]. The Soro copper plate grant of *Mahārāja* Sri Śambuyasaḥ[80] of about 580 A.D. refers to *Uttara* Toṣali. In the Bouda copper plate grant of Tribhubana Mahādevī[81] it is recorded that 'Daṇḍabhukti *maṇḍala*', present Midnapur district in West Bengal, formed a part of *Uttara* Toṣali. The Kaṇās plates[82] of Lokavigraha and the Patiakella plates[83] of Śivarāja refers to *Dakṣiṇa* Toṣali. The former inscription designates its donor as *Aṣṭādaśa-Toṣalidhipati*, i.e. the Lord of Eighteen Toṣalis[84]. The Ervanga copper plate grant[85] of *Mahārāja* Śrī *Śambuyasaḥ*, of A.D. 555 records land grants in *Dakṣiṇa* Toṣali. The Ganjam grant of Mādhavarāja of the Śailodbhava family, dated A.D. 670 speaks of 'Koṅgoda *maṇḍala*' lying between the Bhārgavī-Kuśabhadrā in the north and river Ṛṣikūlyā in the south, which was included in south Toṣali[86]. Inscriptions of Śivakara II[87] of the Bhaumakara dynasty, mention a village Bhubhurudā in Antarudra *viṣaya*, which has been identified with Antarodha[88] in Puri district, being included in *Dakṣiṇa* Toṣali. The early Bhaumakara records speak that those rulers were ruling over Toṣali comprising Koṅgoda, a part of the southern Toṣali[89].

Taking into account the above evidences it can be held that like Kaliṅga, the limits of Toṣali gradually expanded from that of a comparatively small locality around present Dhauli hill. So much so that by the sixth century A.D. it was divided into two distinct parts and engulfed the entire coast land, i.e. from north of the Kaliṅga *janapada* to beyond the present district of Balasore.

Utkala

The *Mahābhārata*[90] refers to Utkala as a distinct *janapada* along with Mekala, Pouṇḍra, Kaliṅga, Āndhra, Niṣāda and Bahlika. In the same literary work Utkal is also mentioned along with other *janapadas*, too[91]. The Utkalas are also mentioned as a clan living in the hilly tracts from Gaya to Orissa along with other clans[92]. In the *Rāmāyaṇa*[93] and the Puranic literatures[94] the Utkalas are associated with the Mekalas.

The *Raghuvaṁśa*[95] of Kālidāsa refers to the Utkala country lying between the river Kapiśa in the Midnapur district of present West Bengal and that of the land of the Kaliṅgas. Scholars have also attributed the river Kapiśa i.e., the modern Kaśāi running through the district of Midnapur as the boundary line between Vaṅga and Utkala[96].

In the *Purāṇas*[97] Utkalas are mentioned as a human race, and some of them[98] locate Utkala in the *Madhyadeśa*. In the *Harivaṁśa* Utkal has been stated as the son of Sudyumna[99] residing in the area of the same name[100] located in the north[101]. The statement in the *Harivaṁśa* regarding the location of Utkala more or less corresponds to that of *Kāvyamīmāṁsā*[102] which states that Utkala is one of those *janapadas* situated to the east of Kāśi.

Somadatta, a king of the Śailodbhava dynasty refers to Utkala *deśa* along with Daṇḍabhukti in his Midnapur plate[103], thus making them adjacent provinces where he was the governing authority. Since the modern district of Midnapur has been identified with Daṇḍabhukti[104] there can be no doubt that Utkala was bordering the province of Daṇḍabhukti. Thus, during the period of Somadatta, the southern portion of present Bankura district of West Bengal, Singbhum and Manbhum districts of Bihar, and Mayurbhanj district of Orissa are identified with Utkala[105]. This hypothesis is more tenable than the identification of modern Orissa with Utkala[106] during the time of

Tīvaradeva. Further, considering another record of Somadatta where the Utkala*deśa* is referred to as Oḍra-*viṣaya*[107], it can be presumed that the district of Balasore was included in the *Litkaladśa.* The reference of Oḍra-*visaya* in the record of the same king which also refers to Utkala*deśa* makes an interesting point to the extent that the same region gradually became known as Oḍra at least from the late half of the seventh century A.D.

Oḍra

In the *Mahābhārata* Oḍra has been referred to as a *janapada*[108], which enjoys a distinct territorial[109] status. As regards the location of this *janapada*, the *Mahābhārata* says that it was situated near the sea[110]. Elswhere, Oḍra has been referred to as a race[111] in the *Mahābhārata*, and yet in another place[112] it refers to the king of Oḍra along with the kings of Pāṇḍya, Kuṇinda, Kirāta, Puṇḍra, etc.

Pliny[113] refers to Oretes as a people of India living near the mountain Mallus. While discussing the above reference, Cunningham[114] has tried to connect these people with that of Oḍra who were living somewhere about the Mahānadī river and its tributaries, with their metropolis at Cuttack in Orissa.

Manu[115] refers to Oḍra as the people associated with the Puṇḍrakas, Ḍrāviḍas etc. On the other hand Varāhamihira[116] gives an independent status to the Oḍra territory as a *janapada* peopled by the Oḍras.

Like the earliest literary documents, the *Purāṇas* also refer to Oḍra as a race[117], and in some other places as a separate geographical unit[118].

Hiuen Tsang refers to U-Cha, corresponding to Oḍra, a country reached by the traveller after 700 li* from Karṇasuvarṇa in a south-western direction[119]. Che-li-to-lo identified with modern Puri[120] was the capital city of the Oḍra country situated on the borders of

* Chinese unit of distance, about one-third of a mile.

the sea[121]. Besides, Hiuen-Tsang mentions a famous monastery called Pu-sie-po-ki-li, i.e., Puṣpagiri on the south-western frontiers of the Oḍra country[122], corresponds more correctly to Ratnagiri near Jajpur[123].

In many medieval inscriptions Oḍra is treated as a *viṣaya*[124]. Thus in the Soro plates of the sixth century, Oḍra-*viṣaya* is mentioned as a part of *Uttara*-Tosali that extended from the river Suvarṇarekhā to as far as the river Vaitaraṇī or Mahānadī[125]. Yet in some other inscriptions Oḍra is referred to as a *deśa*[126]. In the Somavaṁśī records Oḍra has been referred to frequently. The Brahmeśvara temple inscription[127] refers to a battle in which the ruler of Oḍra, identified with Raṇabhañja of the Khiñjali *maṇḍala*, was killed. The inclusion of Khiñjali *maṇḍala* with the Oḍra country is further attested to in the copper plate grant of Yayāti I[128]. Further a grant of A.D. 899[129] depicts Oḍra as a small region in the present Mayurbhanj district. The extent of Oḍra is also ascertained from the Narasimhapur plates of Mahābhavagupta Udyotakeśarī[130], where a village is granted in Airāvata *maṇḍala* which includes half of the bed of the river Mahānadī[131], comprising a part of Oḍra. However, on the other hand the inclusion of both Yamagartta *maṇḍala* comprising the present district of Dhenkanal[132], and Khijjinga *maṇḍala* within the Oḍra territory has been refuted[133].

According to some scholars the modern village Upalada[134] in the Parlakemundi sub-division, corresponding to the village Upalavāḍa mentioned in the copper plate grant of Rāṇaka Rāmadeva (c. 11th century A.D.), was the southern limit of Oḍra. Rājendra Chola's Tirumalai inscription[135] refers to Oḍḍa-*Viṣaya* which was covered by dense forest[136]. The Dīrghasi inscription of Vanapati dated, A.D. 1075[137], a commander of Gaṅga king Rājarāja I, speaks of the defeat of the Kings of Kimedi, Kośala, Oḍra, Utkala, Veṅgi etc.

Scholars have variously identified the Oḍra country. Thus taking into account the ancient literary evidences, it has been identified with northern Orissa[138]. The entire region from the Chilika lake to the Suvarṇarekhā river is also identified with Oḍra[139]. From the sixth and seventh centuries A.D. the whole of coastal Orissa was termed as Oḍra[140]. Others have proposed that the valley of Mahānadī and the lower course of the river Suvarṇarekhā formed the ancient Odra country[141]. From cir. 700-1100 A.D. Oḍra*deśa* was bounded by the Mahānadī river in the north, *Dakṣiṇa* Toṣali in the east, Dakṣiṇa Kośala in the west, and the modern Paralakhemundi region in the south[142].

Thus, before the seventh century A.D. the Oḍra country was lying in-between *Dakṣiṇa* Kośala and Toṣali, and after that the northern coastal Orissa was included and still later the whole of coastal Orissa was known as Utkala.

Dakṣiṇa-Kośala

The Buddhist text *Aṅguttara Nikāya*[143] mentions Kośala in the list of the sixteen *Mahājanapadas*. The *Kalpasūtra* makes a reference to the king of Kośala[144]. The *Mahābhārata* refers to Kośala as a *janapada*[145], to the south of which was *Dakṣiṇapatha*[146]. The *Purāṇas* also mention Kośala as a *janapada*[147]. However, the part of Kośala which was included in ancient Orissa was known as *Dakṣiṇa*-Kośala. Commenting upon the kings of *Dakṣinapatha* who were vanquished by Samudragupta, H.C. Raychaudhuri[148] remarks that "Kośala in *Dakṣiṇapatha*, i.e., south Kośala, comprised the modern Bilaspur, Raipur and Sambalpur districts, and occasionally possibly even a part of Ganjam".

Speaking on southern Kośala, Hiuen Tsang[149] states that from Kaliṅga he went north-west for 1800 li to Kośala, a country which was more than 6000 li in circuit, and its capital was above 40 li in circuit. It has further been noted that the country was called 'south Kośala' apparently to distinguish it from the Kośala in the north[150].

Coming to the epigraphical evidences it is noticed that king Tivaradeva who flourished about the end of the seventh century

A.D.[151] assumed the title of *'Sakalakośa-lādhipati'*[152], obviously which seems to be an honorific title. Apart from this, a number of copper plate grants of the Somavaṁśī rulers found from the region of western Orissa, mention their issuer as the Lord of Kośala[153], while from the time of Mahābhavagupta onward the title *'Trikaliṅgādhipati'* appeared instead of *'Kośalādhipati'*[154]. During the early parts of the tenth century A.D. king Janmejaya I is said to have united both Kośala and Oḍra[155]. Later on the imperial Gaṅga king Devendravarmā Rājarāja conquered both the kingdoms of Kośala and Oḍra, which has been referred to in the Dīrghasi stone inscription[156].

In view of the above references, and that of various place names such as Śrīpura[157], Sarabhapura, Satalma, Suvarṇapur[158] etc., it can be said that the Sambalpur region and particularly the south Mahānadī valley comprising Sonpur, Patna, Sarangarh, and Raipur formed the kingdom of *Dakṣiṇa* Kośala.

Koṅgoda

In the first half of the seventh century A.D. Orissa was divided into three distinct parts, viz., U-ch'a (Oḍra), Kong- yu-t'o (Koṅgoda or Kuṅgada) and Ki-ling-kia (Kaliṅga)[159]. Hiuen-Tsang remarks that Koṅgoda was more than 200 miles from Wu-cha or Oḍra and the country was hilly, stretching from the slopes of the hill to the edge of the sea[160]. Following Hiuen Tsang's statement scholars have held that the Koṅgoda country began from the south of Chilika lake near Chhatrapur[161]. Other scholars have suggested that the region of Koṅgoda possibly extended from the present Kāluparāghāṭ in the north to the Mahendra hills in the south, and from the sea in the east to the boundary of ex-Kalahandi state[162].

By second half of the seventh century A.D. the kingdom of Koṅgoda appeared to have comprised considerable portion of *Dakṣiṇa* Toṣali[163], whereas the later Śailodbhava records suggest that it was a *maṇḍala* in the country of *Dakṣiṇa* Toṣali[164].

The Ganjam plates[165] of Mādhavarāja locate the Koṅgoda country on the bank of the Salima river identified with the river Ṛṣikūlyā[166] in Ganjam district, Orissa. A number of *viṣayas* such as Kṛṣṇagiri, Thoraṇa, Guḍḍa, Devagrāma, Jayapura, Kaṭakabhukti, Khidiṅgahāra etc. referred to in the Śailodbhava records, constitute the Koṅgoda *maṇḍala*[167].

Considering all the evidences it may be suggested that the Koṅgoda *maṇḍala* covered the area between the Chilika lake and the sea in the east to the eastern portion of the present districts of Phulbani and Koraput, and from the lower valley of the river Mahānadī to the Mahendra mountain in the south.

Apart from the various *janapadas* discussed above, a number of smaller separate geographical units existed in different periods in ancient Orissa. These are Śvetaka, Khijjiṅga, Khiñjali, Kodālaka, Taitila etc.

The *Mahābhārata*[168] makes a reference to Śvetaka. During the period of the early Gaṅgas, Śvetaka became prominent; and most of their records were issued from this place. Though most of the plates of the Śvetaka Gaṅgas are undated, generally these were assigned to the seventh century A.D.[169]. Further, Śvetaka probably the capital city, has been identified with modern Chikiti in the district of Ganjam[170]. Others have identified it with the village Sadak[171] near Chikiti.

It the Bhañja copper plates Khijjiṅga is known as Khijjiṅga-*Koṭṭa*. The records of Raṇabhañja[172] refer to some villages situated in *Uttarakhaṇḍa*[173] obviously meaning a division of Khijjiṅga, thereby suggesting that Khijjiṅga was a comparatively big territory. All the Bhañja records referring to Khijjiṅga cannot be traced beyond the tenth century A.D.[174]. This geographical unit has been located in the modern districts of Mayurbhanj embracing also the northern part of Keonjhar[175]. The headquarters of Khijjiṅga, Khijjiṅga-*Koṭṭa* has been identified with modern Khiching in the Mayurbhanj district[176]. This *koṭṭa* or fort of Khijjiṅga is certainly modern Khiching[177], about ninety miles south-west of present Baripada town.

Khiñjali was variously identified with the modern Keonjhar district[178], and Iñjili in modern Anuual[179] of the present Dhenkanal district. These identifications are, however, refuted by some scholars. In the process, place names like Royarā, Jayantamurā, Sivirā, Gandhaṭapaṭi, and etc. of the Bhañja plates have been identified with Rohilā, Janmurā, Subaliā, Gandharāḍi, and etc. in the Sonepur and Baud region[180]. Besides this, rivers like the Tel[181], Vyāghra[182] and Sālankī[183] of the Bhañja plates are known by the same name even today, and that too flowing in the Baud-Sonepur region. The inscriptions of Raṇa Bhañjadeva declare the king as the lord of both the Khiñjalis[184], suggesting thereby the Khiñjali was divided into two parts. Further, the Sonepur grant of Śatrubhañja[185] refers to two Khiñjalis. In this context, it may be noted that whereas the Taspaikerā charter[186] refers to *Uttarapalli*, the Singharā charter[187] makes a reference to *Dakṣiṇapalli*. Hence it has been suggested that probably the river Mahānadī[188] divided the Khiñjali unit into two divisions, a suggestion seems to be tenable.

The copper plate grants of the Śulki kings of Orissa refer to Kodālaka as a *maṇḍala* or district. This *maṇḍala* has been located in the present Midnapur district of West Bengal[189]. The Kodālaka of the inscriptions[190] might have been the capital of the Śulkis. Thus, the find spot of those records may be utilized to locate the place. Hence, it has been identified with the modern Kalau[191], seven miles from Talcher in the present Dhenkanal district. Other scholars[192] have taken it as comprising roughly of the modern Denkanal district. Further it has been maintained that the Nandas who ruled over here after the Śulkis, named it as Airāvatta*maṇḍala*[193]. In any case, it appears more reasonable to suggest that the Kodālaka unit was situated in the modern district of Dhenkanal.

The geographical unit of Taitila finds mention in the *Aṣṭādhyāyī* of Pāṇini[194] as a flourishing trade centre mainly famous for a type of cotton fibre[195]. The *Arthaśāstra* of Kauṭilya[196] refers to Taitila, from where horses of medium variety were being exported to be used in war. A hoard of punch-marked coins datable to the pre-Mauryan period found from Sonepur[197], in the present district of Balangir, indicate that the western Orissa was famous for trade activity during that period[198]. The identification of modern Titilagarh region[199] in the Sambalpur district with that of Taitila seems to be quite probable, and so also the suggestion that the trade centres of the Sonepur-Titilagarh region were connected with other flourishing places of Kaliṅga like Dantapura and Pithuṇḍa[200].

The *janapadas*, thus together constitute ancient Orissa, though significantly expanding and contrasting in different periods, mainly owing to the rise and fall of a number of royal dynasties. Side-by-side comparatively smaller geographical units within the broader outline of ancient Orissa also emerged. Still further, lesser independent geographical units such as Boṇāi, comprising the eastern part of modern Sundargarh district, and a portion of Deoghar region in the Sambalpur district; Khiṇḍiraśṛṅga, comprising the parts of Dharakoṭa, Boḍagaḍa, Seragaḍa and Saraḍā in modern Ganjam district; Cakrakoṭṭā, comprising parts of present Bastar district in M.P. and that of modern Koraput in Orissa also emerged.

References

1. Raychaudhuri, H.C., *Studies in Indian Antiquities*, pp. 35-36.
2. *Dvayanmagadhakaliṅgasuramasādan*. *Aṣṭādhyāyī*, iv. i.70
3. *Kaliṅgāṅgarajāḥ śreṣṭhāḥ Prācyāścedikarūsajāḥ/ Dāśārṇāscaparāntāśca dvipānāṁ madyamāmatāḥ// Arthaśāstra*, Book-ii, cha-ii, slo.-15
4. Majumdar, R.C., (ed) *Mc'Crindles Ancient India as described by Megasthenes and Arrian*, pp. 134-135
5. *Ibid.*, pp. 137, 144

6. Mittal, A.C., *An early History of Orissa*, pp. 24-25
7. *Dīgha Nikāya* (PTS.), II, p. 35
8. *Mahāvastu*, III, p. 364
9. *PTS.*, XXVIII, p. 6
10. *Mahābhārata*, V. 48. 76
11. *Jātakas*, II, pp. 376 ff; *Mahāvastu*, III, 361.
12. *EI.*, XIV, p. 361
13. *JA.*, (1925), pp. 46-47; Bagchi, P.C., *Pre-Aryans and pre-Dravidians in India*, p. 164
14. *Mc'Crindle's Ancient India as described by Potolemy*, p. 63
15. *Mc'Crindle's Megasthenes and Arrian*, p. 144
16. *JA.*, (1925), p. 171
17. Raychaudhuri, H.C., *PHAI.*, p. 79, note no. 2
18. Sen, B.C., *Some historical aspects of the inscriptions of Bengal*, p. 44
19. *JASB.*, XXVIII, pp. 186-ff.
20. *Dīgha Nikāya*, XIV, 36
21. *Sūtrakṛtāṅga*, I, 6. 22
22. Bose, A.N., *Social and rural economy of northern India*, I, p. 213
23. *Jātakas*, III, pp. 376-379; Raychaudhuri, H.C., *PHAI.*, p. 78
24. Law, B.C., *Tribes in Ancient India*, p. 158 ff.
25. *Ayaṁ Kavāte nijaghāna pāṇḍyaṁ/*
    tathā Kaliṅgāndantakūre mamarda//
    Mbh., 5. 47. 70
26. *EI.*, XIV, p. 361
27. *Jātakas*, V, pp. 134, 267 ff.
28. *Ibid.*, III, pp. 3-5
29. *Ibid.*, IV, p. 232 f.
30. *Ibid.*, V, p. 144
31. *Āvaśyaka Niryukti*, 325

32. *Śāntiparva, section IV*, (trans) Roy, P.C., p. 6
33. *Bhavadeva Suri's Pārśvanātha Charita*, pp. 269-70, *ślokas* 155 ff.
34. Raychaudhuri, H.C., *op.cit.*, p. 272; Sircar, D.C., *Inscriptions of Aśoka*, pp. 54-57
35. Sircar, D.C., *SGAMI*, p. 167
36. Rajaguru, S.N., *History of the Gangas*, pt. I, p. 36
37. *Pṛṣthe Kaliṅgāh sāmbaṣṭā Māgadhāḥ Pouṇḍramadrakāḥ/*
Gāndhārāḥ śakuniprāgyāḥ pārvatīyā vasātayaḥ//
Mbh. Droṇaparva, 19. 11
38. *Utkalā Mekalāḥ Pouṇḍrāh Kaliṅgāndhrāśca sunyuge*
Niṣādāśca Trigartāśca Bāhlikāśca jitāstvayā//
Ibid., 4. 6
39. *Saindhavaśca kaliṅgaśca Vikarṇaśca tavātmajaḥ/*
dakṣiṇaṁ pārśvamāsthāya samatiṣṭhanta daṁśitāḥ//
Ibid., 6.2
40. *Duryodhanasamādiṣṭhāh Kunjareiḥ parvatopameiḥ/*
Prācyāśca dākṣiṇātyāśca Kaliṅgapramukhā nṛpāḥ//
Mbh., 93.3369

Kaliṅgānanca sainyena Kaliṅgasya suto raṇe/
Pūrbaṁ pitṛbadhāt Krudho Bhīmasenamupādrabat//
Mbh., 155. 6703
41. *Ete Kaliṅgāḥ Kounteya Yatra Vaitaraṇīnadi*
Yatrāyajata dharmopi devānśaraṇametya vai//
Mbh., 3. 114.4
42. *tataḥ samudratīreṇa jagāma vasudhādhipaḥ/*
Bhātṛbhiḥ sahito vīraḥ Kaliṅgānprati bhārata//
Mbh., 3. 114.3
43. *Setukā sutikāścaiva Kupathā Vajivāsikāḥ/*
Navarāṣtra Mahiṣikāḥ Kaliṅgāścaiva Sarvaśaḥ//
Matsya Purāṇa, 114.37
44. *Kaliṅgadeśapaścārdhe parvate- amarakanṭake/*
Puṇya ca triṣu lokeṣu ramaṇiyā manoramā//
Kurma Purāṇa, 2.38.9
45. Rajaguru, S.N., *IO.*, I, pt. II, p. 58

46. *Ibid.*
47. *EI.*, XXI, p. 23; Rajaguru, S.N., *op.cit.*, Nos. 1-15
48. *EI.*, IV, p. 143
49. *Ibid.*, XXVIII, p. 176
50. *Ibid.*, XXI, p. 25
51. *Ibid.*, XXVI, p. 132
52. Ibid., XXVIII, p. 301
53. Rajaguru, S.N., *op.cit.*, II, p. 330; *CII.*, III, No. 1, text I, 19, p. 7
54. *Ibid.*
55. Others hold the name of the family as Durjaya, *EI.*, XXIII, p. 88 ff.
56. Rajaguru, S.N., *op.cit.*, p. 330
57. *Ibid.*, I, pt. II, pp. 48-53; *EI.*, XXIII, pp. 88-99
58. Cunningham, A., *Ancient Geography of India*, p.435
59. *EI.*, XXIII, p. 65
60. *EI.*, XXV, p. 195
61. *EI.*, XXVI, p. 63
62. *Ibid.*, p. 67
63. Roy, H.C., *Dynastic History of Northern India*, I, pp. 457- 458
64. Kaliṅganagara has been identified with Mukhalingam some twenty miles from Paralakimedi in the Ganjam district - Roy, H.C., *op. cit.*, pp. 448 and 485; with modern Mukhalingam near Srikakulam in present Andhra Pradesh - Sircar, D.C. *op.cit.*, p. 170; with Calingapatam, a sea-coast town in the bay of Bengal about twenty miles from chicacole at the mouth of the river Vaṁśadhārā - *EI.*, XX, pp. 79- 80; with Rajmahendri - Cunningham, A., *op.cit.*, p. 593
65. *EI.*, XXIII, p. 261; *Ibid.*, XXIV, p. 181; *Ibid.*, XXVI, p.167
66. *IO.*, IV, Nos. 17 to 21
67. It is suggested that Trikaliṅga was comprised of Dhānakaṭaka, Andhra and Kaliṅga - Cunningham, A., *op.cit.*, p. 594; was a

Union of Utkala or north Kaliṅga proper and Tel Kaliṅga or south Kaliṅga - *JAHRS.*, VI, p. 203; was formed of kaliṅga or Ganjam dist., south Kaliṅga or Godavari dist. and madhya Kaliṅga or Visakhapatanam dist. - *IHQ.*, VIII, p. 29; comprises of the regions of the Eastern Ghats, from the upper course of the river Mahānadī to about the source of the river Laṅguliā in the south - *JAHRS*, I, pp. 18-19; comprised of Koliṅga proper, Kaṅgoda and Utkala - *JBORS*, XIV, p. 145

68. *CII.*, I. pp. 92-100; *JRAS.*, XII, p. 384; Raychaudhuri, H.C., *op.cit.*, p. 272, fn. 1 (Toṣali variously called Toṣala)
69. Sastri, S.N.M., (ed) *McCrindle's Ancient India as described by Ptolemy*, p. 230; cf. Raychaudhury, H.C., *op.cit.*, p. 256
70. *IO.*, I, part II, p. 148
71. *EI.*, XX, p. 7 ff. (Nāgārjunikoṇḍā Inscription)
72. *Kośalāstosalāścaiva Kaliṅgā Yavanāḥ Khasāḥ/* cha. 13. V. 40
73. *JRAS.*, XII, pp. 384-385
74. See *infra* note No. 147
75. *GOS.*, No. 1, ch. 17, p. 93
76. *OHRJ.*, XIII, No. 2, pp. 1-8
77. *EI.*, XV, p. 3; *Ibid.*, XXIII, p. 197
78. *IO.*, I, pt. II, No. 23, Line-4
79. *EI.*, XV, pp. 1-8
80. *EI.*, XXIII, p. 201
81. *EI.*, XXIX, pp. 210-220
82. *IO.*, I, pt. II, No. 23; *EI.*, XXVIII, p. 331
83. *IO.*, I, pt. II, No. 24; *EI.*, IX pp. 285-288
84. *JKHRS.*, III, p. 261
85. *OHRJ.*, XII, No. 3, pp. 113-122
86. *EI.*, XXIX, pp. 210-220
87. *JBORS.*, XIV, pp. 292-306
88. Mishra, B., *Orissa under the Bhaumakaras*, p. 8

89. *IO.*, I, pt. II, pp. 151-152
90. see *supra.* note No. 40
91. *Chedivatsāḥ Karuṣāśca Bhojāḥ Sindhupulindakāḥ/ Uttamaujā Daśārnaśca Mekalāścotkaleiḥ saha//* Mbh. Bhīṣma parva, X. 39
92. Pargiter, F.E., *Ancient Indian Historical Tradition*, p. 292
93. '*Mekalanutakalamscaiva*' - canto - IV, 41, 9
94. '*Mekalāścotakalai*' - *Matsya Purāṇa*, ch. 114, V. 52
95. *Satirtvā Kapisaṁ sainyair boddha dvirada-setubhiḥ / Utkaladarsita pathaḥ Kaliṅga abhimukhaṁ yayau // Raghuvaṁśa* - IV. 38
96. Sircar, D.C., *op.cit.*, p. 173
97. *Mālavāśca Karusāśca Mekalāścotkalaiḥ saha / Uttamarṇā deśārṇāśca Bhojāḥ Kiskindhakair saha // Matsya Purāṇa*, 113.52
98. *Godhā bhadrāḥ Kaliṅgāśca Māgadhāścotkaleiḥ saha / Madhyadeśyā janapadāḥ prāyaśastatra Kīrttitāḥ // Brahmāṇḍa Purāṇa*, II. 16.42; *Matsya Purāṇa*, XII. 17
99. *Sudyumnasya tu dāyādā strayaḥ parama dhārmikāḥ / Utkalaśca Gayaścaiva Vinatāśvaśca Bhārataḥ // Harivaṁśa*, IX. 15
100. *Utkalasyotkalam rāṣṭraṁ Vinitaśvasya paścimam / Dikpurva tasya rajashre Grayasya tu Gayapure // Ibid.*, X. 19
101. *Utkalasyauttarā rājān Vinataśvasya paścimā/ dikpūrva bharataśreṣtha gayasya tu gayā smṛtā// Ibid.*, IX. 16
102. Chakraborty, N.N., *Rājaśekhara o kāvyamīmāṁsā* (Bengali), p. 269
103. *JASB.*, XI, pp. 7 ff.
104. Majumdar, R.C., *History of Bengal*, I, p. 27
105. *IO.*, IV, p. 326
106. *EI.*, XXXI, pp. 220 f.
107. *EI.*, XXIII, p. 197

108. *Oṣṭrāḥ Puṇḍrāḥ saseirandhrāḥ Pārvatīyāśca māriṣa / athapare janapadā dakṣiṇā Bharatarṣabha // Mbh.*, 6. 10. 56

109. *Utkalā Mekalāḥ Pouṇḍrāḥ Kaliṅgāndhrāśca saṁyuge / Niṣādaśca trigartāśca Bāhlikāśca jitāstvayā // Mbh.*, IV.6. fn. 32 in page 32

110. *Tato yatheṣṭamagamatpunareva sa keśarī / tataḥ samudratīreṇa Vaṅganpuṇḍrānsakeralān // Mbh.*, 14. 83.29

111. *Auḍrāḥ Pouṇḍrāḥ Saisikaṭāḥ pārvatīyāśca māriṣa / athapare Janapadā dakṣiṇā Bharatarṣabha // Mbh., Bhīṣmaparva*, IX, 365

112. *Jatasuro Madrakantasca raja Kuntih Kunindasca Kiratarajah/ tathangavangan saha Pundrakena Pandyodra rajau saha chandhrakena//*

Mbh., 2. 4. 21

113. Bostock & Riley, (trans.), *Natural History*, II, 75

114. Sastri, S.N.M., (ed), *Cunningham's Ancient Geography of India*, p. 586

115. *Pouṇḍrakaścoudrāḍrāvidāḥ Kāmbojā Yavanāḥ Sakāḥ / Pāradāḥ Pahlavāścināḥ Kirātā daradāho Khaśāḥ // Bṛhatsaṁhitā*, XIV.6

117. *Kirātā barbarāḥ sidhā vaidehāstāmraliptikāḥ / Auḍrāmlecchāḥ sasairindrāḥ pārvatīyāśca sattamāḥ // Padma Purāṇa, Svargakhaṇḍa*, 3.53

118. *Bhāgavata Purāṇa*, IX, XXIII.5

119. Sastri, S.N.M., *op.cit.*, p. 584

120. *Ibid.*, p. 585; cf. Banerji, R.D., *op.cit.*, p. 138. Other scholars have located the city in the Mahanadi delta, some sixteen miles south of Cuttack - Mittal, A.C., *op.cit.*, p. 20

121. Beal, S., *Buddhist records of the Western World*, II, p. 205

122. *Ibid.*, p. 205

123. Puspagiri has been wrongly identified with the hills of Udayagiri and Khandagiri near Bhubanesvara- Sastri, S.N.M., *op.cit.*, p. 587;

with Dhauli near Bhubanesvara-Mitra, R.L., *Antiquities of Orissa*, II, p. 59; and with the Phulbani-Ghumsur region - Sahu, N.K., *Buddhism in Orissa*, pp. 49-50. However, the identification of Puspagiri with that of Ratnagiri near Jajpur in Cuttack district seems to be quite probable - Chanda, R.P., *MASI.*, No. 44, p. 6; Banerji, R.D. *op.cit.*, p. 138

124. *EI.*, XXII, p. 202 (Soro Copper plate of Somadatta); *JASB.*, XI, (N.S.) p. 293 (The Talcher grant); *JASB.*, V. (N.S.) pp. 347-350 (The Bengal Asiatic Society grant)
125. *IO.*, IV, p. 364
126. *EI.*, III, p.353; *Ibid.*, VIII, p. 141
127. *JRASB.*, XIII, p. 63
128. *EI.*, III, pp. 351-355
129. *Ibid.*, XXV., p. 159
130. *JBORS.*, XVII, pp. 1-5; *IO.*, IV, pp. 225-234
131. *IO.*, IV, p. 233
132. *Ibid.*, p. 365
133. Sahu, N.K., *UUHO.*, I. pp. 145-146
134. *JAHRS.*, X, p. 166
135. *EI.*, IX, p. 23
136. Sastri, K.A.N., *The Colas*, p. 207
137. *EI.*, IV, pp. 316 f.; Sastri, K.A.N., *op.cit.*, p. 289
138. Benerji, R.D., *op.cit.*, p. 54
139. Mittal, A.C., *op.cit.*, p. 20
140. Sircar, D.C., *op.cit.*, p. 176
141. Mahtab, H.K., *History of Orissa*, p. 2
142. Sahu, N.K., *op.cit.*, p. 147
143. *PTS.*, I, p. 213
144. *SBE.*, XXII, p. 266
145. *Surasenāḥ Pulindāśca bodhāmālāstatheivacaḥ /*
Matsyāḥ kuśalyāḥ Souśalyāḥ Kuntayah Kānti Kośalāḥ //
Mbh., *Bhīṣma Parva*, X. 38; also *Mbh.*, 2. 30. 12

146. *Eṣa panthā Vidarbhāṇāmayaṁgacchati Kośalān /*
ataḥ param ca deśoayaṁ dakṣiṇe Dakṣiṇapathaḥ //
Mbh., 3. 58. 22

147. *Stośalāḥ Kośalāścaiva traipurā vaidiśāstathā /*
Tumurāstumbarāścaiva padgamā naiṣadhai saha //
Matsya Purāṇa, 114. 53

148. Raychaudhuri, H.C., *op.cit.*, p. 475. In this context it is suggested that Kośala to be *Mahākośala* or *Dakṣiṇa*-Kośala, Kośala comprising southern part of the modern Jabalpur dist. and the districts of Raipur and Bilaspur (all in present adjoining Madhya Pradesh) - Banerji, R.D., *op.cit.*, p. 115. Others hold that it was *Dakṣiṇa*-Kośala comprising the modern districts of Bilaspur and Raipur (in Madhya-Pradesh), and Sambalpur in Orissa - Chattopadhyaya, S., *Early History of North India*, p. 185

149. Watters, T., *op.cit.*, II, p. 200

150. *Ibid.*, p. 201

151. *IO.*, IV, p. 347

152. *Ibid.*, plates nos. 3.5.6

153. *Ibid.*, plates nos. 22, 23, 24, 25, 27, 42, etc.

154. *Ibid.*, plates nos. 16, 17, 18 etc.

155. *Ibid.*, p. 245, verse-2; Panigrahi, K.C., *Chronology of the Bhaumakaras and the Somavaṁśīs of Orissa*, p. 6

156. *EI.*, IV, p. 316

157. The capital of *Dakṣiṇa*-Kośala has been identified with Śirpur - Sircar, D.C., *The Successors of the Śātavāhanas*, p. 129

158. The Somavaṁśī kings of *Dakṣiṇa*-Kośala were ruling from Suvarṇapura, modern Sonpur in Balangir dist. - *IO.*, II, p. 345

159. Banerji, R.D., *op.cit.*, p. 136

160. Watters, T., *op.cit.*, pp. 196-197

161. Banerji, R.D., *op.cit.*, p. 139

162. Mishra, B., *Dynasties of Medieval Orissa*, p. 1

163. Sahu, N.K., *op.cit.*, p. 112

164. Banerji, R.D., *op.cit.*, p. 140; Mittal, A.C., *op.cit.*, p. 32

165. *EI.*, VI, pp. 143-146; *IO.*, I, pt. II pp. 157-161
166. *IO.*, I, pt. II, p. 160. Others have identified the said river with that of the Salia rivulet in Banpur (Puri dist.) which flows into the Chilika lake Sahu, N.K., *op.cit.*, p. 112
167. *IO.*, I, pt. II, plates nos. 32, 33, 34, 35, 37, 39 and 40
168. *Mbh, Bhīṣma Parva*, 9.14
169. *JKHRS.*, I, p. 35
170. *JOR.*, XI, p. 58; *EI.*, XYIV, p. 133
171. *EI.*, XXVII, p. 112
172. *IO.*, VI, Nos. 1, 2, 3, 15, 17 & etc.
173. *Ibid.*, Intro. p. XI
174. *Ibid.*, pp. 236-245
175. Sahu, N.K., *op.cit.*, p. 122
176. *IO.*, VI, Intro. p. x
177. Banerji, R.D., *op.cit.*, p. 180
178. *EI.*, XVIII, p. 300
179. Mishra, B., *Dynasties of Medieval Orissa*, p. 34
180. Sahu, N.K., *op.cit.*, p. 120
181. *IO.*, VI, p. 241
182. *Ibid.*, p. 73
183. *Ibid.*, p. 100
184. *Ibid.*, pp. 87, 94, 100; *JBORS.*, II, pp. 167-77
185. *EI.*, XI, p. 99; IO., VI, pp. 51-56
186. *JBORS.*, II, pp. 167-177
187. *Ibid.*, pp. 481-486
188. Sahu, N.K., *op.cit.*, p. 120
189. *JBORS.*, IV, pp. 169 f.; Banerji, R.D., *op.cit.*, p. 196
190. *JBORS.*, II, pp. 394-400; 405-417; *EI.*, XII, pp. 156-58
191. Mishra, B., *op.cit.*, p. 27
192. Sahu, N.K., *op.cit.*, p. 114

193. Mahtab, H.K., *op.cit.*, p. 151

194. *Kurugārhpatariktagurvasūtajaratyaślīladṛḍharūpāparevaḍabā taitilakadruḥ paṇyakambalo dāsībhārāṇañca* // vi.2.42

195. Agrawala, V.S., *India as known to Pāṇini*, p. 62

196. *Prayojñānāmuttamāḥ Kāmbojasaindhavāraṭṭajavānāyujāḥ, madyamā bāhlikapāpeyakasauvīrakataitalāḥ, śeṣāḥ pratyavarāḥ*// Book. 2, ch. 30, ślo. 29

197. *OHRJ.*, I, pp. 123-26

198. Sahu, N.K., *op.cit.*, p. 232

199. Agrawala, V.S., *op.cit.*, p. 63

200. Sahu, N.K., *op.cit.*, p. 233

CHAPTER II

Religious Beliefs of the Early Inhabitants

Religious history of Orissa does not begin with the introduction of Jainism in this land. Evidences, both archaeological and literary, throw light on a sound cultural and religious background of the region. The people who resided in this part of the country left an indeliable mark of their cultural and religious affiliations.

Before reviewing the faiths and beliefs of the original inhabitants of this land, it is to be noted that the hilly regions of Orissa were, and are still the homeland of aboriginal tribes[1], who constitute 23.11% of the present day population. Scholars have suggested the tribal origin of the term Orissa from that of Oḍra, and similarly the term Kaliṅga is said to be derived from a Muṇḍā name[2]. Early literary sources[3] refer to the Pulindas and the Śavaras who were probably the earliest inhabitants of ancient Orissa. Besides the above reference, elsewhere it has been maintained that Utkala, an important and big *janapada* of ancient Orissa was inhabited by the Sudhyumnas[4], who belonged to the proto-Austroloid stock[5]. Apart from this, the various *janapadas* of ancient Orissa were named as Oḍra, Kaliṅga, Utkal and Kośala after the tribes inhabiting this area. As regards the concentration and mobility of these tribes it has been suggested that the geographical factor mainly helped them to remain unsubdued and unconverted, thereby we find today the remnants of these tribes widely scattered[6]. On this score it may be easy to explain the above concentration of tribes in a particular geographical location before the Āryan migration. However, in pre-migration period the social-barriers must have played a dominant role in the non-proliference of the tribal population to other regions, as a result, in the case of ancient Orissa, the coastal belt had been lacking tribal inhabitation.

It has been suggested by the anthropologists that the lower culture in fact "is the basis of human societies"[7], and there is no "human thought so primitive as to have lost its bearing on our thought, nor so ancient as to have broken its connection with our own life"[8]. Hence, for a proper understanding of the composite culture of this region in ancient times, it is essential to go into the origin and gradual developments of some of the important features, contributed both by the pre-Aryans and Aryans, more by the former than by the latter.

It is evident from the existing materials at our disposal that prehistoric men in the palaeolithic age were savage hunters, living in natural caverns and caves. It is also likely that they after some time discovered the use of chipped stones, and towards the end of the period, when they changed their nomadic life, the necessity of protection against wild beasts led them to live in small groups, marked perhaps by crude exogamy, totemism and magic rites including the practice of human and buffalo sacrifices and a rudimentary form of matriarchy. The practice of exposure of the dead is also attributed to them[9]. In the neolithic age men introduced the art of cultivation, various crafts, trade, domestication of animals and pastoral economy, along with the use of polished stone implements. The existence of a joint tribal and family system, based on the patriarchate, has also been suggested[10]. The custom of the burial of the dead along with food and other articles and the practice of the erection of megaliths were well known to them[11]. These customs are still in practice even now by many of the tribal people of Orissa.

With regard to the earliest inhabitants of Orissa, scholars[12] have suggested that the first human inhabitants in Orissa were the hill tribes belonging to the non-Aryan stock, and their descendants have survived till today. Amongst the tribes the Śavaras, variously pronounced as Śavar, Śabar, Saur or Sar; are referred to in the *Aitareya Brāhmaṇa*[13]. These Śavaras had been identified with the Suāri of Pliny and the Śabarai of Ptolemy[14].

In the intervening planes between the sea and the hills the tribes of Oḍras and Utkalas having a comparatively better way of life, were residing; and in course of time moved southward to Kaliṅga[15].

To know the religious beliefs of these early inhabitants, we are not in a sound position, since they have left no records. In the words of Rhys Davids, "Primitive man, whatever the race he belonged to, made no distinction at all between his experiences in everyday life and his experiences in dream. And that was so, not because he looked upon life as a dream, but that he looked upon dreams as realities. .... Now it is suffice to say that the souls outside a man developed into gods. Souls were believed to wander from body to body. Animals had souls, and all things that men feared, and all that moved. The awe-inspiring phenomena of nature were instinctively regarded as the result of spirit action; and rivers, plants, and stars, the earth and air and heavens, become full of ghosts"[16]. And such a system of belief may be summed up as 'Animism', which includes all the conceptions preserved in the works on astrology, magic, and folk-lore relating to god, soul, spirit, ghost etc.[17]

Fetishism in fact formed part of animism, which lay at the root of the various cults in Orissa as well as other places of this country, contributed to in the main by the non-Aryans. This is based on the attribution of spirits to all thing, with which man had a close kinship, for which he felt awe and from which he sought to derive benefit through rites[18]. It is the foundation of every faith and of all people, and in its final analysis, it "includes the belief in souls and in a future state - these doctrines practically resulting in some kind of active worship"[19]. The Aryan worship of the elements of nature, which developed into the worship of images, through a process of anthropomorphism, is based on the same belief; so is the case with the creation of myths, found everywhere among all classes of people[20]. It is also notable in this connection that among primitive and advanced minds "there co-exist the mythical and the religious elements in belief. The rational factor is visible in religion; the irrational is prominent in myth"[21]. The Hindu religion is based on both, or it "is animism more or less tempered by philosophy or magic - The Vedas themselves are one source of the manifold animistic practices, which may now be traced all through popular Hinduism"[22].

During the period before the rise of Jainism, the impact of Vedic religion or Brahmanism must have been a factor in the cultural milieu of the society. Here, it may be pointed out that by this time, the majority of the population were the followers of their own religions, which consisted in beliefs in spells, incantations, charms and spirits. But how far the Vedic religion was alien to the ancient indigenous beliefs has been seriously doubted. Thus it has been said that "Brahmanism was the only form of higher religion in India which could affiliate all the popular cults without any feeling of contradiction"[23]. It seems to be an established fact that Brahmanism could not but flourish assimilating and absorbing the tribal religion which was in currency since time immemorial. To comprehend the nature of the religious life of ancient India it sounds correct to note the remark; that is, like its social life, the religious life of ancient India was a confused total of its local traditions[24], and it expresses itself in harmony with its cultural environment[25]. In this context it has been further observed that ".... the symbols of the higher thought are the awesome physical realities of the peasantry"[26]. At the same time the ancient religion did not at all bear an uniform character. It has been said that "As the tribes pushed on, their language, partly by the ordinary and necessary growth or decay, partly by intercourse with other peoples, continually changed"[27].

Animism flourished among the non-Aryan race vigorously, and from the beginning the common folk seem to have adored the objects, viz., monkey, snake and stone etc. which they supposed to embody their god[28]. By animism the primitive men meant that every object which could affect him in any way was animated by a life and would be like his own [29]. In this form of belief, magic plays a dominant role, and people believed in the malevolent spirits and powers, which influence the destiny of man[30].

Besides the above aspect of the ancient Indian peoples in the field of religion, some other facetes of their beliefs and practices have also come into light. Homage was being paid to deities such as *Yakṣas* and *Nāgas*, which was an obligatory practice for all in the community before the rise of Buddhism and the Bhāgavata religion[31]. The worship of *Yakṣa* seems to have been very popular in those days. Their worship was widespread, and represents on the popular level a continuation of pre-Aryan religion.[32]

Another interesting feature of the ancient mode of worship was the veneration of shapeless stone or block, called as *Grāma Devatī* or *Ṭhākurāṇī*, with simple offerings in the open air[33]. In ancient Orissa such a form of worship has a special significance, since its origin can be convincingly connected with the famous Lord Jagannātha. According to tradition Lord Jagannātha was worshipped in the form of a blue stone by the aboriginal Śavara Chief Viśvāvasu, until Vidyāpati, the minister of king Indradyumna met him and took away the deity[34]. The *Skanda Purāṇa* mentions about the appearance of the deity in the Puruṣottama *kṣetra* (Puri)[35]. In fact, the present day image of Jagannātha and his two associates Balabhadra and Subhadrā display a tribal look and the images resemble more to the aboriginal deities than to any other Aryan deities[36]. On the possible reason behind the making of such peculiar figures which are certainly a result of tribal origin, it has been observed that these figures are not typical of the tribal religion, rather these are typical products of the process of Hinduization[37]. Further, in this connection, scholars[38] have established the said tribal origin by relating it to the Guḍimallam *Liṅga* in present Andhra Pradesh.

It is interesting to note in this connection that when the tribal mode of worship gave way to the civilized Aryan speech, carved image took the place of the blue stone. As a result even in present time the two-fold worship co-exists side-by-side throughout Orissa[39].

Analysing the legend connected with Jagannātha and citing the inscriptional evidence of Śailodbhava dynasty, seventh century A.D., scholars[40] have further suggested that the Mādhava cult which was the faith of the aboriginal Śavara, cited above, was later on absorbed in the cult of Jagannātha.

Another feature of tribal culture in ancient Orissa was the worship of tree from very early times. In tracing the antiquity of Jagannātha, it has been pointed out that the cult of wood (*Dāru*) worship can be traced back to the *Ṛg-Vedic-Sūkta*[41]. Scholars[42] have further concluded that the worship of Puruṣottama or *Dāru Brahma* might have been prevalent in the remote past. However, such a proposition was doubted by the later day scholars[43]. At the same time the worship of tree has been emphasized and related with the worship of Śiva, a pre-Aryan deity. Vedic Rudra has been identified with the pre-Aryan Śiva[44]. One of the popular and important aspects of Śiva cult is the worship of the *Liṅga* or phallus. The antiquity and worship of such a form has been established following the discovery of seals from Mohenjodaro and other places[45]. Further, it has been upheld that the aborigines were the worshippers of the phallus of *Ṛg-veda*[46]. The primitive people were worshipping Śiva in his *liṅga* form which has a resemblance, more or less with the trunk of a tree[47]. The tribal background of *liṅga* worship is manifest in the famous Liṅgarāja temple in Orissa. The *Svayambhū Liṅga* of Liṅgarāja in the temple of Liṅgarāja in Bhubaneswar, represents a natural rock, originally being worshipped under a mango tree; while the *Baḍu* priests of the temple are believed to be the descendants of Śavaras who were originally worshipping the *Liṅga*[48].

The folk and tribal elements had been enriching the religious aspect of the ancient Indian culture. One of the unique contributions in this direction was the cult of *Stambheśvarī* - worship of the mother goddess through the medium of a pillar or wooden post (*stambha*). This cult is believed to have been worshipped by the non-Aryan aboriginal population. Even today *'Stambheśvarī'* known in the name of '*Khambeśvarī*' is being worshipped in the region covering from Ghumsur, Baud and Sonepur in Western Orissa to Anugul and some portion of Dhenkanal[49]. In the *Vedas* there are a number of passages in which trees are invoked as deities[50]. The *Jātakas* refer to the worship of tree goddess with animal sacrifies and sometimes, with human sacrifice also[51]. Thus, there can be no doubt in the fact that the worship of the cult of *Stambheśvarī* has its origin in the tree worship of the aborigins of Orissa.

Apart from the above general observation, we now discuss the religious beliefs and practices of some important aborigins of ancient Orissa. The native wild tribes of India belong to two great classes, such as Kolarians and the Dravidians[52]. In the context of ancient Orissa, the tribes have been broadly divided into two broad groups. Firstly, the pre-Dravidian group consisting of tribes such as the Kandha, Goṇḍa, Orāon, Kolha, Koyā, Gadavā, Baṇḍā etc., while the second group comprising the Sāntāla, Juāṅga, Muṇḍā, Ho, Śavara etc., is known as the Negroids[53].

The Śavaras are one of the earliest tribes of ancient Orissa, referred to in ancient literature[54]. Their most famous deity was the malevolent *Ṭhākurāṇī*, spouse of the male *Ṭhākura*, who was invoked through human sacrifice[55]. The association of Śavara with Jagannātha at Puri has been referred to above[56].

Another tribe that inhabited ancient Orissa were the *Bhūiyāns*, who claim to be the son of the *Bhūmi* (earth). They have been divided into a number of septs and totemistic castes[57]. The *Nāga* (cobra), *Bāgha* (tiger), and *Sūrya* (sun), three important totems, were evoked, and it seems that the religious beliefs and faith of the Bhūiyān tribe was concentrated and revolved around these totems. They also believe in spirits, witch-craft, and ancestor worship; and offer *pūjā* to their gods through priest known as *Dehuri* selecting them out of their own tribe[58].

The Orāons mostly reside in the modern districts of Mayurbhanj and Sambalpur in Orissa. This tribe is said to have been joined with the *Vānara* army in favour of Rāma in his war with Rāvaṇa[59]. Perhaps this was the reason of their not killing any species of monkey. Like the Khonds, this tribe recognises a supreme god in the sun, but at the same time they do not worship him since he does not do any harm to them[60]. The Orāons do not believe in the idea of a future life in heaven, however, believe in a sort of metempsychosis, i.e., if a man is eaten by a tiger, he becomes a tiger[61]. Further, amongst this tribe the mouse totem is found which is the *vāhana* of Gaṇeśa[62]. They also believe in malignant spirits, to whom their supreme deities, viz., *Dharma, Sūraja-Deotā* etc. cannot control or protect[63].

The Orāons worship the mother goddess called *Devīmā* in a thatched house known as *Devī-maṇḍā*, through some symbols. Inside the *Devī-maṇḍā* the symbols are the lumps of earth numbering three, five and seven, in the form of small cones which seem to represent the breast of the mother goddess. Scholars[64] have suggested that this idea of mother goddess with their symbolic representation is the original conception of the Orāons. In this connection it may be noted that in the Bachelor's dormitory (*Dhumkuriās*) of the Orāons, we find a wooden plank upon which female breasts are carved, and at the same time in one of the wooden posts supporting the roof there are representation of the female genetal organ[65].

"The tract of country in the province of Orissa lying south of the Mahanuddee in the belt of hills facing the Bay of Bengal, is inhabited by the Khonds, an aboriginal race which from time immemorial has maintained its primitive language, habits, and superstition[66]. The Kandhas worship sun as their chief deity[67]. They have a great devotion to the oral traditions in the field of religion. These traditions are being sustained through various rites, invocations and rituals[68]. The chief rite of the Kandhas is the human sacrifice offered to the earth-goddess 'Tari'. Some scholars maintain that the offering was made to the 'male earth god as ancestor[69]'. Yet others hold that the fertility of their fields depended on her (earth goddess) favour, which could be secured only by the sacrifice of human life[70]. The victims are called 'meriāhs'[71]. Although the victims are generally obtained by purchase, often acquired by violence also. This practice of human sacrifice is an interesting feature in the Indian cultural scene. Scholars have traced the prevalence of such sacrifices in the Indus Valley Civilization, pointing out to a seal which represent seven victims for sacrifice[72]. The Vedic literature also testify to this sacrifice[73]. The *Mahābhārata*[74], and *Aitareya Brāhmaṇa*[75] mention about such type of sacrifice. Though the Kandhas believe in a chief divinity they also revered other gods such as the river-god, rain-god, spring, wealth, hill-god, small-pox-god, boundary-god, judgement-god and etc.[76].

Another important tribe is the Goṇḍas inhabiting the present districts of Ganjam, Phulbani, Sambalpur, Keonjhar and Mayurbhanj. Like the Kandhas, they worship the representation of sun, offering human sacrifices[77]. The sun apart, they worship the moon and stars and use stones for idol. Another important aspect of their religious beliefs, is the annual feast and the worship of the snake[78]. One of the most distinctive features of the religious practices of the Goṇḍas is, however, the cult of phratry, in which the clan deities were described by the generic term persapen[79]. In the early stage this tribe had no mythology, no priest; but later on they started worshipping Hindu gods such as

Jagannātha, Rāma, Kṛṣṇa; simultaneously with their own Jaṅgdeo, Liṅgadeo, and Jhulan *Devi*[80].

The Sāntāls, described as one of the finest specimens of the native savage[81], inhabit mostly the present districts of Balasore and Mayurbhanj, and belong to the Kolarian group. They worship spirit of every sort, and regards beasts as divine. While the sun represents the highest spirit, their race-god is the 'Great-Mountain'. To the mountain-god (*Buruboṅgā*) they are said to have offered human sacrifices[82].

The Barbarians belonging to the lowest substratum of the population are the Muṇḍā type, who speak Austro-Asiatic tounge. These Muṇḍās live mostly in the districts of Sundargarh and Mayurbhanj. The religion of this tribe is based on totemism. The members of this group associate themselves with the actual life of vegetable or animal species, and the beliefs and practices are characterised by blood sacrifice[83].

Of course, there are several other religious practices and/or faiths and beliefs of these tribal communities but all these minute details are not needed to record here for our study. However, it is probable that all the elements of the cult of fertility, head-hunting, human sacrifice, faith in reincarnation, ancestor worship and the rites connected with the dead, belief in heavenly bodies, magic and sorcery are based on the same animistic belief. The existing material so far discovered from this region explain these cults.

References

1. Even today there are as many as sixty-two tribes belonging to three different ethnic groups : Austric, Drāvidian and Indo-Aryan, reside in Orissa - vide Appendix, pp. A-B., Mohapatra, K., (ed.), *Tribal language and culture*; Mishra, B., *Ādivāsī Samāja O Sanskṛti* (Oriya), p. 14

   Austric group - Binjhiā, Blumij, Boṇḍa, Ḍidāyi, Gadbā, Ho, Juāṅg, Jurāyi, Khariā, Kol, Karmāli, Koḍa, Lodhā, Māheli, Muṇḍā/Muṇḍari, Pareṅgā, Sāntāl, Sorā.

Dravidian group - Dhārwa, Goṇḍ, Jatāpu, Kiśān, Koṇdh, Koṇḍā Dorā, Koyā, Māriā, Mirdhā, Orāon, Olari, Parjā, Pengu.

Indo-Aryan group - Bagatā, Bāthudi, Bhuyān, Bhatra, Halbā, Jhariā, Kurmi, Lariā, Matiā, Omonatyā, Pentiyā, Sāunti.

Very Primitive tribes - Boṇḍa, Khariā, Mānkiḍiā, Kutiā Kondh, Dongriā, Kondh, Lanjiā, Sorā, Pāuri, Bhuyān, Birhor & Didāyi.

2. Behera, K.S., *et al.*, *Tribal Language and Culture*, p. 37
3. *Aitareya Brāhmaṇa*, VII. 8.; *Vāmana Purāṇa*, Ch. XIII, 48-49
4. *Harivaṁśa*, IX. 15. also see *supra*. p.17
5. Pragiter, E.F., *Ancient Indian historical tradition*, p. 295; Chattopadhyaya, S., *Racial Affinities of Early North Indian Tribes*, p. 67
6. *JRAS.*, XIII, p. 216
7. Hodson, T.C., *The Primitive Culture of India*, p. 128
8. Tylor, E.B., *Primitive Culture*, II, p. 452
9. Aiyangar, P.T.S., *Stone Age in India*, pp. 10-24 ff.
10. *Ibid.*, pp. 26 ff.
11. *Ibid.*, pp. 26-39
12. Hunter, W.W., *A History of Orissa*, I. (ed.), Sahu, N.K., p. 52
13. *Aitareya Brāhmaṇa*, VIII. 18
14. Cunningham's *Ancient Geography of India*, (ed.), S.N.M. Sastri, p. 509
15. *BODG.*, (Puri), p. 22
16. Rhys Davids, T.W., *Buddhism, its history and literature*, pp. 10-11
17. *Ibid.*, p. 36
18. Tiele, C.P., *Outlines of the History of Religion*, p. 9; Tylor, E.B., *op.cit.*, I, pp. 285 ff., 417-426; II, pp. 184 ff.; Lang, A. *Myth, Ritual and Religion*, I, pp. 52-59.
19. Tylor, E.B., *op.cit.*, I, pp. 426-27
20. Lang, A., *op.cit.*, I, pp. 163 ff, 238 ff, 254

21. *Ibid.*, pp. 328 ff.
22. Risley, H., *Census Reports of India*, 1901, I, pp. 350 ff.
23. Law, B.C., *India as described in early texts of Buddhism and Jainism*, pp. 202-203
24. Oursel, P., Masson *et al.*, *Ancient India and Indian Civilization*, p. 117
25. Pande, G.C., *Studies in the Origin of Buddhism*, p. 318
26. Wheeler, M., *The Indus Civilization*, p. 83
27. Rhys Davids, T.W., *op.cit.*, p. 19
28. *IGI.*, I, p. 432
29. *Ibid.*, p. 431
30. Majumdar, D.N., *Races and Cultures of India*, p. 423
31. Agarwala, V.S., *India as known to Pāṇini*, p. 481
32. Coomaraswamy, A.K., *Yakṣas*, pt. I, p. 36
33. *BODG.*, (Puri), p. 82
34. For the Indradyumna legend in connection with the Lord Jagannātha, betraying his tribal origin see - *Skanda Purāṇa*, vii, 16 ff.; *Brahma Purāṇa*, 42, 16-84; *Padma Purāṇa*, 5, 17, 38-5, 22, 55. The legend as given in *Mādalā Pāñji*, the palm-leaf chronicles of Lord Jagannātha, see - *BODG.*, (Puri), pp. 97-98. For the legend with its Oriya folk version see - Sāralā Das's *Mahābhārata*, (Oriya), *Mūṣalī parva*, *Adhyāyas*, vi, pp. 50-62; viii, pp. 74-78; ix, pp. 78-87; x, pp. 87-93; xii, pp. 105-117; xiii, pp. 118-120; *Vanaparva*, pt. II, *Adhyāya*, vi, pp. 171-193; Kṛṣṇna Das's *Deula Tolā*, (Oriya), pp. 191-235. Also cf. *Caitnya maṅgala* of Jayānanda (a Bengali biographical work in verse), *Prakāśas*, 1/146 and 4/25
35. *Skanda Purāṇa*, *Puruṣottama- māhātmya*, VII, 16 ff;
36. Sahu, B., *Jagannātha cetanāra Udbhava O Vikāśa* (Oriya), *et al.*, *Āma Jagannātha : Āma Sāhitya*, (Oriya), (ed.), Adhikari, P., pp. 183-184
37. Eschmann, A., *et al.*, *The Cult of Jagannātha and the Regional Tradition of Orissa*, p. 100
38. Jash, P., - *History and Evolution of vaiṣṇavism in Eastern India*, pp. 214-215

39. *BODG.*, (Puri) p. 82
40. Behera, S.C., *et al.*, *op.cit.*, p. 49
41. *Ṛg-veda*, X, 155, 3
42. Sāyaṇācārya, *Ṛg-Veda-Saṁhitā*, *Sāyaṇabhāṣya*, vaidika Saṁśodhana Maṇḍal, pp. 841; Kane, P.V., *History of Dharmaśāstra*, IV, pp. 692-93; *OHRJ.*, VII, no. 1, pp. 15-16
43. Mishra, K.C., *The Cult of Jagannātha*, p. 71; Jash, P., *op.cit.*, p. 209
44. Jash, P., *History of Śaivism*, p. 1
45. Marshall, J., *Mohenjodaro and Indus Civilization*, III, pp. 59 ff.; Vats, M., *Excavations at Harappa*, I, pp. 369-71
46. Jash, P., *op.cit.*, p. 5
47. Behera, S.C. *et al.*, Mohapatra, K., (ed.), *op.cit.*, pp. 46-47
48. Behera, K.S. *et al.*, *Ibid.*, p. 42
49. *Utkala Sāhitya* (Oriya), Vol. XXVI, pt. III, p. 80
50. Macdonell, *Vedic Mythology*, p. 154
51. *Jātakas*, III, p. 160, V, pp. 472, 474, 488
52. Hopkins, E.W., *The Religions of India*, p. 525
53. Mishra, B., *op.cit.*, p. 14
54. *Supra*, p. 38
55. Hopkins, E.W., *op.cit.*, p. 535, Hopkins has made these statements in connection with the Śavaras or Saurās of the Deccan.
56. *Supra*, p. 43
57. *GIO.*, (Mayurbhanj), p. 130; *Ibid.*, (Sambalpur), p. 118
58. *Ibid.*, (Mayurbhanj), p. 131
59. Roy, S.C., *The Orāons of Chotanagpur*, pp. 3-4
60. Hopkins, E.W., pp. *op.cit.*, p. 532
61. *Ibid.*
62. *Ibid.*
63. Rowney, H.B., *The Wild Tribes of India*, p. 82
64. Roy, S.C., *op.cit.*, p. 53

65. *Ibid*.
66. Marshman, J.C., *(The) History of India*, III. pp. 107-108
67. Hopkins, E.W., *op.cit*., pp. 528-32
68. *JRAS*, XIII, p. 222
69. *JRAS*, (1942), p. 172
70. Marshman, J.C., *op.cit*., p. 109
71. *ERE*, VII, p. 649
72. Marshall, J. *op. cit*, I, PL. XII
73. *Saptāsyāsan-paridhayastriḥ sapta samidhaḥ Kṛtāḥ* / *Devā Yatyajñan tanvānā abaghnan puruṣan paśuṃ* // *Ṛg-veda Saṁhitā*, 10.90.15
74. *Jarāsandhavināśaṁ ca Rājñān ca parimokṣaṇam* / *Yadi Kuruyāma Yajñārthaṁ Kiṁ tataḥ paramambhavet* // *Mbh*., 2. 15.14
75. *Etān rājasūyān yajñakratun provāca tametamabhisecaniye puruṣān paśumālebhe* // *Aitareya Brāhmaṇa*, VII. 3.3
76. Hopkins, E.W., *op.cit*., pp. 528-529; cf. *JRAS*., XIII, p. 227
77. Hopkins, E.W., *op.cit*., p. 526
78. *Ibid*., p. 527
79. Haimendorf, C.V.F., *The Goṇḍas of Andhra Pradesh*, p. 426
80. *ODG*. (Mayurbhanj), *1967, p. 131*
81. Hopkins, E.W., *op.cit*., p. 532
82. Risley, H., *The People of India*, p. 447
83. Oursel, P. and Others, *op.cit*., p. 119

CHAPTER III

Historical Account of Jainism

I

Rise of Jainism :

Jainism is a religion with a distinct form and philosophy of its own. It is also regarded as one of the most ancient monastic organisations of ancient India. It cannot be now regarded as a reaction to the existing Brahmanic religion which was the most dominant faith during those days; or an off-shoot religion of the same. Its antiquity is well ascertained when we find that both the religion and its culture have been known by different names and epithets in different periods and places, viz., Ṛṣabha cult, *Ahiṁsā dharma, Yogamārga, Vrātya, Arhat, Śramaṇa* or *Nirgrantha Dharma*, the *Sarākas, Śrāvakas*, Jaina, etc.[1]

The *Kalpasūtra*[1], which is supposed to have been composed in its original form by Bhadrabāhu, shows the early stage in the development of Jainology, while it speaks of the tradition of four *Jinas*, viz., Ṛṣabhadatta, Ariṣṭanemi, Pārśva and Mahāvīra. Thus, according to this text, the tradition of twentyfour *īrthaṅkaras*, was a later development. According to the Jainas their system is the eternal truth[2] being revealed in every age by successive *Tīrthaṅkaras*. S. Radhakrishnan[3] has made a reference to *Yajur-Veda* where he finds the names of three *Tīrthaṅkaras*, namely Ṛṣabha, Ajitanātha and Ariṣṭanemi. However, it s very difficult to trace these names in the *Yajur-Veda* as denoting *Tīrthaṅkaras*. To determine the actual age and historicity of the first twenty-two *Tīrthaṅkaras*, it has been an odd proposition, which seem to be completely mythical and have no historical validity[4] inasmuch as they are all separated from each other by 'astronomical figures'. At the same time what is revealed about them in the Jaina traditions, are far as the contemporary evidences go, the twenty-third *Tārthaṅkara*, Pārśvanātha, besides the twenty-fourth, Mahāvīra, was a historical personage.[5] It should be noted here that Jainism of the early historical period was a religion of a comprehensive Jaina order of the whole bodies of Jaina saints, that was established rather than reformed by the last and the twenty-fourth *Tīrthaṅkara, Vardhamāna* Mahāvīra.

The Jainas believe tha theirs' was a religion revealed time and again, and would continue to be revealed in every one of these endless succeeding periods of the world by innumerable *Tīrthaṅkaras*[6]. The twenty-third *Tīrthaṅkara* is believed to have lived for one hundred years[7], and died two hundred and fifty years before Mahāvīra[8]. He is said to have been born in Banaras (U.P.) about 817 B.C.[9]. The parents of Mahāvīra are believed to have been the worshippers of Pārśvanātha[10]. The hill of Sameta-śikhara[11] was the centre of activities of Pārśvanātha, which in subsequent periods became one of the greatest *Tīthas* (place of pilgrimage) for the Jainas. Jaina texts unanimously speak that on the eve of his *Nirvāṇa*, Pārśvanātha came to this hill and achieved *mokṣa*[12]. After this event, the hill came to be known as the mount Pārśvanātha[13]. Buhler[14] has shown that including Pārśvanātha, twenty of the *Tīrthaṅkaras* died or obtained *mokṣa* (deliverance in bliss) on Sametaśikhara. According to the *Kalpa Sūtra*, Pārśvaātha's order consists of 16,000 Śramaṇas, 38,000 nuns, 164,000 laymen, and 327,000 laywomen. Apart from these he had a number of monks as disciples who were well versed in the *Pūrvas* and destined to obtain liberation in that very birth[15]. The monk community of Pārśvanātha was divided into eight groups under the head of eight *gaṇadharas* viz., Subha, Subhaghosa, Visiṭṭha, Bambhayārī, Soma, Siridhara, Vīrabhadra and Jasa[16].

Vardhamāna Mahāvīra, the twenty-fourth and last *Tīrthaṅkara* was born at Kuṇḍagrāma[17] a suburb of Vaiśālī, modern Basarh in the Muzaffarpur district of Bihar[18], in 599 B.C.[19]. Therefore, he was called Veśālie (Vaiālika), an inhabitant of Vaiśāli. His father was the *Kṣatriya* Siddhārtha head of a warrior clan called the *Jñātrikas*[20], and mother *Kṣatriyāṇī* Triśalā was the sister of king of Vaiśālī[21]. Mahāvīra was known to his contemporaries as *Jñatiputra*, *Nātaputta* (in Sanskrit and Pāli respectively), while the Buddhists call him *Nigantha Nātaputta*[22]. "Mahāvīra had lived thirty years as a householder, more than full twelve years as a state inferior to perfection, something less than thirty years as a *Kevalin*, forty-two years as a monk and seventy- two years on the whole"[23].

In the thirteenth year of his wandering after he renounced the world, Mahvīra attained "the complete and full, the unobstructed unimpeded, infinite and supreme, best knowledge and intuition, called *Kevala*"[24]. Thus in forty-two years of his age he "was recognised as omniscient, as a prophet of the Gainas, or a *Tīthaṅkara*, and had titles, *Gina*, Mahāvīra ..."[25]. Thereafter for the rest of thirty years of his life he had been teaching his religion and organising his order of ascetics till he obtained *Nirvāṇa* at the age of seventy-two at Pāvā[26], modern Pāvāpuri in nalanda district of Bihar[27].

Jainism, it is suggested, was but a development of the older proto-Jainism of Pārśvanātha, the twenty-third *Tīrthaṅkara*[28]. It is generally agreed that Mahāvīra founded his order upon a loose group of ascetics, who were not strict to their chastity, and were wearing clothings. These early Jaina monks were called *'acela'*, a term used to refer to any unclothed ascetic[29]. However, they were not completely nude, and used to wear a *Kaṭibandha* or *Kolapaṭṭaka to cover the privities*[30]. *This kind of modification ordained upon the followers of Pārśvanātha took place when Vardhamāna* attained the highest knowledge[31], and appeared as a prophet in the thirteenth year of his wandering.

In some Buddhist texts[32], *Nigantha Nātaputta* (Mahāvīra) is mentioned along with five other heretical leaders viz., Purāṅa Kassapa, Makkhali Gośāla, Ajita Kesakambala, Pukuḍha Kaccāyana and Sanjaya Belaṭṭaputta as "the leaders in religious life who are heads of companies, of disciples and students, teachers of students; well known, renowned, founders of schools of doctrine, esteemed as good men by the multitude"[33]. Besides these six important heretical sects, a number of other heretical sects are also referred to[34]. Elsewhere, only five sorts of *Śamaṅas* viz., the *Niganthas*, the *Śākyas*, the *Tāpasas*, the *Gairikas*, and the *Ājīvikas* are mentioned[35]. Whatever might have been the case, the existence of such heretical schools was either the result of broken away groups from the Vedic tradition, or grew up in isolation from and in opposition to it[36]. The identification of Nigantha Nātaputta with Mahāvī has been upheld by several scholars[37]. H. Jocobi holds that while the teachings of *Nigantha Nātaputta* was not an accurate or exhaustive description of the Jaina creed it contains nothing alien from it[38]. J.G. Buhler[39] has pointed out that the *Nirgranthas* were recognised as an opposite sect of that of the Buddhist. Thee *Nirganthas* are described as founders of schools and doctrines and were esteemed as good men by all[40], of which sect *Nātaputta* (or *Jñātiputra*) was the leader. According to Jaina scriptures, Jaina *Sādhus* were known as *Nirgranthas*, etymologically meaning 'without any tie, without restraint'[41]. This fact is also apparently corroborated by Buddhist literature and other evidences[42]. The seventh pillar edict of Aśoka also refers to the *Niganthas*[43]. *Elsewhere it has been maintained that the similarity between these words and the names of the family, to which Vardhamāna* belonged is apparent, and this *Nātaputta* or *Jñātiputra* is the same person as *Vardhamāna*, the descendant of the *Jñāti* family and founder of the *Nirgrantha* of the Jaina sects[44].

In this connection we may take note of the fact that the Buddhist writings had never spoken of these *Nirgranthas* as a newly-risen sect, nor of the *Nātaputta* as the founder of that sect. They seem to imply that the *Nirgranthas* were probably an old sect at the time of Buddha and that *Nātaputta* was only the reformer of the faith[45]. Further, it is commonly accepted that *Vardhamāna* Mahāvīra was a contemporary of Gautama Buddha, and that the Jainas had already gained the status of an important faith during the period when the Buddhist faith was being founded[46]. Secondly, an analysis of their philosophical speculations also shows that Jainism is older than Buddhism. The Jainas or immovable and celestial or terrestrial possesses the soul[47]. This belief had been the dominant feature in the life of almost all the acquired and accumulated their inspirations from the primitive animism, this form of belief must have existed extensively in the society when Jainism was first organised[48]. The above belief of the Jainas, a fact missing in Buddhism seems to be quite probable. A new faith in all likelihood would tend to accept and assimilate, though not fully, the existing religous beliefs and practices of the mass. Here it is worth mentioning that rise of Buddhism coincided with a wide array of changes especially in social and economic fields. The changes gave a death blow to the tribal mode of society, as such demand for reorganisation of society was quite urgent. This eventually fostered a new religion and philosophy devoid of rituals[49] - the exploiting device - which dominated the religious scene by then.

The antiquity of Jainism has been further traced to the development of metaphysical thought. In common with the oldest Brahmanical philosophies, Vedānta and Sāṁkhya; the ancient Jaina texts usually speak only of substances (*dravyas*) and their development or modification (*paryāyas*)[50].

Like philosophy, also in the field of magical rites, the Jainas belieed in the force of magical syllables which had its roots in the primitive stages of mankind. Although it is common to both Jainism and Brahmanism, it is hard to believe that the jainas borrowed this idea from the Brahmanical system[51].

A more significant point in favour of our contention needs to be emphasized i.e., while the Buddhists had considered the *Nirgranthas* as an important sec, the latter did not make any kind of reference to the former[52]. Thus it suggests the prevalence of Jainism much before the advent of Gautama and *Vardhamāna* Mahāvīra[53].

In the field of practical ethics, Jaina literature itself shows that Mahāvīra only added the fifth vow tothat of the *cāujjāma dharma*[54] or the four-fold religion of Pārśvanātha. Pārśvanātha had laid down the four-fold morality (four great vows) viz., *Ahiṁsā* (non-killing), *Sunṛta* (truthful speech), *Asteya* (not stealing), and *Aparigraha* (renouncing of all illusory objects) for his followers; to which Mahāvīra added the vow of *Brahmacarya* (chastity)[55]; and all these vows collectively known as *Pañcajāma dharma*[56].

It is to be noted that Mahāvīra's rules for his followers were different from that of Pārśvanātha[57], who was the preacher of the *cāujjāma dharma*[58].

Though the Jainas believe that the *Pūrvas* were the oldes sacred lierature[59] of their faith dating back to Ṛṣabha, the first *Tīrthaṅkara*, the historical records and the Jaina canon do not support such a view. Hence it has been rightly suggested that the *Pūrvas* were taught by Mahāvīra himself to his followers, whereas the *Aṅgas* were composed by his *Gaṇadharas*[60].

Mahāvīra was not responsible in any way for the establishment of a new religion, instead he improved upon the religion of Pārśvanātha by reforming it, and by giving new philosophical orientations to it. Thus by all acounts, there seems to be no doubt regarding the antiquity of Jainism prior to the age of Mahāvīra.

Just to suffix our contention we may refer to the meeting of Keśi, a disciple of Pārśvanātha with Gautama that of Mahāvīra, where the latter is said to have brought about the union between the old and new Jainism[61]. This event clearly suggests the antiquity of Jainism and the historical standing of Pārśvanātha.

The sixth century B.C. marked a turning point in the annals of Indian religious history. The social, economic and political factors worked simultaneously at the root of such a great change. As a result, what was known of Jainism, got transformed, modified into a more socially-oriented movement by Mahāvīra, who himself was a product of that age.

Jainism was not a product of a sudden reformation in the sixth century B.C., but it was a religious movement that was under process of development for a long time.[62] It has been observed that the germs of the opposing sects such as Jainism and Buddhism were contained in the institution of the fourth *āśrama*, and that the latter was the model of the heretical sects[63]. Thus from the sacrifical creed of the Vedic religion, and from the Upaniṣadas, the heretical sects drew their inspiration, and built up their own systems by their own rational thinking completely independently[64]. In the light of the above discussions it seems to be wrong to hold that "the rise of Jainism like all orthodox and heterodox Hindu communities was due to the favour of princes", as suggested by Max Weber[65].

In this era of stiff ritualism and dogmatic teachings of the Vedic Brāhmaṇas, the heretical sects more particularly, Jainism and Buddhism owed their success to the politics of the day; and the former is most important because of its priority and lasting character[66]. The socio-religious conditions of this age has been generally described[67] as the worship of the elements to please the gods and goddesses for their own benefits and well- being. Such a system which was the monopoly of the Brāhmaṇas of the day invited serious questions and thus the heretical sects secured their own ground for an uprising. The great ascetic leaders - Mahāvīra and Gautama Buddha - were the products of this age of social formate of the tribes. Two very important factors provided the base for their rise. Firstly, there was no deep penetration of Brahmanism into the tribal areas to the north of

Magadha; and secondly, the free democratic tribes were themselves breaking up[68]. This process was one of the several processes that were going on simultaneously along with the decayof the older Aryan tribes, rise of autocracies, of new religions, and greater volume of trade[69]. In this connection it should be pointed out that the rise of the heretical sects was continued by the rising civilization in the Gangetic valley, when political power was rapidly consolidated[70].

The intellectual life of India during this age was going through a process of ferment, and the only seems to have been concentrated on the truth[71]. The development of organised states in the place of old tribal structure, and the advent of material culture seem to have worked on the root of much confusion and research[72]. Hence the movements of the period, as has been rightly pointed out[73], was not the result of *Kṣatriya* protest agaist the caste exclusiveness of the Brāhmaṅas, rather a result of natural growth. The submersive desire took a definite form with the aid of social and material changes, mentioned above, and became increasingly prominent in this particular age. Hence Jainism rejected the Vedic-learnings, its rituals, the existence of any supreme deity, the Vedic gods and goddesses, but retained the doctrine of soul in contrast to that of Buddhism. Now they laid stress on *'Karma'*, i.e., a man's action, not his caste, was of supreme importance. Thus it is stated that "By conquering love, hate, and wrong belief he exherts himself for right knowledge, faith, and conduct, then he will cut off the fetters of the eight-fold *Karman*, which are productive of delusion; (then) the five kinds of obstruction to right knowledge, the nine kinds of obstruction to right faith and the five kinds of obstacles (called *Antarāya*) : the last three remnants of *Karman* he destroys simultaneously; afterwards he obtains absolute knowledge and faith, which is supreme, full, complete, unchecked, clear faultless, and giving light (or penetrating) the whole Universe."[74]

II

Jainism in Orissa before Khāravela

The antiquity of Jainism in Orissa has not yet been definitely ascertained. It is generally believed that Orissa witnessed some activites of the Jaina *Tīrthaṅkaras* prior to Mahāvīra, the twenty-fourth or the last *Tīthaṅkara. Thus Aranātha the eighteenth Tīrthaṅkar* is said to have received his first alms in city of Rāypur[1] (Rājpura), one of the metropolis of the Kaliṅga country. This Rājpura is further mentioned as the capital city of Kaliṅga in the *Mahābhārata*[2].

The twenty-third *Tīrthaṅkara*, Pārśvanātha's connection with Kaliṅga has also been referred to in the Jaina literaturre[3] in the context of the marriage of Pravāvatī, daughter of king Prasenjit of Kusasthalapura with Pārśvanātha. The Kaliṅga king is said to have intervened in the above affair, but subsequently withdrew himself at the cite of Pārśvanātha, who prevailed upon the Kaliṅga king, thereby forcing the latter to retreat from the scene. It is possible that the Kaliṅga king after having moved by the above act got attracted towards the religion of Pārśvanātha. This fact is corroborated by the sculptural representation of P‹200rśvanātha in the caves of Udayagiri and Khandagiri near Bhubaneswar. The identification of this Kaliṅga king is still near Bhubaneswar. The identification of this Kaliṅga king is still shrouded in mystery, and at present it is not possible to identify him due tothe lack of the archaeological evidences.

Some scholars, on the basis of Jaina *Kṣetra- Samāsa* have tried to show the possible route through which Pārśvanātha entered Orissa. It is held that from Tāmralipta, Pārśvanātha entered into Kopakata or Kopakataka, where on the second day of hismeditaion he broke his fast in the house of Dhānya[4]. Later on this place came to be known as Dhānyakataka which has been identified with modern Kopri in the present district of Balasore in north Orissa[5]. This place must have developed as a sacred shrine and attacted the people to the religion of Pārśvanātha.

Karakaṇḍu, the ruler of Kaliṅga, and a contemporary of Pārśvanātha, wasprobablya follower of the Janina religion[6]. Several jaina texts[7]furnish us with an interesting story relating to his birth, growth (both in odd circumstances) and in circumstances in which Karakṇḍu was coronated as the king of both Campāpura (his father Dadhivāhana's kingdom), and Kaṅcanapura, where Karakaṇḍu was living along with his foster parents. Further, the texts, in continuation of this story, says how eventually Karakaṇḍu intiated himself into the Jana faith and converted to a Jaina. Campāpura of the story seems tohave been rightly identified with modern Charampa[8] near the Bhadrak town in the Balasore district of Orissa from where a large number of jaina antiquities have been bound. According to the *Uttarādhyayana Sūtra*[9] and the Jātakas[10], the Kaliṅga king along with Gandhāra had adopted the Jaina faith after having placed their sons on the respective throne of their kingdom. Further the *Jātaka* mentions that Karakaṇḍu was living in a cave along with Dummudho and Naggaji, after entering the ascetic order[11]. Elsewhere in the *Jātakas* [12], it is further stated that a king of Kaliṅga named by Kāliṅga, renounced the world and entered into the ascetic order, while ruling from the city of Dantapura[13].

Both the Jaina tradition and *Jātaka* accounts refer to Karakaṇḍu, while in some other places the *Jātakas* refer to Kaliṅga as the king of Kaliṅga. Here, it is interestng to note that the time and context in all the traditions seem to suggest the same event. Hence, on the question of identification of both names of the kings, it has been rightly suggested that both of them were one and the same person[14], who was a subordinate to king Dandaki of Dandaka in the south[15].

Thus, the literary evidences mentioned above indirectly reveal that both karakaṇḍu and his son and successor were the followers of the Jaina faith. If webelievethe traditions referredtoin the Jaina *Sūtra* and the *Jātakas* the fact seems to be clear that the son of Karakaṇḍu who was placed on the throne in order to facilitate the latter's initiation into the Jaina faith, must have been a follower of the same faith.

It may be noted in this connection that during the days of Karakaṇḍu, Jainism ormore secifically the religion of Pārśvanātha, whose followers were known as the *Nirgranthas*, had made considerable headway into the Kaliṅga country as reflected in the literary texts.

Jainism in Orissa during the age of Mahāvīra makes an interesting study. Various Jaina texts refer to Mahāvīra's connection with Kaliṅga. It is stated that Mahāvīra in the eleventh year of his monkhood, left Śrāvasti[16] for his southern sojourn. After reaching Sanulaṭṭhīyagāma, heproceeded towards Daṇḍabhūmi[17], probably situated in the Singhbhum district of south Bihar in the name of Dalbhum. From Daṇḍabhūmi, via Peḍhālagāma[18] and some other places, he proceeded to Hatthasīsa[19], situated probably in northern Kaliṅga[20], which was a centre of trade and commerce[21]. In the course of his sojourn he reached Toṣali[22] identified with present Dhauli near Bhubaneswar[23]. In this connection it may be noted that Toṣali has been mentioned as a Jaina centre where an image of *Jina* was installed and guarded by king Toṣolika[24]. Thus it seems that before Mahāvīra's coming to this region it had already developed into a famous centre of religion of Pārśvanātha. This is further proved by the fact that on his return journey from Mosali[25] situated further south-west to Toṣali, Mahāvīra again visited Toṣali for a second time, on his way to Siddhāattapura[26]. On both the occasions Mahāvīra was taken to be a robberand washit hard, and during his return visit he was about to be hanged[27]. Hence it is gathered that during Maāvīra was taken to be a robber and was hit hard, and during his return visit he was about to be hanged[28]. Hence it is gatheredthat during Mahāvīra's visit, the Kaliṅga people had been the followers of Pārśvanātha; and till that period the religion of the former did not establish itself in Kaliṅga.

Some other Jaina texts also testify to the visit of Mahāvīra to Kali‹215ga. According to the *Haribhadrīya Vṛtti*, when Mahāvīra visited Kaliṅga, the then king of Kaliṅga was a friend of the former's father[29]. In the same text it is further recorded that following the invitation from the Kaliṅking, Mahāvīra paid his visit. Another tradition recorded in the Jaina *HarivaṁŚa Purāṇa*[30]*, describes Mahāvīra as a friend of the Kaliṅga king.*

Judging by the above evidences, it can be supposed that the royal house of Kaliṅga was very much friendly with Mahāvīra and must have accorded their support to the cause of the Jaina religion. It is also possible that Jainism spread in the region with the royal support.

The Hāthīgumphā īnscription of king Khāravela belonging to the second half of the first century B.C.[31], further upheld the visit of Mahāvīra to kaliṅga. The line-14[32] of the ibnscription proclaims that Mahāvīra had preached his religion on the Kumārī hill, identified with Udayagiri near Bhubaneswar[33]. Though the inscription does not make any clear reference to the author of the act, Mahāvīra may well be related to have revolved the whell of victory from that place[34]. Further in thisconnection, the practiceof letting the wheel of *Dharma*in action by Gautama Buddha may be cited, which has been widely portrayed in the early Buddhist art Sāñcī, Bodhgayā, and at a slightly later date at Sārnāth and other ancient Buddhist sites.

After this famous event Jainism spread more rapidly in Orissa. Here it should be noted that after the sixth century B.C., Jainism,a refined and modifiedform of the religion of PārŚvanātha, was steadily gaining ground. The existence of some Jaina centres in Orissa to which the Jaina pilgrims frequented, prove the spread of Jainism. One of these centres was Pihuṇḍa[35], a port city, identified with PṚthudaka[36].Others have identifiedit with Pithuṇḍa[37], asea-coast town, whichwasthe Pityundra metropolis of Ptolemy[38], located by the latter in the countryof Maisolia[39], i.e., between the delta of the river KṚṣā and Mahānadī[40]. Elsewhere[41], it is contended that the city was situatednot very farfrom Amarāvatī in the heart of ancient Āndhrapatha. Although it is difficult to identify Pihuṇḍa definitely, the foregoing discussion suggests that it was in the present day Andhra portion ofancient Kaliṅga.

The spread of Jninism in Orissa during the age of Mahāvīra has further been alluded to in the *Sūtra* literature and the *Mahābhārata* indirectly. Thus the *Baudhayana Dharma Sūtra*[42] speaks of Kaliṅga along with Puṇḍa, Sauvīra and Vaṅga as impure countries, and prescribed the *'VaiŚvānara haviḥ'* (sacrificial fire)[43] for the purification of the Aryan people, visiting these impure countries[44]The *Mahābhārata* regards the people of Kaliṅga along with the Karashkaras, the Mahisakas, the Keralas, the Karkoṭakas etc. having no religion, and thereby should be avoided[45]. Thus, it seems clear that the people of Kaliṅga had been the followers of anti-brahmanical faiths and possibly for that they were treated in derogatory manner in the Brahmanical literature[46]. Futher considering the popularity of Jainism in the region, it may be supposed that there were a considerable number of Jaina followers.

So far as the extant archaeological evidences are concerned relating to the early history of Jainism in Orissa, the edicts of AŚoka Maurya reveal the earliest information. The line-4 of Rock Edict-XIII[47], states that therelived everywhere *Brāhmaṇas, Śramaṇas* and people belonging to other sects. This edict describes the Kaliṅga war which was fought between Aśoka and dthe Kaliṅga country in the eighth regnal year of the former. In this connection it is interesting to note that amongst the set of fourteen Rock Edicts, Edict-XIII alons with that of XI and XII did not find a place at Dhauli and Jaugaḍ (the places within Orissa where Aśoka's Edicts are found); the capitals of northern and southern parts of Kaliṅga resectively after its conquest by Aśoka. In their place two separate Edicts had been inserted.

The occurrence of the term *Śramaṇa* in the Edict, as well as the absence of Edicts - XI, XII and XIII are very much significant in the present context. Further, both the facts, of course, with the knowledge and direction of Aśoka, seem to be interrelated.

The proper identification of the term '*Śramaṇa*' has not yet been satisfactorily met.with. The *Ṛg-Veda*[48] refers to the wandering ascetics and yogis as '*Munis*'. Pāṇini in his *Aṣṭādhyāyi*[49] mentions *Śramaṇs* belonging to both the sexes. Baudhāyana[50] uses the term '*Śramaṇa*' for the *munis*. The *Bṛhadāraṇyaka Upaniṣad*[51] mentions both'*Śramaṇa*' and '*aśramaṇa*'. Megasthenes[52] had traced the distinction between the '*Śramaṇas*' and the '*Brāhmaṇas*'. The Buddist literature *Aṅguttara Nịkāya*[53] refers to two separate classes of ascetics calling them *Parivrājaka*,i.e., '*Brāhmaṇas*' ; and '*Annatittiyas*', i.e., other non-brah-manical ascetics. Patañjali commenting on Pāṇini's *sūtra*[54] refers to the '*Śramaṇas*' and the *Brāhmaṇas* as two eternal antagonistic groups[55]. The distinction between '*Brāhmaṇa*' and '*Śramaṇa*' seems to be clear when the former treats the latter calling them '*muṇḍakas*' and '*vasalas*'[56]. Thus, it is probable that the *Brāhmaṇas* had recognised the '*Śramaṇas*' as a group outside their domain, and regarded them inferior as well. The term '*Śramaṇa*' corresponds to both the Jaina and Buddhist ascetics. For their Buddhist affiliation the *Jātakas*[57] may be noted, where Bodhisattva Gautama has been alluded to.

Simultaneously, the Jaina ascetics were also known as *Śramaṇas*. According to the *Kalpa Sūtra* the *Arhat Pārśvanātha had lived full seventy years as a Śramaṇa*[58], and had a community of sixteen thouand *Śramaṇas* with Āryadatta[59] as their head. In this context the dialogue between king Nemi who had already renounced the household life and adopted the Jaina faith, with Sakra the king of gods is noteworthy. In the *Uttarādhyayana Sūtra*[60] it is found that Sakra advised king Nemi to organise elaborate rituals and to feed the *Śramaṇas* and *Brāhmaṇas*. Here it is to be noted that since king Nemi was a Jaina follower, Sakra advises the former to satisfy the *Śremannṇas* (Jaina followere) first of all.

Thus, it follows that during Aśoka's Kaliṅga conquest there were considerabloe number of Jaina followers inhabiting the land. One of the reasons to explain the absence of Rock Edict XIII in Kaliṅga is indicated by the fact that during the Kaliṅga war a good number of people belonging to the Jaina faith had been killed, and for that Aśoka felt it wise to avoid engraving it in the periphery of the Kaliṅga couuntry. As regards the Rock Edicts XI and XII and XIII, it may be noted that, while in the former Aśoka advocates liberality to the *Brāhmaṇas* and *Śramaṇas*; in the latter he honours men of all religious communities irrespective of whether they are ascetics or householders[61]. Hence it seems to be clear that while a number of Jaina followers had been killed in the war it could not become possible on the part of Aśoka to engrave the Edicts inwhich he has shown liberality and hounour to the Jainas along with other communities..

It may be noted in this connection that the first important penetration of jainism into the southern part of India occurred during the time of Candragupta Maurya, when the great famine of Magadha caused the jaina pontiff Bhadrabahu to migrate along with the emperor and with a vast following into the present Karnataka state, and settled at Śrāvaṇa Belgolā[62]. The *Mahāvaṁśa*[63] indicates that Jainism was prevalent in the island of Ceylon during the fourth century B.C. Moreover, the Hāthigumphā inscription of king Khāravela informs that during the period of the Nandas Jainism was one of the important religions prevalent in Kaliṅga[64].

In this connection some scholars have noted that the origins of south Indian Jainism were laid by Mahāvīra during the sixth century B.C. in the Kaliṅga has been further attested by the existence of ancient Jaina rock-carvings and inscriptions in the hills of the north Arcot district in northern Tamil Nadu.

Thus, it seems clear that there was a connecting land- passage between Magadha and south-India via Kaliṅga through which Jainism traversed. Dantapura the ancient capital of Kaliṅga was linked up conveniently with many other historically imporatant places of the adjoining kindgoms by land rout[65]. It has been shown that the city of Kāñcanapura in in north Orissa, which was one of the metropolises of Kaliṅga, was a great centre for commerce and trade, carrying free trad with Ceylon[66]. The Pāli literature mentions about land route that passed throught Bodhagayā to Kaliṅga. Thus at Bodhagayā, two merchants from Utkal,viz., Tapussa and Bhallika were said to have met Lord Buddha, while they were proceeding towards Rājagṛha[67] This land-routs, possibly had been used by the Kaliṅga king Brahmadatta[68] who is said to haye brought the tooth relic of Gautama Buddha to Kaliṅga. In this connection it may be recordedthat the Utkalas, who had been occupying the northern portion of Orissa were coming to Gaya in connection with trade and commerce[69].

It is possible that northern Orissa had been connected with Bodhagayā through the south-west part of present-day West Bengal. In all probability the followers of Jainism, particularly those of Pārśvanātha, had utilised this tract of land to traverse into the Kaliṅga country. In thios connection it may be pointed out that both the Ājīvikas and *Nirgranthas* had been living in the south-western part of Bengal before the *Jina*-hood of Gośāla,the Ājīvika leader[70]. Mahāvīra is said to have spent one rainy season in Paṇitabhūmi[71] which is the same was a division of the country of Lāḍha or western Bengal[72].It is frther noted that both Gośāla and Mahāvīra lived together for a period of six years in Paṇiyabhūmi[73]. In the *Kalpa sūtra*[74] it has been stated that Tāmraliptika *śākhā* which is one of the four *śākhās* of the *Godāsa gaṇa* was founded by the Jaina monk Goḍāsa. This shows the popularity of Jainism in the Tāmralipti retion which is situated in the Midnapur district of West Begal.

The south-western part of West Bengal, i.e. the present districts of Midnapur and Bankura, thus witnessed some important happenings pertaining to the Jaina relegion. The proximity of this region with northern Orissa and the connecting land-route suggest suggest that the Jaina monks had taken their southern course of souour through this region and entered into Orissa.

III

Jainism and Khāravela

The reign of the Cedi king Khāravela[1] was a glorious and significant period in the history of Jainism in Orissa. The faith had made a great headway and prospered quite flourishingly in this age. The famous Hāthīgumphā inscription[2] of Khāravela is the first epigraphical record throwing light on the early history of Jainism. The inscription suggests that the Cedi king along with his family members had a definite leaning towards Jainism. Jainism seems to have re-established its supremacy over Kaliṅga, being directly patronised by its overlord, Khāravela. While narrating the accounts of the first thirteen years of the reign of Khāravela, the inscription simultaneously speaks of various activities of the king relating to his affinities with the Jaina religion, and with the Jaina communities residing in the Kaliṅga country in those days. This, in turn, clearly suggests the royal support accorded to the Jaina cause.

To understand and evaluate the history of Jainism during this period the following lines of the inscription need to be discussed exhaustively.

Line one :

> *(- [3] Swastika symbol) Namo Arahaṁtānaṁ[4] namo savasidhānaṁ Aireṇa mahārājena Māhāmeghavāhana[5] Cetirāja[6] - vasa[7] - vadhanena pasatha - subha - Lekhanena[8] caturanta Luṭhita[9] guṇa upetena[10] Kaliṅgadhipatinā Sirikhāravelena* /

The record opens with invocations to the *Arahats* and the *Siddhas*. Such kind of appeal to the *Arahats* and *Siddhas* corresponds to the beginning of the five-fold forms of homage used by the Jaina followers[11]. Further, in this connection it may be noted that such appeals in the Jaina inscription found from Mathurā belonging to the first century B.C.[12]. Thus the contemporary epigraphical evidence clearly records the usual practice which had been followed by the

Jainas in engraving their inscriptions. In this line, it is further clear that Khāravela who bears royal titles such as *Kaliṅgādhipati, Mahārāja, Ārya* and *Mahāmeghavāhana*, highlighted the glory of the Cedi family by offering his salutations to the Jaina *Arahats* and *Siddhas*.

The term *Arahata* was common to both the Jainas and the Buddhists. Some scholars have expressed view that the caves (locally called *gumphā*) at Udayagiri and Khaṇḍagiri, (the Hāthī*gumphā* on the Udayagiri bears the inscription of Khāravela) might be of Buddhist affiliation[13]. We shall, however, endeavour to show on the basis of text of the inscription that these caves were of Jaina affiliation.

In the line nine of the inscription, Khāravela is said to have entertained the Brāhmaṇas, house-holders, Arahatas and Śramaṇas with gifts as a token of this victory, and at the same time ensured the gifts to be universal.

Line nine :

> Sava dharāvāsa parivesane[14] sava gahanaṁ ca Kārayituṁ baṁhaṇānaṁ jayaparihāraṁ dadāti[15]/ *Arahatānaṁ samaṇānaṁ ca satasahasehi*[16]/

In this line of the record it is clear that though he was a devout Jaina, on special occasion of celebration, he used to proclaim his secular attitude. At the same time one point should be noted in this connection that in course of his exhibiting secular favour, he had given prominence to the *Arahata-śramaṇas* (Jainas).

Khāravela has been credited to have carried out two expeditions against Magadha : the first[17] in his eighth regnal year, and the second in his twelfth. The twelfth year of his reign had marked the culminating point of his career as a campaigner. This time the attack against Magadha had been undertaken with a clear motive in view, which is immensely important for the present study. To strengthen our contention, the following lines (eleven and twelve) of the inscription are worth noting :

Bārasame ca vase ....[18] *satasahasehi*[19] *vitāsayati utarāpadha rājāno .... Māgadhānaṁ*[20] *ca vipulaṁ bhayaṁ janeto hatisaṁ*[21] *Gaṅgāya*[22] *pāyayati / Māgadhāṁ ca rājānaṁ Bahasatimitaṁ pāde vaṁdāpayati Naṁdarāja nitaṁ*[23] *ca Kaliṅgajinaṁ*[24] *sarnivesaṁ*[25] *Magadhato rāja gaharatanaṁ parihārehi*[26] *Aṅga-magadha vasuṁ ca nayati*[27]/

During the course of his second expedition in north India, Khāravela is recorded to have humiliated the Magadhan king Bahasatimita[28] and brought back the Kaliṅga-*Jina* to Kaliṅga, which had been earlier carried away by the Nanda king[29] of Magadha. In this connection it is sometimes contended that Khāravela had led his expedition against the kings of north-western frontier provinces[30]. But the terms Aṅga and Magadha mentioned in the record in connection with his expedition, certainly do not mean the region in the north-western frontier provinces. The attack was directed into the heart of the Magadhan capital on the banks of the river Ganges. In course of his attack Khāravela caused great fear amongst the people of Magadha by defeating their ruler and brought the Kaliṅga-*Jina* along with the riches from Aṅga and Magadha. The Magadhan king is also recorded to have payed obeisance at the feet of king Khāravela, while the latter had camped his army numbering a hundred thousands on the banks of the Ganges (symbolically alluded in the record as '*hatisaṁ gaṅgāya pāyayati*').

The recovery of the image of Kaliṅga-*Jina* and its eventual reinstatement in Kaliṅga, so also its identification are not free from doubt. However, a close scrutiny of some of the expressions in the record affords us to identify the Kaliṅga-*Jana* with some amount of certainty. The expression of the record '*Nandarāja nitaṁ ca Kaliṅga-jinaṁ sannivesaṁ*', has been variously read and interpreted, e.g., *Nadarāja-jita-Kaliṁga-jana-saṃnivesam*[31] meaning Khāravela '(did something in connection with) the settlements of the Kaliṅga people subjugated by king Nanda'[32]. Both the reading and its interpretation are hard to accept. Here it is interesting to note that the Nandas' attack over Kaliṅga had occurred in the second half of the fourth century B.C., and according to this interpretation, it would mean that Khāravela who belonged to the second half of the first century B.C. helped the subjugated people of Kaliṅga resettle after such a long interval. Further, if this line of argument is accepted, the stubborn resistance of the people of Kaliṅga against Aśoka-Maurya who attacked Kaliṅga in 261 B.C.[33] would remain unexplained. On the other hand, the war with Aśoka would only mean that the people of Kaliṅga had already overcome the defeat inflicted upon them by the Nanda king well before the age of Aśoka.

The term *Sannivesam* has been variously interpreted. It stands for an assemblage, site, place, form, figure or an open space near a town[34]. Some scholars have understood that '*saṁnivesa* ...., probably *saṁniveśayati*', meaning thereby setting up an image[35]. Yet others have read the term as *Jināsanam*[36] obviously denoting the seat, or throne of Jina and not an image of Jina. At one time K.P. Jayaswal[37] had suggested that the Kaliṅga *Jina* was the statue or foot-marks of the First *Jina* Ṛṣabha. Later on, however, he proposed the view that it was 'the image (saṁnivesaṃ), known as the *Jina* of Kaliṅga'[38]. Elsewhere it has been pointed out that "images preceded footprints in the history of Jaina worship", and that the 'Jainas worshipped or honoured the remains of their prophets and raised monuments on the relics which they called *Nishidi* (resting place)[39]. In this connection it may be noted that the more appropriate term would be *Kaliṅgajinaṁ sannivesam* - evidently an image of the *Jina* of Kaliṅga. This image of the Kaliṅga *Jina* must have been a most attractive and life-like image, the very look of which must have highly desired, and for that it had been taken away by the Nanda king[40].

The Kaliṅga-*Jina* must have been a sacred object associated with the people of the land much deeply. Therefore Khāravela had to wage military expedition twice against Magadha to recover the same.

In this context it is to be noted that after having defeated the Magadhan king, Khāravela did not think of including that region with Kaliṅga, instead he simply returned back to Kaliṅga with that coveted image of the Kaliṅga-*Jina*, and of course, with some riches, suggesting thereby that the sole intention of Khāravela's military campaign against Magadha was to recover the lost glory of Kaliṅga – the image of the *Jina*.

The inscription does not record the name of any *Tīrthaṅkara*, instead it records only the *Jina* of Kaliṅga. In this context it has been observed that it was a practice to designate a particular Jaina *Tīrthaṅkara* image after the name of the locality, where the iamge had been set up[41]. Thus for instance, the first *Tīrthaṅkara* at Satrunjaya is called 'the Satrunjaya-*Jina*' ; the image at Abu is called 'the Arbuda- *Jina*' ; the *Jina* at Dhulew (Mewar) is called 'the Dhulew-*Jina*'[42]. Hence the *Jina* in Kaliṅga was called the Kaliṅga-*Jina*.

Many theories have been put forward with regard to the identification of the Kaliṅga-*Jina*. One scholar has identified the *Jina* to be Śitalanātha, the tenth *Tīrthaṅkara*[43]. This supposition is advanced following a tradition which avers that Śitalanātha was born at Bhādalpur[44], the same place as Bhadrapuram or Bhadrachalam in the Godavari district of Andhra Pradesh, which was included in the ancient Kaliṅga country. This view is also endorsed by other scholars[45]. Another scholar has preferred to identify the Kaliṅga-*Jina* with Mahāvīra, the twenty-fourth and the last *Tīrthaṅkara* on the basis that Mahāvīra had been widely worshipped in the north-eastern *Janapadas*[46]. Some other scholars yet think that the Kaliṅga *Jina* was Ṛṣabhanātha, the first *Tīrthaṅkara*[47]. In favour of this contention attention is drawn to the Culla-Kaliṅga-Jātaka where the god of Kaliṅga had been represented by a white bull, which is incidentally the cognisance of Ṛṣabhanātha[48].

The above attempts to identify the Kaliṅga-*Jina* seem to have not been backed by any definite and categorical evidences. A scrutiny of both the traditional and archaeological sources helps us to identify the Kaliṅga-*Jina* with a far greater degree of certainty. According to the Jaina traditions three *Tīrthaṅkaras*, viz., Aranātha, the eighteenth; Pārśvanātha, the twenty-third and Mahāvīra, the twenty-fourth are said to have paid their visit to Kaliṅga[49]. In this connection it seems reasonable to deduce that any one of these *Tīrthaṅkaras* would have been the *Jina* of Kaliṅga described in the Hāthīgumphā record. As far as Aranātha is concerned no sculptural remains are extant, and thereby suggesting a less popular position amongst the Jainas of Kaliṅga. On the other hand the images of Pārśvanātha and Mahāvīra had been found more or less in equal numbers from different parts of Orissa[50]. In this context it is interesting to note that the tradition relating to Pārśvanātha and *Vardhamāna* Mahāvīra along with that of Ṛṣabhanātha and Neminātha was specially glorified in the *Kalpasūtra* of the fourth century B.C. More importantly the rock-out caves in the Udayagiri and Khaṇḍagiri hills (near Bhubaneswar in the district of Puri, Orissa); one of the earliest examples of the Jaina art clearly exhibit the prominence of Pārśvanātha, the twenty-third *Tīrthaṅkara*[52]. Hence the *Jina* of Kaliṅga might well have been Pārśvanātha, whose image was being worshipped in Kaliṅga during the Nanda attack against the land in the second half of the fourth century B.C.

Furthermore the prevalence of image worship in Kaliṅga during the age of the Nandas is attested to in the Hāthīguṁphā inscription. The practice of image worship in Kaliṅga during the age of the Nandas, in turn, speaks of the popularity of Jainism in this region even before that age.

According to the Jaina legends[53] the practice of image worship in Jainism is as old as the religion itself. Elsewhere it has been pointed out that like the Buddhists, the Jainas also worship their prophets like gods and erect statues in their temples[54]. Archaeological evidences relating to the temples of Jaina images have been discovered at Mathura, which prove its existence as early as B.C. 600[55]. The prevalence of image worship during the sixth century B.C. has also been referred to in the *Aṣṭādhyāyī*[56]. The practice of image worship is further alluded to in the *Arthaśāstra*[57]. In this connection it may be pointed out that amongst the earliest round-figure-sculptures belonging to the Mauryan period, one naked torso of a Jaina *Tīrthaṅkara*[58] has been found from Lohanipur near Patna in Bihar.

Thus, the practice of image worship among the followers of the Jaina religion seems to have been quite old, though it is difficult to trace the exact period as to when it started. The Hāthīgumphā inscription, however, evidently suggests its prevalence at least in the age of the Nandas.

The line fourteen of the inscription further states explicitly the support and patronage that had been accorded to the Jaina *Arahats* by the Cedi king :

> *Terasame ca vase supavata vijaya cake Kumārīpavate arahato*[59] *parinivasatahi*[60] *Kāyanīsidiyāya yāpa-ñāvakehi*[61] *Rājabhātihi*[62] *Cinavatāni*[63] *vasāsitāni*[64] *pūjānurata*[65] *uvāṣaga*[66] *Khāravela siriṇā jīvadehasayika*[67] *parikhātā*[68]/

Many interesting details can be gleaned from this particular line which unmistakably speak that Khāravela was a Jaina follower. After the period of his military campaigns, Khāravela, it is recorded, caused to have evolved the wheel of victory in the *Kumārī Parvata*, in his thirteenth regnal year. This act refers to the fact that the Jaina religion was preached and promulgated in this hill. After this, he is further said to have carried out various religious activities for the Jaina monks. In the record Khāravela is called *upāsaka* (a devout worshipper) of the Jaina monks who were wearing fine cloths, and carried out excavations for them[69] along with brothers as a part of his victory celebrations. These excavations were dedicated to the Jaina monks to be used as residence during the period of the rainy season. Near the *Kumārī parvata* (Udayagiri) he had also dedicated some excavations to the Jaina monks for the purpose of crimatorium. In this context it may be noted that at the top of the Khaṇḍagiri hill remnants of pillars have been found which were interpreted to have been commemorative ones in memory of Jaina monks who died at this place[70]. On the other hand for the expression of *jīvadehasayikā* some scholars[71] have suggested that after finishing the layman's vow Khāravela realised (experienced) the distinction between *jīva* (soul) and *deha* (matter), two vital principles of the Jaina philosophy. But nowhere in the Hāthīgumphā inscription Khāravela is said to have taken a layman's vow. Besides, in his career of war and plunders it was hardly practicable on his part to realise the Jaina philosophy. On the other hand it seems possible that only after the period of his campaigns and particularly after the recovery of the *Jina* of Kalinga, Khāravela had realised the Jaina philosophy.

Furthermore, this line provides certain informations regarding some Jaina sects residing in the Kaliṅga country. The term *Yāpa-ñāvakehi* may well stands for *Yāpanīyaka*, who were recognised as belonging to a sect of Jaina religious system. In this context, the explanations given in the *Nītisāra*[72] where five different sects of the Jainas have been referred to along with the *Yāpanīyakas*; may be noted.

The line fifteen of the record which offers some other grounds as to the inclination of Khāravela towards the Jaina religion is worth-noting :

> .... *sakata*[73] *samaṇa suvihitānaṁ ca savadiśānaṁ*[74] *yatinaṁ*[75] *tapasaṁ*[76] *issinaṁ*[77] *leṇaṁ Kārāpayati*[78] *Arahata nisidiyā samipe pābhāge*[79] *varākāra samuthāpitāhi aneka yojanāhitāhi panatisāhi*[80] *satasahasāhi*[81] *silāhi silathambhāni*[82] *ca cetiyāṁ*[83] *kārāpayati*[84]/

Thus it is gathered that near the dwelling-cells of the Jaina *Arahats*, Khāravela had carried out further excavations for the *Śramaṇas* and *Yatis* (Jaina monks), *Tapasas* and *Ṛṣis*. He had also caused to erect some *śilāsthambhas* (possibly commemorative pillars) for the Jaina monks, and also a *Caitya* hall[85], collecting valuable stones from far off places at the cost of 35,00,000 coins. The erection of the *Caitya* shrine further suggests that possibly he had been carrying out regular philosophical discourses with other religious sects for better understanding of his own faith - Jainism.

Besides Khāravela, his chief queen is also recorded to have donated caves to the Jaina monks. In this connection the Svargapurī cave inscription[86] which is found inscribed on the raised space between the second and third doorways in front is note-worthy :

> *Arahaṁta-pasādāya Kaliṅgānam samanānaṁ lenaṁ kāritaṁ Rājino Lalākasa /*
> *Hathisihasa papotasa dhutunāyā Kaliṅga-cakavatino Siri Khāravelasa /*
> *agamahisiya kāritaṁ /*[87]

Thus, to satisfy the *Arhats* of Kaliṅga, the chief queen, who was the daughter of Lalāka, the great-grandson of Hatisiṁha, caused to excavate temple for the *Arhats* and cave for the *Śramaṇas*. In this context the remarks of some scholars is quite interesting to note. It is observed that in the noble task of serving the Jaina religion Khāravela always associated himself with his chief queen[88], whose name unfortunately has not been recorded in the inscription.

IV

Jainism on the Wane

The period of the Cedi king Khāravela marked the glorious phase of the history of Jainism in ancient Orissa. During this period Jainism had gained the royal status and surpassed in its glory all the other phases in the history of Jainism in this land. But the succeeding period witnessed a conspicuous decadence of Jainism in Orissa, although scholars still hesitate to make out any positive reason or reasons behind the prevalence of Jainism in its low ebb. Evidences at our disposal are not sufficient enough to reconstruct the history of this faith in Orissa properly; but an idea of the existence of this religious system in Orissa can be formed with the help of antiquities and textual references of the later periods.

It is needless to say that after the downfall of the Mahāmeghavāhanas (the dynasty to which the Cedi king Khāravela belonged), Jainism did not seem to have enjoyed royal patronage in the early centuries of the Christian era. "Yet the religion continued to flourish, as it was greatly popular among the mass who kept the fire of the faith ablaze. The political changes through which the country passed hardly affected the faith for many centuries"[1]. In fact, there are several occasions where political changes played a vital role in transforming the course of a particular faith. It might be a fact that even if a religious belief spreads amongst the mass in general, it cannot flourish successfully unless and until it enjoys active patronage from the royal house.

Regarding the prevalence of Jainism in this period it has been reported that in the town of present-day Aska, situated some twenty-five miles to the north of the city of Brahmapur in the Ganjam district, there exists a very old temple known as Tribidheśvara. In the *garbha-gṛha* there is one circular stone bearing three signs which serves the purpose of a deity. In front of the main temple, the *Jagamohana* (the immediate adjunct of the main temple) contains an image of *Vṛṣabha* carved out of stone. On the second adjunct of the main temple there is an inscription found engraved on one of the black quadrangular stone slab. On the basis of all these, and further by making reference to the Jaina *triratna*, it is suggested that it was a Jaina temple belonging to the time of Khāravela[2]. The bull in the *Jagamohana* has been identified with the mount of Ṛṣabhadeva (Ṛṣabhanātha), the first jaina *Tīrthaṅkara*.[3] Further, in this context, after citing a legend it is stated by the same scholar that perhaps the Jaina *Ṛṣis* used to offer *pūjā* to the deity[4]. Unfortunately, by the time it is reported the temple was in a dilapidated condition, and had been converted to a Hindu temple in the name of *Vicitra*-Tribidheśvara.

Following the above observations it may be mentioned that the southern part of Orissa thus witnessed some activities by the Jaina followers probably in the early centuries of our era. In this connection it is interesting to note that during this period the Kols and the Kandhas of the southern part of Orissa had been believing in the fact that they had defeated and drove away the earlier population of the region called as Jainas and Bhūyāns. It has been suggested that the Kadambas[5] who had considerable influence over this part of Kaliṅga were the Jaina followers who subsequently went down to the Kols and the Kandhas. The capital of the Kadambas was Palāsikā corresponding to the present day Palasa in the district of Ganjam. Subsequently, the Kadambas were succeeded by the early Gaṅgas of Kaliṅganagar during the last quarter of the fifth century A.D.[6] In the late period of their history the Kadambas had been ruling as subordinate to the early Gaṅgas from Jayantipura, identified with the village of the same name in the Ganjam district[7]. Quoting the family titles of the Kadambas such as : Candra, Māñcī, Bhogī, Pilāka, Deva and Pāka, it is suggested that they were the followers of Jainism who originally hailed from south India.[8]

The early Gaṅgas before coming to occupy Kaliṅganagara were worshippers of the image of Jaina *Tīrthaṅkara* in the remote hill tract of Phulbani district. Some Jaina sculptures bearing the Gupta style of the fourth century A.D. have been discovered from Phulbani[9], thus attesting to the above suggestion. One of these sculptures now housed in the Orissa state museum at Bhubaneswar, has been identified with Pārśvanātha[10]. These evidences may be cited as corroborative of the popularity of Jainism in the remote hill tract of the district of Phulbani.

A gold coin belonging to the third century A.D., which clearly imitates the coin type of Vāsudeva I (Kuṣāṇa dynasty) on the obverse, and bearing a Roman head on the reverse with a legend *Maharaja rajadhasa Dhamadamadharasa*, has been found during the excavation at Śiśupālagarh[11] situated in the south-eastern part of Bhubaneswar. On the basis of this coin it has been contended that the king Dharma Dāmadhara was a Jaina follower belonging to the Muruṇḍa family which was ruling a portion of Bihar and also of Orissa[12]. The discovery of a single coin, however, does not conclusively prove any Muruṇḍa occupation over parts of Orissa as suggested by some scholars[13]. This problem in general and problem of their homeland, in particular has generated a lot of controversy[14]. In the present context, leaving aside the controversy, it may be suggested that the king Dharma Dāmadhara who was a subordinate to the parent Muruṇḍa lineage had a considerable sway over Kaliṅga and subsequently issued coins of his own. The issue of such coins otherwise called Puri-Kuṣāṇa coins by subordinate rulers seems numerous[15]. Further it may be suggested that since the rulers of the main Muruṇḍa lineage were followers of Jainism[16], the Muruṇḍa king ruling in Orissa might have been a Jaina follower[17].

The spread of Jainism in parts of northern Orissa, during the early centuries of the Christian era is attested by a stone inscription discovered from the village Asanpat in Keonjhar district[18]. This inscription provides us with some important information regarding the state of Jainism in this region. It refers to one *Mahārāja* Śatrubhañja of the Nāga dynasty, the king of Vindhyavati who defeated the *Devaputras* in many battles. The *Mahārāja* is said to have donated wealth to various *maṭhas*, to *Bhikṣus, Carakas, Parivṛājakas*, and *Nirgranthas*. This liberal act shows his catholic approach to Buddhist *Bhikṣus* as well as Jaina *Nirgranthas*, though he was a Śaivite by faith. Thus the followers of the Jaina religion must have been inhabiting this region in large numbers so that they had been referred to in the record of a *Mahārāja*. This fact is further strengthened by the discovery of a considerable number of Jaina images and relics from this part of the land. An ancient Jaina temple at the Bāulā mountain range is still to be found in the district of Keonjhar. Besides, a large number of Jaina relics and monuments are scattered all over the district even today[19].

The Jaina lexicon *Abhidhāna Rājendra*[20] refers to a *Ṛṣi-taḍāga* (holy pond) in Selapur under Toṣali *Viṣaya*, where a Jaina festival was conducted every year for a period of eight days. The same text further says that the inhabitants of Anandapura (in Keonjhar district) had also been observing the same festival for a period of eight days on the bank of Prācinavāhanadī which joined with Saraśvatī[21]. Some scholars[22] have identified the river Prācinavāha with that of Vaitaraṇī, and Saraśvatī with river Brāhmaṇī, which seems to be accurate for the present day Anandapur town is situated on the bank of river Vaitaraṇī.

From the first quarter of the fourth century A.D. to the first quarter of the sixth century A.D., the Māṭhara dynasty had held its sway over the southern part of Kaliṅga. Two rulers of this dynasty, viz., Umāvarman[23] and Nandaprabhañjana Varman[24] issued their grants from the victorious Vardhamānapura, identified with the town at the foot of the Mahendra mountain[25]. The naming of the headquarter of the royal house as Vardhamānapura apparently in honour of Vardhamāna Mahāvīra is interesting. In this connection it may be noted that the region which was ruled by the Kadambas, the Jaina followers,was subsequently dominated by the Māṭharas. Thus it might be a fact that at least these two rulers of the Māṭhara dynasty had developed a leaning towards the Jaina faith.

V

Resurrection of Jainism

From the first half of the seventh century A.D., Jainism seemed to have regained gradually its lost glory. Both archaeological and literary sources including the foreign accounts suggest that Jainism enjoyed quite a significant position during the seventh century A.D, The paucity of materials during the early centuries of the Christian era has been one of the major hindrances for the study of Jainism during those centuries. Simultaneously the political factors also played their role to worsen the above problem. During the early centuries of our era, Orissa was disintegrated into various petty kingdoms having no interaction in the field of politics, society, religion, art, etc. But the situation gradually improved with respect to the later periods, and particularly from the seventh century A.D. we are in a better position to reconstruct the general history of this region as well as that of Jainism in ancient Orissa.

By this time the early Gaṅgas had made their inroads into the heart of the Kaliṅga country and made Kaliṅganagara[1] their capital. According to their family traditions, they were advised by a Jaina monk named Simhanandi to establish two kingdoms; one at Kaliṅga and the other at Gaṅgavāḍi in ancient Mysore state; and so Daddiga proceeded to Mysore, while Mādhava settled in Kaliṅga[2] to establish his kingdom. Both the kings accepted the Jaina faith as their religion and adopted elephant[3] as the sacred emblem. Subsequently, however, the early Gaṅgas of Kaliṅganagara adopted Śaivism as their faith. Yet the early Gaṅga king Devendravarmana had the elephant emblem in his Bangalore copper plate instead of bull which is usually found in all the copper plates of the Gaṅgas of Kaliṅga[4]. We are not sure under what circumstances the Gaṅgas of Kaliṅga changed their faith, but at the same time it can be said without any doubt that the early rulers of this dynasty had professed Jainism. This fact has been further corroborated by the discovery of some Jaina sculptures from Phulbani[5]. These images had evidently been worshipped by the early Gaṅgas before they eventually occupied the heart of the Kaliṅga kingdom.

In the accounts of Hiuen-Tsang, the Chinese pilgrim, who visited Orissa in about A.D. 639, we get some interesting information regarding the position of Jainism in ancient Orissa. In Koṅgoda, comprised of the present day Puri and Ganjam districts roughly, which was one of the major *janapadas* of ancient Orissa, the Chinese pilgrim saw *Deva* temples numbering more than one hundred, and the *Tīrthikas* of about ten thousands in number[6]. Obviously then the region of Koṅgoda was a stronghold of Jainism during the first half of the seventh century A.D. Elsewhere, it is noticed that with very many unbelievers of different sorts, numerous *Nirgranthas* were residing in Kaliṅga country[7]. Thus the reference to the Jaina followers in the foreign accounts both in Kaliṅga and Koṅgoda speak not only of the popularity of the faith, but also of their vast numbers amongst the non-brahmanical followers. In this connection it may be noted that the two dynasties who ruled in Orissa during this period, viz., the early Gaṅgas and the Śailodbhavas[8] were the followers of Brahmanical religion. Thus, though Jainism did not enjoy the royal support, this faith was not disfavoured by the royal house either; instead, their relatively high proportion amongst the co-religious groups is well indicated in the contemporary records.

The Bāṇapur copper plate grant of Dharmarāja[9] (c. 695 A.D. - 730 A.D.) of the Śailodbhava dynasty, makes some important and interesting revelations, thereby helping to trace the history of Jainism. Śrī Kalyāṇadevī, the queen of Dharmarājadeva is the donor of this grant. In the charter the names of the two donees, viz., *Darhadācārya* Nāsicandra and his disciple *Ekaśāṭa* Prabuddhacandra are mentioned. The grants were made at the villages of Rāṇḍa, Suvarṇaraloṇḍi, and Madhuvāṭaka falling within the Thoraṇa *viṣaya*, which forms a part of Koṅgoda. From the expression[10] in line 44(a) it is gathered that to meet the expenses of the ceremonial worship of an image, possibly of a goddess, the grant was made. In the same line[11] of the grant it is noticed that *Ācārya* Nāsicandra who was an *Arhat* and his pupil Prabuddhacandra have been described to wear only a piece of cloth[12]. On this point some scholars[13] have suggested that the Digambara sect of Jainism was prevalent in Orissa. However, the practice of wearing one piece of cloth shows that they were Śvetāmbara group of monks. To make the point more clear we have to take into consideration the implication of the term *Arhat*. Here it should be noted that though the term *Arhat* denotes both to the Jaina and Buddhist monks, in this context we see no objection in applying the term to the Jaina monks[14]. In the *Bṛhatsaṁhitā*[15], the god of the *Arhats* has been described as *Digvāsaḥ*. Thus *Arhat* signifies Jaina saints who move naked. To substantiate the contention we may take into consideration a number of Jaina bronze images discovered from Achutrajpur which is located near the find spot of the present inscription. This place became a prominent Jaina centre from the eighth to the eleventh centuries A.D. and a number of Jaina images such as those of Ṛṣabhanātha, Candraprabha, Vāsupūjya and Āmrā have been found from this place.[16]

At about the same period, in the far south of the present-day Orissa a stone inscription has been found on the outer wall of a temple, which stands on the top of a hill near the villages of Padmapur and Jagadamba in the Gunupur sub-division of Koraput district. At the fort of the hill there are some small caves. The inscription bears the name of Dharmakīrtti, who is said to have defeated Kumārila Bhaṭṭa[17] in philosophical discourses, and further, entering into controversies with the Jainas, tried his best to propagate Buddhism in Kaliṅga[18]. Hence it can be argued that during this period the followers of the Jaina religion were numerous, and possibly there had been some close competition among the then prevailing sects for supremacy. In this connection if we refer back to Hiuen-Tsang's account mentioned earlier, the situation would become more clear. Thus the entire Koṅgoda region along with its adjoining areas in the Koraput district witnessed the activities of the Jaina followers, who were seemed to be quite large in number.

Yet another epigraphical record provides some interesting details with regard to the popularity of Jainism in and around the region of Kaliṅganagara, the capital city of the early Gaṅgas. The record in question is the Andhavarmam plates of Indravarman[19], discovered near the village of Andhavarmam on the left bank of the Vaśundharā river in Srikakulam district, Andhra Pradesh. The plates had been issued from Kaliṅganagara in the Gaṅga era 133, corresponding to A.D. 789/790 [20]. The expression in line 19 reads as follows :

Tumvuru Vaṁśa Rājya samvatsarāṇā

The term 'Tumvuru' denotes the disciple of the fifth Jaina *Guru*[21]. The king Indravarman, who issued this record, and is said to be belonging to the Tumvuru family might have been an ardent follower of the Jaina religion. It is in fact interesting to note that this is the only record where a Tumvuru-era has been mentioned. As such it has rightly been concluded[22] that it is not possible to identify this era. On the other hand it is probable that the said record refers to the existence of a Jaina community, which necessitated the introduction of Jaina hierarchial order amongst them.

During the early medieval period, Jaina sculptures and monuments have been found in large number in various parts of Orissa, which in its own term speak of the popularity and wide prevalence of the Jaina faith in this land. We shall now turn our attention to these evidences.

The village Podasingi, about 15 km. away from Anandapur in Keonjhar district has yielded a number of figures of Jaina *Tīrthaṅkaras, Yakṣas, Yakṣiṇī* etc. Some of the sculptures are found buried, a few others are damaged. From this place a large image of Mahāvīra has been found. This site has been surrounded by the Bāulā-hill-range on one side while on the other side remnants of a damaged wall is traced. From Podasingi the earliest inscribed Jaina image[23] has been found. This image depicted in a meditative pose is seated on a lotus pedestal with a bull below. A short inscription in two lines is engraved near the right hand of the image which says that the Ṛṣabha-bhaṭṭāraka image was donated by one Iḍhaka (?)[24]. The various Jaina figures found here exhibit the characteristic features of the sculptural idiom of the post-Gupta period, and can therefore be assigned to the seventh-eighth century A.D., and certainly not the Gupta tradition as has been supposed by some scholars[25]. At present most of the sculptures have been preserved on cement platform in front of the Pañca-Bhavana in Anandapur. Out of the findings the image of Ṛṣābhanāth is prominent suggesting that the worship of Ṛṣabha-cult was popular in this area. Besides the image of Ṛṣabhanātha, Pārśvanātha, Mahāvīra, Ambikā Śāsanadevī of Neminātha are also found from this Jaina centre.

The village Kosali situated some twenty-nine km south-east of the present Baripada town in Mayurbhanj district, revealed the existence of an entire foundation and a portion of the ground floor of an ancient Jaina temple. The relic suggests that the temple had two adjuncts, viz., *garbhagṛha* and a *Jagamohana* facing the north. Among the findings the image of Pārśvanātha[26] (See Plate)which stands on a serpent and with a serpent hood, is most interesting.

During the time of the early Bhañja kings, Khijiṅga-Koṭṭa, identified with modern Khiching[27] in the Mayurbhanj district, situated fifty-two km. north of present Keonjhar town, was a famous Jaina centre. Several images of Ṛṣabhanātha, (See Plate) Pārśvanātha and Mahāvīra, all are in *Kāyotsarga* pose, which have been discovered from this area, are housed in the Khiching museum.

Baripada, the district headquarters of Mayurbhanj district, has yielded a number of *Jina* images. Among the images found from Baripada those of Ṛṣabhanātha, Nemināthа, Pārśvanātha, and Mahāvīra, are most important. At present many images have been set against the wall of the inside gate of the present Jagannātha temple. A fine sitting image of Pārśvanātha (See Plate) is noteworthy.

Badasahi, a big village situated nearly twenty-seven km south-east of the Baripada town, has also yielded a number of Jaina images.

Ranibandha, a village situated at a distance of nearly five km to the west of Badasahi, has yielded an image of Mahāvīra. The religious offerings to the image was being performed by the *Dehuries*. It is suggested that formerly the *Sarākas*, identified with *Śrāvakas* used to come to this village to perform *pūjā* (offerings) to the image[28]. In this context it is interesting to note that one *Sarāka* tribe had been living in the Singbhum district in Bihar. Scholars have suggested that in the later stage of their existence the *Sarākas* of Mayurbhanj had accepted Buddhism as their faith[29]. Others, on the other hand, have believed them to be Jaina followers[30]. Further, it is to be noted that at various Jaina centres in the district of Mayurbhanj there existed *Sarāka* ponds believed to have been dug by the *Sarāka* tribe.

During the early medieval period Charmpa, situated some three km to the north of Bhadrak town in Balasore district, was a flourishing centre for Jainism. So many images pertaining to Jaina religion have been discovered from this village. Out of these images those of Ṛṣabhanātha, Ajitanātha, and Śāntinātha[31] are stylistically developed images, and are housed at present in the state museum at Bhubaneswar.

The above remains have been assigned to the seventh century A.D.[32], while some others have placed them to the ninth-tenth century A.D.[33]. Yet another scholar assigned them to the tenth-eleventh century A.D.[34]

Another area of Jaina importance is the Pundala village situated some eighteen km to the north-west of the Balasore town. Here a beautiful image of Pārśvanātha has been recovered from the adjacent Sona river bed. It is believed that the Jaina priests had thrown this image into the river to protect it from the onslaught of the iconoclasts[35]. The image stands on a *Padma-pīṭha* in the *Kāyotsarga* posture (See Plate)[36], and is known as 'Ananta' to the local people.

Many stone images of Mahāvīra[37] have also been found in the village Bhimapur situated at a distance of thirteen km to the south-east of the Balasore town. Among all those images, the image of Mahāvīra (See Plate)[38] is a beautiful one. At present a number of small images of Mahāvīra are being worshipped under the trees, which further shows that the worship of the Mahāvīra cult was popular here.

It has been reported[39] that Pāṇḍavaghāṭa, an ancient place on the sea-shore, four km away from Bhimapur, had been frequently visited by the Jaina merchants to worship a big stone bearing foot-prints, which they believed to be those of *Jinas*. Owing to the proximity of this village to other Jaina centres it may be presumed that this was a Jaina centre in the ancient days, and the foot-print marks are the commemorative marks of the Jaina saints. It may be noted in this connection that the worship of foot-print of the Jaina saints are uncommon among the Jaina followers. We have enough evidence of *Viṣṇu-pada* and *Buddha-pada*, and we are also aware of the Śiva's foot-print (*Śiva-pada*)[40], but not of *Jina-pada*. This particular object makes us to believe that the worship of foot-print was also in practice among the Jainas.

Another site of Jaina importance was the area of Ayodhya, situated nearly eighteen km to the north-west of the Balasore town. From this village a standing image of Pārśvanātha has been found,[41] which has been assigned to a period later than the ninth century A.D.[42]

The region of Jaleswar some forty-nine km to the north of Balasore town has also yielded a number of images of Jaina faith belonging to the tenth century A.D. The images of Śāntinātha, a *caumukha*, and of Supārśvanātha, of this site, are at present housed in the Orissa state museum, Bhubaneswar.

Apart from the districts of Keonjhar and Mayurbhanj, some sites, important for the study of Jaina religion, in the district of Cuttack have also been identified. The village of Jhadesvara situated at a distance of about thirty-nine km to the north-east of the Cuttack city, is important in this connection. It has been reported[43] that some very important and valuable relics found here belong to the glorious period of Jainism. The images of *Tīrthaṅkaras* (See Plate)[44], Gaṇadharas, Pūrvadharas, Śrāvakas and *Śrāvikās* found at the site are of chlorite stone, and very beautiful and striking.

The ancient Virajā-*kṣetra*, on the bank of river Vaitaraṇī known as Jajpur in the district of Cuttack, was once a famous Jaina centre. Some of the images found from this region are at present kept in the premises of the Ākhaṇḍaleśvara temple; situated at the town of Jajpur. A well carved small image of a naked Jaina *Tīrthaṅkara* with a placid countenance was found on the temple wall itself. Besides Jajpur proper, in the adjoining villages such as Narasimhapura and Hatadiha the Jaina images are found.

In the Cuttack city proper, there are twenty-five Jaina images mostly of stone, housed in the Digambara Jaina *mandira* (temple), located at Chaudhury Bazar. The images are mostly of *Tīrthaṅkaras* such as Ṛṣabhanātha and Pārśvanātha. Apart from these *Tīrthaṅkara* images some panels bearing Jaina themes are also kept here. Scholars have assigned these images to the period of twelfth century A.D. or even later[45].

From the bed of the Kāṭhajoḍi river, a tributary of the river Mahānadī, three *Tīrthaṅkara* images, one of Pārśvanātha, and two of Ṛṣabhanātha, were found. One of them is missing, while the other two are now under the custody of a local monk at Pratapnagar, situated some ten km from Cuttack.

Apart from the above - mentioned places where Jaina images are found in the district of Cuttack, some other regions such as Chaudwar,

Chatia, Candola, Udayagiri and Ratnagiri, also yielded some *Tīrthaṅkara* images.

A number of Jaina images have been found from the Prāchī-valley area, which speak the popularity of the Jaina faith in this region. This region, consisting the border area of the present districts of Cuttack and Puri in the Mahānadī delta, through which the river Devī, a tributary of Mahānadī, and river Prāchī, which was also originally a tributary of Mahānadī; flow into the Bay of Bengal.

This region has yielded architectural and sculptural remains belonging to Brahmanism, Buddhism and Jainism, which range from the period of seventh century A.D. to eleventh century A.D. It was one of the most flourishing and famous centres of Jainism. Various images of *Tīrthaṅkaras*, *Yakṣas*, and *Yakṣiṇīs* are found in different places of this valley.

At the village of Adasapur in this valley region, a beautiful image of Ṛṣabhanātha (measuring 21" × 11") has been found and kept inside the ruined Swapneśwar (Śiva) temple.[46] While describing the above image it has been argued that Ādinātha was the temple cult of the region, and a temple might have existed in the vicinity of the Swapaneśwar temple, where the image of Ādinātha (Ṛṣabhanātha) was housed. Since ancient relics and images found from this valley are in plenty, the above suggestion has been made; but it cannot be definitely ascertained unless fresh evidences are found.

Another image found in the same village is without its lower portion. However, the *prabhā* resembles that of the earlier image which is referred to above. This image has been identified with that of Mahāvīra[47]. It has been further argued that the practice of worshipping both the images jointly was prevalent in ancient Orissa. For this the relief in the Jaina temple at Cuttack has been cited as an example[48]. The Victoria Albert Museum, London, also preserves one such stele which has been collected from Orissa.[49]

A miniature Ṛṣabhanātha image is noticed in the Viśvāmitra *Āśrama* near Kākaṭpur village, while a similar type of a small damaged image was found lying near the Bharadvāja *Āśrama*. Another beautiful image of Pārśvanātha is found inside the temple of Gramesvara in this valley area about five km from Nayahata.

Besides these images, a number of images are also found from various sites of this valley. *Yakṣa* and *Yakṣiṇī* figures are also found in several sites of this valley. An image of *Yakṣa* associated with Neminātha, is kept in the Antarvedi *Maṭha* situated near Banamalipur, the confluence spot of three rivers namely Prāchī, Sarasvatī, and Maṇikarṇikā. All these evidences unmistakably suggest that the Prāchī valley was a famous centre for the activities of the Jaina followers in the early medieval period.

Koraput, the southern most district of Orissa, has also been once influenced by the Jaina religion. A village named Bhairavasinghpur in the Jeypur region was a great centre for the activities of the Jainas. A number of Jaina images, of varying heights from one foot to five feet have been found from this village. An image of Ṛṣabhanātha has been found lying in a precarious condition in the village area. A Śiva temple in this village also contains a number of Jaina images on the interior wall. Another village in this district, Nandapur has yielded a Jaina image.[50]

Besides the stray sculptures, some Jaina shrines have also been found in the district of Koraput. One such Jaina shrine is located at the village Subei. Near this village a Jaina monument is traced in the midst of the scrub forest. Within an oval enclosure having a low wall all around is a series of some ten small shrines. The entire complex has been seriously damaged, and only two of them are still standing. It has been argued that these monuments belong to the earliest phase of temple building in Orissa[51]. However, because of the delapilated condition of the monuments, it is difficult to ascertain the date of this group of monuments.

The reign of Udyotakeśarī[52] of the Somavaṁśī dynasty, who ruled Orissa between C. 1040 A.D. - 1065 A.D., marks an interesting period in the history of Jainism in Orissa. During his reign building activities started once again at Khaṇḍagiri for the Jaina followers of the land, and the glory of Khaṇḍagiri-Udayagiri was revived. The Lalāṭendukeśarī, Navamuni caves bearing inscriptions, and the Bārabhujī cave are the latest group of caves excavated on Khaṇḍagiri. It is generally believed that all these caves had been excavated during the reign of Udyotakeśarī. However, the inscription does not provide any proof to the effect that the caves were excavated during his reign. On the other hand, there is reason to believe that these caves were renovated by him to serve the purpose of sanctuaries.

Udyotakeśarī though an ardent follower of Brahmanical religion was catholic enough to patronise Jainism, and also to protect the Jaina establishment at Udayagiri and Khaṇḍagiri. Further, in his fifth regnal year the king started the work of renovation of the decayed tanks and temples. On this hill cave he had also set up the images of twenty-four *Tīrthaṅkaras*. All these facts are clearly attested in the Lalāṭendu Keśarī cave inscription[53]. It is stated in the record that Udyotakeśarī donated the caves on the *Kumāra-parvata*[54] (Khaṇḍagiri) which were further reconditioned by him to the twenty-four *Tīrthaṅkaras*. In this cave a group of Jaina images of the Digambara sect numbering eight were also scooped out on the backwall. All the figures are nude and depicted in standing pose in the niches on the wall. Five of these figures first, third, fifth, sixth and eighth from the left - are crowned with seven hooded serpants, while the coil of the snakes are shown behind the figure sculptures.

Another epigraphical record[55] in stone found lying at the village Bhogapuram in Bhimalipatam taluk, in Visakhapatnam district, Andhra Pradesh, in the *Śaka* era 1100, corresponding to 1178 A.D., throws some valuable light on the history of Jainism. In line seven[56] of the inscription it is clear that the Jaina temple, Rājarāja-*jinālaya* was probably built under the patronage of king Rājarāja alias Devendravarman, a follower of Brahmanical religion, who ruled in the period A.D. 1070-1077[57]. Again, in line eighteen[58] of the same inscription we come across a reference to Ambikā, the *Yakṣiṇī* of Jaina *Tīrthaṅkara* Neminātha[59]. Further, in this connection it may be noted that a certain merchant named Kannama Nāyaka constructed a Jaina *maṭha* called Rājarāja-jinālaya at Bhogapur in Bhilipatam Taluk of Visakhapatnam district, in the eleventh regnal year of the eastern Gaṅga king Anantavarma, *Śaka* 1109. This event has been recorded in an inscription at Bhogapuram[60]. This Kannama Nāyaka, a devout worshipper of *Jina*, and a subordinate to the Utkala king, had installed the sacred image of *Jina* at Remaraniagiri (the modern Ramatirtham) in the *Rājarāja Jinālaya*, for which the merchants of Bhogapura have donated lands for the burning of a perpetual lamp[61].

In the light of these evidences one may assume that Jainism regained its lost glory in this region in the early medieval period.

VI

Date of Khāravela

Admitting the role of Khāravela in the spread and development of Jainism in India, especially in Orissa, it is a prerequisite to discuss critically about his date. The object is more critical and problematic because of the non-existence of any positive contemporary references relating to the date of Khāravela's accession to the throne or to his activities. To ascertain the period of the Cedi king various theories have been propounded by various scholars.

Without deciphering the name of Khāravela in the Hāthīgumphā inscription, it was once held that king Aira (apparently referring to Khāravela) flourished in the fourth century B.C.[1]

Some other scholars place Khāravela in the last quarter of the third century B.C. Taking the fifth regnal year of Khāravela as corresponding to the year 103 after the year which marks the end of the Nanda rule, it has been propounded that Khāravela's accession took place in the year 223 B.C [2].

Another group of scholars take first half of the second century B.C. as the period of Khāravela. It is held by these scholars that the Hāthīgumphā inscription was issued in the thirteenth regnal year of Khāravela corresponding to the 165th year of the Maurya era which began in 324 B.C., and hence the accession of Khāravela took place in the year 172 B.C.[3]. Others[4] have suggested the year 154 B.C. as the coronation year of Khāravela, advancing the calculation that the eleventh regnal year of the king coincided with the year 113 after Aśoka's Kaliṅga conquest in 256 B.C. . Yet another scholar apparently belonging to this group places the ascendancy of Khāravela to the beginning of the second century B.C.[5]

Some scholars place Khāravela in the last quarter of the second century B.C. According to one scholar Khāravela had ascended the throne of Kaliṅga in 103 B.C. [6] after taking the fact that the thirteenth regnal year of Khāravela corresponds to the 165th year of the Maurya era which starts from 225 B.C. , i.e., the date of Aśoka's conquest of Kaliṅga. Another scholar[7] has suggested that Khāravela had ascended to the throne in the second half of the second century B.C.

A host of scholars further suggest that Khāravela had flourished in the second half of the first century B.C.[8] These scholars do not accept the reading of the term *Muriya-kāle*[9] in line sixteen, which was the main source for the earlier scholars to locate Khāravela in second or third century B.C. Besides all these, another scholar has placed Khāravela in the first century A.D.[10]

The Hāthīgumphā inscription is the sole source of information to know about Khāravela. Therefore, it is necessary to weigh carefully all the internal and circumstantial evidences, which are available in the inscription and in the caves of Udayagiri and Khaṇḍagiri respectively for ascertaining the date of Khāravela. In line four of the inscription, Khāravela's association with Sātakaṁni has been referred to. Further, in line six, it is told that in his fifth regnal year Khāravela caused to dig the canal into the city, which was dug by the Nanda-*rāja* in the year either 103 or 300 years before the period of Khāravela. Again in line twelve it is recorded that after defeating Bahasatimita, the king of Magadha, Khāravela brought back the Kaliṅga-*jina* to Kaliṅga. Keeping these three points in view the date of Khāravela may be ascertained with a greater degree of certainty.

Thus, in his second regnal year Khāravela led his expedition daringly (*acitayitā*, in Sanskrit *acintayitvā*) towards the west against Sātakaṁni[11]. There is no doubt in the fact that this Sātakaṁni was the contemporary of Khāravela. Once the date and identification of Śātakarṇī are settled, it would be easy to ascertain the period of Khāravela. Śātakarṇī of the record apparently belongs to the Śātavāhana dynasty and can be identified with Śātakarṇī I, the third ruler of the dynasty, who is further identified with his name sake mentioned in the Nānāghāṭ inscription of Queen Nāganikā[12] and Śātakarṇī I of the *Purāṇas*[13]. The name Śātakarṇī also finds mention in a Sāñci epigraph apparently suggesting the same person of the Nānāghāṭ record. However, some scholars have tried to identify Śātakarṇī of Hāthīgumphā inscription with his name sake in the Sāñci epigraph, and differentiate between Śātakarṇī of both the Nānāghat and Sañci and records[14]. It has been satisfactorily shown that the foundation of the Śātavāhana dynasty was laid in the year 30 B.C.[15], and that Śātakarṇī I had started his reign in the year 12 B.C., which corresponds to the second regnal year of Khāravela. Thus it is gathered that Khāravela had ascended to the Kaliṅga throne in the year 14 B.C.[16].

In determining the age of Khāravela, the line six of the Hāthīgumphā record is crucial[17]. In this line it is clear that in his fifth regnal year Khāravela caused to dig a canal into the city, which was earlier dug out by a certain Naṁda-*rāja*[18] some *ti-vasa-sata* before the age of Khāravela. Hence both the identification of the Naṁda-*rāja*; and the meaning of the expression *ti-vasa-sata*, the latter indicating the time interval between the Naṁda-*rāja* and Khāravela, are significant for the present purpose.

K.P. Jayaswal[19] has identified the Naṁda-*rāja* of the record with Nandivardhan. E.J. Rapson[20] identifies the Naṁda-*rāja* with a local king of Kaliṅga "called Nanda who was reigning over Kaliṅga before its annexation by Aśoka". R.D. Banerji[21], on the other hand, has identified the Naṁda-*rāja* of the record with Mahāpadma Nanda and observes that "It would be more natural to suppose that a great conqueror, Mahāpadma Nanda, to whom the *Purāṇas* ascribe the subversion of all Kshatriya Kingdoms put an end to the Kshatriya monarchy in Orissa also". Yet, scholars like B.M. Barua[22] followed by K.C. Panigrahi[23] tried to identify the Naṁda-*rāja* with that of Aśoka Maurya.

Nandivardhan cannot be identified with the Naṁda-*rāja*, for neither he nor any other member of the royal family who belonged to the Śaiśunāga dynasty appear to have attacked Kaliṅga[24]. Similarly the second suggestion that Naṁda-*rāja* was a local ruler, does not stand its ground. Earlier[25] it has been shown that the *Jina* which was carried out after a conquest of Kaliṅga had to be recovered by Khāravela following his successful campaigns against Magadha.

The view that Aśoka Maurya was the Naṁda-*rāja* of the present record is unwarranted likewise. Although Aśoka had made his conquest over Kaliṅga, nowhere it has been mentioned that he had either taken away the *Jina* of Kaliṅga, or dug a canal into the capital city. Besides, Aśoka belonged to the Mauryan dynasty[26], and not to the Nanda dynasty to which Naṁda-*rāja* is said to have belonged in the inscription.

In this connection it is to be pointed out that the identification of the Naṁda-*rāja* with that of Mahāpadma Nanda, which has been suggested and supported by many scholars[27] seems to be more convincing. The Naṁda-*rāja* mentioned twice in the record belonged, no doubt, to the Nanda dynasty. Keeping this in view it should be noted here that according to the *Purāṇas*[28], of all the kings of the Nanda ruling house Mahāpadma Nanda was the only king who is credited as the destroyer of all the Ksatriya races including those of Kaliṅga[29]. In this connection it may be observed that no other Nanda king was recorded to have carried out any kind of welfare activities such as digging of canals. This kind of exercise may only be attributed to Mahāpadma Nanda who was a great and powerful ruler of those days.

The above identification, further, appears to have been substantiated by another internal evidence. The expression *ti-vasa-sata* in line six may be explained either as *trayodhika-varsa-śata* or *tri-guṇa-vasa- sata*. If the first reading is accepted, then the reign of Khāravela would coincide with the period of Aśoka, which cannot be accepted at the present state of our knowledge[30]. On the other hand, if the second reading is accepted, then, the Naṁda-*rāja* of the record could be identified with Mahāpadma Nanda[31]. Admittedly the extant evidences do not permit us to exactly fix the year in which Mahāpadma Nanda carried out his campaign against Kaliṅga. Yet, we may broadly assign it to the later half of the fourth country B.C.

While attempting to determine the age of Khāravela, some scholars, pointing out to a reference in line twelve[32] of the Hāthīgumphā inscription, have concluded that Khāravela had defeated Puṣyamitra who is referred to in the record as Bahasatimita[33]. This inference, however, does not stand scrutiny. Bahasatimita has been identified with his namesake mentioned in he Pabhosā inscription as the son of the sister of Āṣāḍhasena, and in the Morā inscription as the father of the queen of a Mathura king[34]. Others have traced that the above two records belonged to two different periods, and the person mentioned in them could not be one and the same person[35]. Bahasatimita has further been identified with Bahasatimita II[36]. In this connection it is to be noted that while *Divyāvadāna* distinguishes between the kings named Vṛhaspati and Puṣyamitra, and mentions Pāṭliputra as the residence of the latter; Khāravela's Magadhan rival was possibly called '*Rājagahanapa*' who was apparently residing in the city of Rājagṛha[37].

Bahasatimita may possibly be identified with his name sake either in the Pabhosā inscription, or in that of the Morā inscription. Further, his association with Magadha and the discovery of his coins from Kausambi[38] suggest his authority over Magadha, which was extended up to the Kausambi region. In the present state of our knowledge, Bahasatimita of our record may be identified with a ruler of the Mitra dynasty, and definitely not with Puṣyamitra.

Apart from the internal evidences just mentioned, some of the circumstantial evidences are also needed for the purpose.

On palaeographical considerations it has been suggested that the Hāthīgumphā inscription could be safely placed later than the Besnagar inscription of Heliodorus, which is assigned to the close of the second century B.C.[39], and the Nānāghāṭ inscription of queen Nāganikā which is assigned to the early quarter of the first century B.C.[40]

The relief panels on the facade of the Mañcapurī and Svargapurī caves (this is a double-storeyed cave : the lower one is called Mañcapurī and the upper Svargapuri)[41] which belong to the age of Khāravela[42] also provide some clues to determine the age of Khāravela. It has been pointed out by competent authorities that the execution of the sculptural friezes "displays a decided advance on the work of Bhārhut (second century B.C.)"[43].

It is, of course, admitted that the Hāthīgumphā inscription does not bear any date, and as a result, a sharp controversy regarding the date of Khāravela still continues. But the evidences at our disposal tend us to believe that the Cedi king established his hegemony at the second half of the first century B.C. over present day Orissa and extensive parts of Bengal and Andhra Pradesh.

References

1. *IA.*, XXX, p. 280; Dutta, N., *Early Buddhistic Monachism*, pp. 120 f.; *Modern Review*, (1929), Calcutta, p. 499; *JBORS.*, V, pp. 554-558
2. In its present form it is compiled in A.D. 454 during the reign of Dhurvasena, King of Gujrat - Law, B.C. - *Some Canonical Jaina sūtras*, p. 97. The text of *Kalpasūtra* is translated by H. Jacobi, in *SBE.*, XXII. Besides this, there is also another *Kalpasūtra* known as the *Old-Kalpasūtra* dealing with monastic rules, has edited by W. Schubring.
3. *Utt.* Su., II, 45, (trans.) Lalwani, K.C.
4. *History of Indian Philosophy*, I, p. 287
5. Majumdar, R.C., Pusalkar, A.D. and Majumdar, A.K., (eds.), History and Culture of the Indian People, II, *The Age of Imperial Unity*, p. 411
6. Shah, C.J., *Jainism in North India*, p. 2
7. *Abhidhānacintāmaṇi*, (Devādhidevakāṇḍa), Verses. 50-57
8. *SBE.*, XXII, pt. I, p. 274
9. *SBE.*, XLV, pt. II, p. 119, note - 3; p. 122, note - 3; *IA.*, II, p. 261
10. Schubring, W., *The Doctrines of the Jainas*, p. 29
11. *SBE.*, XXII, pt. I, p. 194
12. Situated in the Hazaribagh district of Bihar, it is a holy place for the Jainas. It is said to be visited by pilgrims from the remotest corner of India - Colebrooke, H.T. *et al.*, *Miscellaneous Essays*, II, p. 213. On the top of the hill there is at present a temple of Pārśvanātha.
13. SBE., XXII, pt. I, p. 275; Hemacandra's *Triṣaṣṭhī salāka*, parva, IX, V. 316
14. Stevenson, S., *The Heart of Jainism*, p. 49
15. *On the Indian sect of the Jainas*, p. 65

16. *SBE.*, XXII, pt. I, p. 274; also see *Samvāyaṅga*, pp.316, 65a, 101b, 103a, 104b
17. *Samvāyaṅga*, p. 13b. The commentary further holds that though the number of *gaṇadharas* is ten in some other texts, the last two *gaṇadharas* must have been short-lived - *Ibid.*, p. 14b
18. *SBE.*, XXII, pt. I, intro. pp. X-XI; pp. 189-191
19. Kuṇḍagrāma has been identified with Basukuṇḍa near Vaiśālī, and Vaiśālī with modern Basarh - *ASI.*, 1903-1904, p. 82; Dey, N.L., *The Geographical Dictionary of Ancient and Medieval India*, p. 107; Majumdar, R.C., and Pusalkar, A.D., (eds.), *op.cit.*, p. 413; Law, B.C., *Mahāvīra: His Life and Teachings*, p. 19
20. Shah, C.J., *op.cit.*, pp. 27-28; also cf. Stevenson, S., *op.cit.*, p. 8. Though the Jaina tradition places the birth of Mahāvīra in 599 B.C., scholars are not unanimous on the issue. Since Mahāvīra had lived seventy-two years, scholars argue upon the date of his decease to fix his date of birth. For the details see Shah, C.J., *op.cit.*, pp. 27-34; Jain, K.C., *Lord Mahāvīra and his Times*, pp. 74- 88. At the present state of our knowledge it is difficult to settle the issue with absolute certainty, and for our purpose we refer to the traditional account keeping in view that Mahāvīra was an elder contemporary of Gautama Buddha - cf., Nahar, P.C., and Ghosh, K.C., *An Epitome of Jainism*, intro. p. 8; Schubring, W., *op.cit.*, pp. 37-39
21. *SBE.*, XXII, pt. I, p. 191; also cf., Rapson, E.J., (ed.), *CHI.*, I, p. 140
22. *SBE.*, XXII, pt. I, intro. p. XLI
23. *Ibid.*, intro. p. XV and note-1
24. *Ibid.*, p. 269
25. *Ibid.*, p. 201, 'Kevala' corresponds to 'Bodhi' (enlightenment or supreme knowledge) of the Buddha.
26. *Ibid.*, intro. p. XV
27. *Ibid.*, p. 269
28. Majumdar, R.C., Pusalkar, A.D. and Majumdar A.K., (eds.), *op.cit.*, p. 415
29. *ERE.*, I, p. 265; also see, Rapson, E.J., *op.cit.*, p. 193

30. *Ibid.*

30. *The Commentary on the Dhammapada*, I, pp. 308-309; also cf. *Prakrit Text Series*, VII, p. 19

31. *SBE.*, XXII, pt. I, p. 73 and note-2

32. *Ibid.*, p. 201

33. *Dīgha Nikāya*, I, *Sāmaññaphala Sutta*, pp. 45-51; *Sutta Nipāta, Mahāvaggha*, 6, pp. 91-92

34. *SBB.*, III, pp. 165-166

35. The other heretical sects are mentioned as Muṇḍasāvakas, Paribhājakas, Magaṇḍikas, Tedaṇḍikas, Aviruddhakas, Devadhammikas, Piśāchillikas, Achelakas and Ekasāṭikas, etc. *SBE.*, II, pp. 220-222; also cf., *The Saṁyutta- Nikāya of the Sutta-Piṭaka*, pt. I, ch. II, 3 - *Tena Kho pana samayena satta ca jatila satta ca nigantha satta ca acela satta ca paribbajaka parulha-kaccha-nakha-loma kharividham adaya Bhagavato avidure atikkamanti* //

36. quoted by Jacobi, H. in *SBE.*, XXII, pt. I, p. 128, note-1

37. Jayatilleke, K.N., *Early Buddhist Theory of Knowledge*, p. 21

38. Shah, C.J., *op.cit.*, p. 6

39. *SBE.*, XIV, pt. II, intro. p. XX; also cf., Rapson, E.J., (ed.), *The Cambridge History of India*, I, p. 143

40. *Op.cit.*, p. 29

41. *SBE.*, XI, p. 106

42. *SBE.*, XLV, pt. II, p. 52 and note-2, pp. 73-75

43. *Dīgha Nikāya*, I, *Sāmaññaphala Sūtra*, pp. 50-51; *SBB.*, III, p. 166; *Bṛhat Saṁhitā*, Li, 21; *Abhidhānacintāmaṇi*, V. 76

44. *EI.*, II, pp. 272 f. Apparently the original form of the word *Nirgrantha – SBE.*, XLV, pt. II, intro. p. XIV, note-8

45. Buhler, J.G., *op. cit.*, p. 29; cf. Basham, A.L., *History and Doctrine of the Ājīvikas*, p. 17

46. *SBE.*, XXII, pt. I, intro. p. XXXIV

47. *Ibid.*, XXLV, pt. II, Intro., pp. XIV-XV

48. Schubring, W., *op. cit.*, p. 15; Colebrooke, *Miscellaneous Essays*, II, p. 276
49. *SBE.*, XLV, pt. II, intro. p. XXXIII
50. Kosambi, D.D., *An introduction to the Study of Indian History*, p. 129
51. *SBE.*, XLV, pt. II, intro. p. XXXIII-XXXIV
52. Schubring, W., *op.cit.*, p. 16
53. *IA.*, IX, p. 161
54. Shah, C.J., *op.cit.*, p. 7
55. *Nāyādhammakahāo*, pp. 139, 218; *Ṭhāṇaṅga*, p. 457b; *Bhagavai*, p. 455a; *Uttarādhyayana Sūtra*, 23.12
56. *Kalpa sūtra, Subodhika-Ṭīkā*, p. 8
57. *Bhagavai*, pp. 136 ff.; also cf. Motilal, B.K., *The Central Philosophy of Jainism* (*Anekāntavāda*), p. 3. According to some other traditions Pārśvanātha's four vows were of non-killing, non-lying, non-stealing and chastity; and that it was '*aparigraha*', added by Mahāvīra - Stevenson, S., *op.cit.*, p. 49
58. *Ācāraṅga sūtra, śrūtaskandha*, II, VV, 12-13
59. For Pārśvanātha's '*cāujjāma dharma*' see *supra* note 55, also cf., Schubring, W., *op.cit.*, p. 30
60. Shah, C.J., *op.cit.*, p. 9
61. *SBE.*, XXII, pt. I, intro. p. XLV, note-1
62. *SBE.*, XLV, pt. II, pp. 119-129
63. *Ibid.*, XXII, pt. I, intro. p. XXXII
64. *Ibid.*, intro. p. XXXII
65. Dasgupta, S.N., *A History of Indian Philosophy*, I, p. 210
66. *The Religions of India*, p. 202
67. Hopkins, E.W., *Religions of India*, pp. 280-283
68. *PIHC.*, (1938), p. 35; R.G. Basak in *J.N. Banerjea volume*, p. 44
69. *JBBRAS.*, 27, pt. II, pp. 181-182

70. *Ibid.*, p. 183
71. Basham, A.L., *op.cit.*, p. 4
72. *The Mahā Bodhi*, XVI, (1955), No. 6, p. 256
73. Basham, A.L. in the *Sources of Indian Tradition*, complied by Bery, T. *et al.*, p. 40
74. Shah, C.J., *op.cit.*, p. 17
75. *SBE.*, XLV, pt. II, p. 172

II

1. *Āvaśyaka Cūrṇi*, p. 324
2. *Śāntiparva*, Sec. IV, p. 6. (trans.), Roy, P.C.
3. *Pārśvanātha caritra of Shri Bhava Deva Suri*, Ślokas-155 f.. pp. 269-270
4. Basu, N.N., *Archaeological Survey of Mayurbhanj*, p. XLIII
5. *Ibid.*, p. XLII
6. Karakaṇḍu has been described as a Jaina Sage :*Paia-sada-Mahāññava*, p. 227
7. *Āvaśyaka Cūrṇi*, II, pp. 204-207; *Uttarādhyayana Cūrṇi*, p. 178; *Uttarādhyayana Vṛtti* by Santi Suri, p. 299 ff; *Niśithasūtra Cūrṇi*, II, p. 231; *Abhidhāna Rājendra*, III, on Karaṇḍu, pp. 357-359
8. Das, H.C., *Cultural Development in Orissa*, p. 206
9. *SBE.*, XLV, pt. II, Lect. XVIII, 45, 47
10. *The Jātakas*, III, pp. 376-379
11. *Ibid.*
12. *Ibid.*, V, p. 137
13. for the identification of Dantapura see *supra.*, pp. 3-5
14. Sen, B.C., *Studies in the Jātakas*, p. 8
15. *Ibid.*, p. 6
16. *Āvaśyaka Niryukti*, 495
17. *Ibid.*, 496
18. *Ibid.*, 497
19. *Ibid.*, 507

20. Mittal, A.C., *An Early History of Orissa*, p. 121
21. *Nāyādhammakahāo*, p. 20
22. *Āvaśyaka Niryukti*, 508
23. Sircar, D.C., *Successor of the Śātavāhanas in the lower Deccan*, p. 30
24. *Vyavahāra Bhāṣya*, 6. 115 f.
25. *Āvaśyaka Niryukti*, 508
26. *Ibid.*, 510
27. *Ibid.*, 508, 510
28. *Haribhadrīya Vṛtti*, pp. 218-20; *JBORS.*, VIII, p. 223
29. *Harivaṁśa Purāṇa*, iii, 4; cf.; *EI.*, XX, No. II, p. 88
30. See section on data of Khāravela
31. *EI.*, XX, p. 80
32. *Ibid.*, III, p. 166; *JBORS.*, VIII, p. 246
33. Desai, p. B., *Jainism in South India and some Jaina Epigraphs*, p. 18
34. *SBE.*, XLV, pt. II, Lect. XXI, 3
35. Law, B.C., *Some Jaina Canonical Sūtras*, p. 182
36. *IA.*, LV, p. 145; *JA.*, (1925), pp. 57-58
37. Sastri, S.N.M., *Mc Crindle's Ancient India as described by Ptolemy*, p. 187
38. Gerini, G.E., *Researches on Ptolemy's Geography of Eastern India*, p. 668
39. Sastri, S.N.M., *op.cit.*, pp. 68, 185, 386, 387
40. Yazdani, G., (ed.), *The Early History of the Deccan*, p. 56
41. *Avaṭṭān Kāraskarān Puṇḍrān Souvīrān vaṅgān Kaliṅgan Prānūnaniti Ca gatvā punastomena yajeta sarvapṛṣthayā vā* /i, 1. 30;

    Padvyāṁ sa Kurute pāpaṁ yaḥ Kaliṅgan prapadyate ṛṣayo niṣkṛtim tasya prāhurvaiśvānaraḥ haviḥ/ *Ibid.*, i, 1, 31
42. Apte, V.S., *The Practical Sanskrit English Dictionary*, pp. 1024, 892

43. Bagchi, P.C., *Pre-Anyan and Pre-Dravidian in India*, pp. 73-74

44. *Karṇaparva*, Ch. 44, p. 113, (trans.), Roy, P.C.

45. In this context we may note that the river Vaitaraṇī which is flowing through Kaliṅga was described as a holy river for the performance of religious rites - *Mhb.*, 3.114.13. Others have recorded that the Aryans were visiting Kaliṅga, Vaṅga and Aṅga for the purpose of pilgrimage only - Bagchi, P.C., *op.cit.*, p. 74. It shows that before Orissa had become considerably Aryanised the holy place of the bank of the river Vaitaraṇī had been often frequented by the Aryans. Here it may be noted that the conception of the holy-place (*tīrtha*) was pre-Aryan, which seems to be indicated by the existence of pilgrim spots in non-Aryan territories, to which place the Aryans were advised not to visit except on pilgrimage - *JAIH.*, VI, pts. 1-2, p. 319

46. Sircar, D.C., *SI.*, p. 37; Sen, A.C., *Aśoka's Edicts*, p. 99; Basak, R.G., (ed.), *Aśokan Inscriptions*, p. 64

47. *Ṛg-Veda Saṁhitā*, VI, (ed.), Max Muller, X. 136, 4.5

48. '*Kumāra śramaṇādibhiḥ*', ii, 1, 70

49. Śrautasūtra, 16, 30

50. IV, iii. 22

51. Majumdar, R.C., (ed.), *Mc Crindle's Ancient India as described by Megasthenes and Arrian*, pp. 97-98

52. Part. IV, sec. XXXIX, pp. 34-37

53. *Aṣṭādhyāyī*, ii, 4, 9

54. *Yeṣām ca virodhaḥ śāśvatikaḥ ityasyāvakāśaḥ śramaṇabrāhmaṇayoḥ//*
Bhāṣya II on sūtra II, IV, 12

55. Pande, G.C., *Studies in the Origin of Buddhism*, p. 260

56. *Jātakas*, III, 40

57. *SBE.*, XXII, pt. I, sūtra. 168

58. *Ibid.*, sūtra. 161

59. *Jaittā viule jagge bhoittā samaṇamāhaṇe* /
Lalwani, K.C., *op.cit.*, IX, 38

60. Sircar, D.C., *Inscriptions of Aśoka*, pp. 48-49
61. The Jaina tradition recorded in *Rājāvalikathe* averse this - *IA*., XXI, p. 157. also cf., Majumdar, R.C., and Pusalkar, A.D., (eds.), II, *The Age of Imperial Unity*, p. 419
62. Geiger, W., (trans.), Intro. p. XXXVI and p. 75
63. see *Infra*., pp. 96pp.
64. Desai, P.B., *op.cit*., p. 3
65. *The Jātakas*, III, p. 3
66. Mittal, A.C., *op.cit*., p. 119
67. *Mahāvagga*, i. 4; *Vinaya Piṭaka*, I. 4
68. Rājaguru, S.N., *History of the Gaṅgas*, pt. I, p. 185 ff; see also *supra*., p. 4
69. *JAHRS*., II, no. 1, p. 26
70. Barua, B.M., *The Ājīvikas*, pt. I, p. 57
71. *Kalpa Sūtra, SBE*., XXII, pt. I, sutra-122
72. Vajjabhūmi may be taken to correspond to the modern district Midnapur in south-western Bengal - Law, B.C., *Historical Geography of Ancient India,* p. 254
73. *SBE*, XXII, pt. I, p. 84, note-1
74. Jain, K.C., *Lord Mahavira and his Times*, p. 47
75. *SBE*., XXII, pt. I, p. 288

III

1. The date of Khāravela is a matter of keen controversy among the scholars. Generally two theories propounded by two groups of scholars have been put forward in order to ascertain the date - the first one holds that the Cedi ruler flourished in the first half of the second century B.C., while the second group maintains his existence in the second half of the first century B.C. For a detailed discussion see section on data of Khāravela
2. This famous and significant inscription of the first century B.C. has drawn the attention of several scholars who have analysed it from various perspectives, viz., political, socio-economic , religious etc. See - Prinsep, J., *JASB*., VI, pp. 1075- 1091; Cunningham, A., *CII*., I, pp. 27 ff., pp. 98-101, pp. 132 ff.; Mitra, R.L.,

Antiquities of Orissa, II, pp. 31- 55; Fleet, J.F., *JRAS.*, (1910), pp. 242 ff., p. 824; Luders' list - No. 1345; jayaswal, K.P., *JBORS.*, III, pp. 425-472, IV, pp. 364-403, XIII, pp. 221-246; XIV, pp. 150-151; Thomas, F.W., *JRAS.*, (1922), pp. 83 ff.; Jayaswal, K.P. and Banerji, R.D., *EI.*, XX, pp. 71-89; Barua, B.M., *OBI.*, pp. 1-47, *IHQ.*, XIV, pp. 459-485; Sircar, D.C., *SI.*, I, pp. 213-221; Mittal, A.C., *An Early History of Orissa*, pp. 395-400; Sahu, N.K., *UUHO.*, I, pp. 397-409; Shastri, D.G., *Khāravela- Śilālekha* (Oriya), pp. 6-23

3. Sircar, D.C., *op.cit.*, p. 214, *Śrīvatsa*; Mittal, A.C., *op.cit.*, p. 395, *Crown*; Sahu, N.K., *op.cit.*, p. 399, *Baddha maṅgala*
4. *EI.*, XX, p. 79; Barua, B.M., *OBI.*, p. 7, *Arihaṁtānaṁ*
5. *IHQ.*, XIV, p. 461; and Sircar, D.C., *op.cit.*, p. 214, *Mahāmeghavāhanena*
6. Barua, B.M., *op.cit.*, p. 7, *Cetarāja*
7. Barua, B.M., *op.cit.*, p. 7, *vaṁśa*
8. *IHQ.*, XIV, p. 461, *lekhaṇena*
9. Barua, B.M., *OBI.*, p. 7, *caturamta-rakhaṇa*; Mittal, A.C., *op.cit.*, p. 395; and Sahu, N.K., *op.cit.*, p. 399, *luṭhaṇa*
10. *EI.*, XX, p. 79, *guṇapahitena*; Sircar, D.C., *op.cit.*, p. 214, *upitena*
11. *ṇamo arihaṁtānaṁ ṇamo siddhāṇaṁ ṇamo āyariyāṇaṁ ṇamo uvajhāyāṇam namo loesavvasāhūṇaṁ, emo yaṁcaṇamukhāro* — *Kalpa Sūtra*, sūtra-1, also cf. Buhler, J.G., *On the Indian Sect of the Jainas*, p. 39
12. Buhler, J.G., *op.cit.*, p. 41
13. Mitra, R.L., *op.cit.*, pp. 67-70
14. *EI.*, XX, p. 79, *sava gharāvāsa parivasane agiṇathiyā*
15. Barua, B.M., *OBI.*, p. 17, *sava-gharāvāsinam ca sava-rājabhatakanāṁ ca sava-gahapatikanam ca sava-bāmhaṇānaṁ ca pāna-bhojana dadāti*
16. *EI.*, XX, p. 79, *Arahato va --- giyato*
17. In line seven and eight it is recorded that in his eighth regnal year, Khāravela carried out his first north-Indian expedition and attacked Magadha with a vast army. He fought at Goradhagiri (modern Barābār hills in the Gaya district, Bihar), and threatened

the metropolis Rājagṛha (modern Rajgiri in the district Nalanda, Bihar). Some scholars have argued that Khāravela had killed a king named Gorathagiri and looted his capital Rājagṛha - Sircar, D.C., *et al.*, *The Age of Imperial Unity*, p. 214. The above conclusion seems to have been drawn following the suffix 'giri' (the Jaina literature speaks of two Jaina apostales, viz., Mahāgiri and Siṁhagiri - *JDL.*, XIV, p. 5). It is hard to accept such a supposition only because of Goradhagiri has the suffix 'giri'. At any case Gorathagiri is the ancient name of modern Barābar hills - *JBORS.*, I, p. 159

18. *IHQ.*, XIV, p. 467, *sikanam*
19. *EI.*, XX, p. 79, *hasa ke (saha) - sehi*; *IHQ.*, XIV, p. 467, *sahasehi*
20. *Ei.*, XX, p. 80, *Magadhānam*
21. *EI.*, XX, p. 80, *hati*;
    Sircar, D.C., *op.cit.*, p. 217, *hatasam*
22. *EI.*, XX, p. 80, *suganigiyam*
23. Mitra, R.L., *op.cit.*, p. 44, *Naṁdarājani tato*;
    IHQ., XIV, p. 468, *Nadarāja-jita*
24. Mitra, R.L., *op.cit.*, p. 44, *agajanasara* ....;
    IHQ., XIV, p. 468, *Kaliṅga-jana*
25. Barua, B.M., *OBI.*, p. 22, *Kaliṅga-jināsanam*;
    Sircar, D.C., *op.cit.*, p. 217, *samnivesa*
26. *EI.*, XX, p. 80, *padīharehi*;
    IHQ., XIV, p. 468, *nipunehi*
27. *EI.*, XX, p. 80, *neyāti*;
    IHQ., XIV, p. 468, *niyati*
28. for the identification of Bahasatimita see section on data of Khāravela
29. for the identification of the Nanda king see section on data of Khāravela
30. Banerji, R.D., *History of Orissa*, I, p. 80
31. *IHQ.*, XIV, p. 468. Others have read *nandarajani tato agajanasara* Mitra, R.L., op.cit., p. 44; *Naṃda- rāja-nitāni Aga-jinasa .... naga* - *JBORS.*, III, pt. IV, pp. 457-458

32. *IHQ.*, XIV, pp. 479-480
33. The Rock Edict XIII of Aśoka contains a detailed account of the Kaliṅga war which took place in his eighth regnal year corresponding to B.C. 261, cf. *EI.*, II, pp. 246 ff., *CII.*, I, pp. 66 ff., Sircar, D.C., *op.cit.*, pp. 35 ff. Other scholars think that the Kaliṅga war was fought in the year B.C. 262-Chattopadhyaya, S., *Bimbisāra to Aśoka*, p. 116
34. Apte, V.S., *Practical Sanskrit-English Dictionary*, p. 958
35. *EI.*, XX, p. 88, note 9
36. Barua, B.M., *OBI.*, p. 22
37. *JBORS.*, III, pt. IV, p. 433
38. *Ibid.*, XIII, pt. III, pp. 232-233
39. *Ibid.*, IV, pt. IV, p. 366
40. *PIHC.*, (1952), p. 97
41. *JBORS.*, IV, pt. IV, p. 386
42. *Ibid.*, p. 386
43. *EI.*, XX, p. 85
44. *IA.*, II, (reprint), p. 136; The birth place of Śitalanātha is known as Bhadrikāpura or Bhadillapura and also Madrapura - Bhattacharya, B.C., *The Jaina Iconography*, p. 46
45. Das, M.N., *Yuge yuge Utkaliya Dharma O Sāhitya* (Oriya) I, p. 101
46. Mittal, A.C., *op.cit.*, pp. 145-146
47. Sahu, N.K., *op.cit.*, p. 228
48. *Ibid.*, p. 228, note-2
49. see *supra* pp. 73-75, 77-79
50. see *infra.* pp. 129ff.
51. *SBE.*, XXII, pt. I, pp. 217-285
52. see *infra.* p.
53. *Śrutvā sakāśād bharateśvaroapi kailāsabhūdhre maṇiratnacūrṇaiḥ* /
Dvāsaptatim Jainapamandirāṇāṁ nirmāpya cakre jinabimbasaṁsthāṁ //

Tataḥ prabhrutyeva mahādhanaiḥ svaṁ pratiṣṭhāya dhanyatamaṁ vidhāya /

Saṁrakṣyateanādijinendracandramukhodgataṁ stāpanasadvidhānaṁ //

Pratiṣṭāpāṭha, 62, 63

54. *SBE.*, XXII, pt. II, intro. p. XXI
55. Bhattacharya, B.C., *op.cit.*, p. 24
56. *Jivi kārthe cāpaṇye* - *Aṣṭādhyāyī*, v, 3, 99
57. Kauṭilya while describing about a well-arranged *Durga* (fort) refers to the settlement of the Brāhmaṇas, and the installation of the chief deity of the fort in the northern direction - *tataḥ param nagararājadevatālohamanikāravo brāhmaṇāścottrāṁ diśamadhivaseyuḥ* /

    ch. 22, p. 55
58. *JBORS.*, XXII, pp. 130-132. Other scholars however, assign this sculpture to a later date - Roy, N.R. *et al.*, *The Age of the Nandas and Mauryas*, pp. 379-380
59. *IHQ.*, XIV, p. 468, and Sircar, D.C., *op.cit.*, p. 217, *arahate*
60. *EI*, XX, p. 80, and IHQ., XIV, p. 468, p *akhiṇa saṃsitehi*
61. Barua, B.M., *OBI.*, p. 25, *rāja-bhatakehi*; *IHQ.*, XIV, p. 468, *Yāpujāvakehī*;

    Sircar, D.C., *op.cit.*, p. 217, *yāpujāvakehī*
62. *EI.*, XX, p. 80, and Sircar, D.C., *op.cit.*, p. 217, *rājabhitini*; Mittal, A.C., *op.cit.*, p. 399, *rājamitini*
63. Barua, B.M., *OBI.*, p. 25, *rāja-ñātihi*
64. *Ibid.*, p. 25, *rāja-putehi*
65. *IHQ.*, XIV, p. 468, *pūjāyarata*

65/66. Barua, B.M., *OBI.*, p. 25, *rājamahisihi*67.

67. EI., XX, p. 80, *sirikā; IHQ.*, XIV, p. 469, *jivadeha - ? ka*

67/68. Barua, B.M., *op.cit.*, p. 25, *satadasa- leṇasataṁ kārāpitaṁ*

69. Some scholars after reading the missing letters in the beginning of the line fifteen suggested that Khāravela had excavated altogether 117 caves - Shastri, D.B., *op.cit.*, p. 21
70. see *infra*. p. 111

71. *JBORS.*, XIII, pt. III-IV, p. 234
72. *Gopucchakaḥ śvetāvāsā drāviḍo yāpanīyakaḥ* /
niḥpicchikaśceti pañcaite jaināhbhāsāḥ prakrirtitāḥ //
Vidvadraratnamālā, I, p. 132
73. *EI.*, XX, p. 80, *sukatā*
74. *IHQ.*, XIV, p. 469, *sata-disānaṁ*
75. Sircar, D.C., *op.cit.*, p. 218, *ñānīnaṁ*;
Mittal, A.C., *op.cit.*, p. 399, *aninaṁ*
76. *EI.*, XX, p. 80 and Sircar, D.C., *op.cit.*, p. 218, *tapasī*; Barua, B.M., *OBI.*, p. 26, *tāpasa*
77. Sircar, D.C., *op.cit.*, p. 218, *hasina*
78. *EI.*, XX, p. 80, *saṁghayanaṁ*;
IHQ., XIV, p. 469, *ña?naṁ(sama)pasi(naṁ)(bhi)-saṁghiyanaṁ*;
Sircar., D.C., *op.cit.*, p. 218, *saṁghiyanaṁ*
79. *EI.*, XX, p. 80, and *IHQ.*, XIV, p. 469, *pābhāre*; Sircar, D.C., *op.cit.*, p. 218, *pabhare*
80. *IHQ.*, XIV, p. 469, *pakva-sisehi*
81. *EI.*, XX, p. 80, *pa si o ....*
82. *EI.*, XX, p. 80, *siṁhapatha*;;
IHQ., XIV, p. 469, *sipaja-thabhani*
83. Barua, B.M., *OBI.*, p. 26, *cetiyāni*
84. *EI.*, XX, p. 80, *rañi-si(ṁ) dhulāya nisayāni*
85. see *infra.*, p. 210
86. for the inscription see EI., XIII, p. 159; *IHQ.*, XIV, p. 159; Sircar, D.C., *SI.*, I, pp. 221-222
87. Sircar, D.C., *op.cit.*, pp. 221-222
88. Shah, C.J., *Jainism in North India*, p. 156

IV

1. Mitra, D., et al., *Orissa Review (monument special)*, p.15
2. *Utkal Sāhitya*, (oriya), XXI, pt. III. (1917) p. 134

3. *Ibid.*, p. 134
4. *Ibid.*,
5. yangar, M.S.R., and Rao, B.S., *Studies in South Indian Jainism*, p. 65
6. Other scholars place the beginning of the Gaṅga-era at 626-27 A.D., see *IO.*, I, pt. II, p. 59
7. Rajaguru, S.N., *History of the Gaṅgas*, pt. I, p. 208
8. *Ibid.*, p. 212; *IO.*, II, pp. 360-362
9. *IO.*, II, pt. II, p. 345
10. Rajaguru, S.N., *op.cit.*, p. 193
11. *Ancient India*, no. 5, January, 1949, p. 97; *JNSI.*, XII, pp. 1-4
12. Gupta, P.L., *Geographical names in ancient India Inscriptions*, p. 90
13. *JNSI.*, XXXII, pp. 31 f.
14. Some scholars place them somewhere in central India - *Purāṇa*, XVIII, no. 1, pp. 88-92; Ptolemy has placed them in the territory which comprised Tīrhat and the country southward on the east of the Ganges bordering with Gaṅgariḍae - *IA.*, XIII, p. 377
15. Guhaśiva, a Kaliṅga king believed to have been among the issuer of the Puri-kuṣāṇa coins - *JNSI.*, XII, p.1
16. *Abhidhāna Rājendra*, II, pp. 726-727
17. also cf., Gupta, P.L., *op.cit.*, p. 90
18. *OHRJ.*, XIII, no. 2, pp. 1-8
19. *JKHRS., III, pp. 225-227*
20. quoted by Sahu, N.K., *Oḍiā Jātira Itihāsa*, (Oriya), p. 356
21. *Ibid.*, p. 356
22. *JKHRS.*, III, p. 227
23. *IO.*, II, pt. II, plate No. 2
24. *Ibid.*, plate no. 12A
25. *Ibid.*, p. 62V

1. For the identification of Kaliṅganagara see *supra*. p. 11
2. *EC.*, VII, intro. p. 16 ff. For a slightly differed another tradition see, *EC.*, IX, intro. pp. 9f.
3. Elephant is the *Lāñchanā* of Ajitanātha, the second *Tīrthaṅkara*
4. *IO.*, II, pp. 113, 342
5. Rajaguru, S.N., *Ibid.*, p. 193
6. Phys Davids, T.W. and Bushell, S.W., - (ed.), *Watters on Yuan Chwang's Travels in India*, II, p. 196
7. Beal, S., (trans.), *Buddhist records of the Western World*, II, p. 208
8. *IO.*, I, pt. II, pp. 163 ff.
9. *EI.*, XXIX, pp. 38-43; *JAHRS.*, I, p. 52; *IO.*, I. pt. II, no. 43
10. *Va(ba)li-sa(sa)ttra-charu-pravarttanāya/*

    bhaga va tī śrī-Rājñī
    EI., XXIX, p. 43
11. *d-arhat-ā(d-ā)chārya-Nāsichandra //*

    tad-śi(ch-chhi)shya eka-śāṭa-Pravu(bu) ddhachandra yāva (t) jīvati / EI., XXIX, p. 43
12. It has been suggested that the term *ekśāṭa* possibly means one who has taken a vow to wear one piece of cloth - *EI.*, XXIX, p. 40. Since the term *śāṭa* is formed being added with the suffix 'ghañ' to the root *śaṭ*, meaning cloth, the reference here means only one piece of cloth, and not to make a vow to wear one piece of cloth.
13. Behera, K.S. *et al.*, *Bābu Chhoṭelāl Jaina Smṛtigrantha*, p. 170
14. Pāṇini (III, 2, 133) speaks of "*Arhaḥ praśaaṁsāyām*". The term '*Arhat*' has been described in two different senses, firstly meaning person of wisdom, and secondly as honourable person - *Bāla Manoramā on Sidhānta Kaumudī*, pt. IV, p. 120. He who attains arhathood is called as '*Ārhantya*': '*Arhato muṃ ca*' - *Gaṇasūtra*, V, 1, 24
15. *Bṛhatsaṁhitā*, ch. 58, V. 45
16. Mitra, D. *et al.*, *Orissa review (Monument special)* p. 16

17. A compilar of Dharmaśāstra, flourished in the seventh and eight century A.D cf., De, S.K., *History of Sanskrit literature* I, intro. p. XXV
18. Subramaniam, K.R., *Buddhist remains in Andhra and Andhra History*, pp. 62-63.
19. *OI.*, II, No.9
20. It is generally accepted that the Gaṅga-era was started in A.D. 498-*EI.*, XXVII, p. 192. However, Rajagura, S.N. (*IO*,II, Appendix, I) did not accept the view and suggested A.D. 626/627 as the starting point of Gaṅhs-era, after thoroughly reviewing the question afresh.
21. Tumburu 'attendant of the fifth *Arhat*of the present *Avasarpiṇi*', Jain - Williams, M., *A Sanskrit- English Dictionary*, p. 450
22. *IO.*, II, pp. 41-42.
23. see *infra.* p.239 for description of the image.
24. Ghosh,A., (ed.) *Jaina Art and Architecture*, I, p. 159. The findings from Poḍāsiṅgi has been discussed in *OHRJ.*, X, pt.III, pp. 74 ff.,*Ibid.*, pt. IV, pp. 30 ff. *Orissa Review (Monument special)*,pp. 15-18. For further discussion see *infra.* pp.239-241.
25. Ghosh, A., *Ibid.*, pp. 159-160.
26. see *infra.* p. 241.
27. *OI.*, VI, *intro.* p.x; Chanda, R.P., *Bhañja* dynasty of Mayurbhanu and their ancient capital Khiching, p.17.
28. Basu, N.N., *op.cit.*, p. 48
29. *JBORS.*, XII, pt.III, p. 447
30. Mohanty, S., and Das, G., (eds.), *LaxminārM200yaṇa Granthāvalī*, pt. I (Oriya), p. 271.
31. for discussion see *infr.* pp. 243-245.
32. *OHRJ.*, I, no. 4, p. 264.
33. Ghosh, A., (ed.), *op.cit.*, p. 160
34. Mitra, D.,*op.cit.*, p.16
35. Vasu, N.N., *op.cit.*, p. XIiv
36. for further description see *infra.* p.245

37. Vasu, N.N., *op.cit.*, p. XIV
38. for discussion see, *infra*. pp. 246-247
39. Vasu, N.N., *op.cit.*, p.108
40. Jash, P., et al., *JIH.,LVII*, pt. I, p.25
41. for discussion see *infra*. pp.245-246.
42. Fabri, C.L., *History of the Art of Orissa*, p. 178
43. Vasu, N.N., *op.cit.*, p. XIvi
44. for further discussion see *infra*. pp.247-248.
45. Ghosh, A., *op.cit.*, p. 163.
46. for description see *infra*. pp. 248-249.
47. Mohanty, S., and Das, G., (eds.), *op.cit.*, pp. 360- 361
48. *Ibid.*
49. Chandra, R.P., *Medieval Indian Sculpture*, p.71
50. *Koraput district Gazetteer*, 1945, p.22
51. Dehejia, V., *Early stone temples of Orissa*, p.103
52. Udyotakeśarī, also known as Latāṭendu Keśarī, one of the most profound rulers of the Somavaṁśī dynasty, was
53. *Oṁ śrī Udyotakeśarī vijayarājya saṁvat 5 /*

    Śrī Kumārapavvaıastāne jinna vāpījirnnaīsaṇa/

    Udyotita tasmin thāne caturviṁśati tīthakara/

    stāpita pratiṣṭhā (kā) le ha (ri) opa jasanandika-/

    nndatidrathā śrīpāraśyanāthasya karmmakhayaḥ//

    IO., IV, no,36, p. 236-37; cf. *EI.*, XIII, p. 167; Panigrahi, K.C., *Chronology of the Bhaumakaras and Somavamsis of Orissa*, pp.52 ff.
54. Thus in line second of this inscription it is clear that Khaṇḍagiri's ancient name was *Kumāraparvata*. Likewise, the Hāthīgumphā inscription, in line fourteen mentions *Kumārīparvata*, wich was the ancient name of Udayagiri.
55. *Śrī Kurman inscription, IO.*, III,pt. II, no. 27υ
56. *Seṭi yettimocina śrī Rājarāja (ji) nālayam....*

57. *IO.*, III, pt. II, p. 316, fn.2
58. *Śrī Ambikādeviki nivedyamunaku....*
59. Bhattacharya, B.C., *The Jaina Iconography*, pp. 103-104
60. *IMP.*, III, p. 1665; also cf. *IO.*, III, pt. II, p. 329.(The inscription is quoted by S.N. Rajaguru, in *ISBJ*)., p. 164.
61. Rajaguru, S.N., *ISBJ.*, p. 164.

VI

1. Mitra, R.L., *op.cit.*, pp. 11, 16 f.
2. Smith, V.A., *Early History of India*, p. 207; also cf. *EI.*, X, pp. 160-161.
3. *EI.*, XX, pp. 74-77; Banerji, R.D., *History of Orissa*, I, pp. 91-92.
4. JRAS., (1910), pp.242 ff.
5. Rapson, E.J., (ed.), *CHI.*, I pp. 112-113
6. Indraji, B.L., *op.cit.*, pp. 152-177.
7. *JAS.* (Letters), XIX, no. 1,pp.25-32
8. Raychaudhuri, H.C., *PHAI.*, pp.331-336, 357-372; *IHQ.*, v.p. 597; Majumdar, R.C., (ed.), *Age of Imperial Unity*, pp.215 f; Ghosh, N.N., *Early History of India*, pp.189-194; Sircar, D.C., *op.cit.*, pp. 206 ff; Chattopadhyaya, S., *Early History of North India*, pp. 56- 59; Mittal, A.C., *op.cit.*, pp. 264-281; Sahu, N.K., op.cit., kpp. 303-326; Ganguly, D.K., *HGDHO.*, pp. 129-135
9. *JBORS.*, (1917), p. 459
10. Barua, B.M., *OBI.*, p. 277
11. In line four of the Hāthīgumphā record itis stated that : *Dutiye ca vase acitayitā sātakaṁniṁ pachima disaṁ haya-gaja-nara-radha Vahulaṁ daṇḍaṁ paṭḍaṁ paṭhāpayati/*
12. Rapson, E.J., (ed.), *CHI.*, I, p. 482; Sircar, D.C., *op.cit.*, p. 194, note-1
13. *EI.*, II, pp. 88-99; also cf. Raychaudhuri, H.C., *PHAI.*, pp. 367-368; Rapson, E.J., *Catalogue of Indian Coins*, pp. XVii-XXiv. Others have, however, identified him with Śātakarmī II of the puranic list - *IA.*, (1919), p. 217.

14. Barua, B.M., *OBI.*, pp. 145-153.
15. Majumdar, R.C.,(ed.), *The Age of Imperial Unity*, pp. 195 ff. Chottopadhaya, S., *Early History of North India*, pp. 34-35, has suggested that Śātakarṇī had ruled either at the end of the 1st century, B.C., or at the beginning of the 1st century A.D.
16. cf. *OHRJ.*, III, no. 2. p. 86
17. *Pañcame ca dānī vase Naṁda-rāja ti- vasa=sata oghāṭitaṁ tanasuliya vāṭā paṇādiṁ pavesayati..../*
18. The present record also refers to Naṁda-*rāja* for a second time in line twelve.
19. *JBORS.*, I, p. 80
20. Rapson, E.J., (ed.), *op.cit.*, I, p. 484
21. *Histoy of Orissa*, I, p. 60
22. *OBI.*, p. 281
23. *JAS.* (Letters), XIX, no 1, pp. 25-26
24. Raychaudhuri, H.C., *op. cit.*, p. 134
25. see *supra*. pp. 96-98.
26. *EI.*, VIII, pp.42 f.
27. *MASI*; no. I. p. 12; Raychaudhuri, H.C., *op.cit.*, pp.334-335; Mittal, A.C., *op.cit.*, pp. 128-129. Sahu, N.K., *op.cit.*, pp. 215-224; Ganguly, D.K., *op.cit.*, p. 134.
28. Pargiter, E.R., *Dynasties of the Kāli Age*, pp. 23-24
29. Some scholarsdo not accept any Nanda conquest over Kaliṅga on the basis of a reference to Kaliṅga as *avijita* (meaning remained unconquered) land in the Rock Edict XIII of Aśoka; and further suggest that Kaliṅga was not conquered till the 7th year of Aśoka's reign when the Rock Edict was supposed to have been engraved - *IHQ*; XIV, p. 476; On the other hand, it may be held that the term *avijita* might simply refer to the fact that kaliṅgawas not included within the limits of the *Vijita* (empire) or *Rāja- viṣaya* (Royal dominions) - Raychaudhuri, H.C., *op.cit.*, p. 335, note 2
30. The inscription of Aśoka mentions that under the suzenainty of Aśoka Kaliṅga was governed by a Maurya *Kumāra* and not by

a local Kaliṅga King, Raychaudhuri, H.C., *op.cit.*, p. 202, note 1.

31. According to scholars the Śśśunāga dynasty was supplanted by the line ofthe Nandas in B.C. 345 - Raychaudhuri, H.C., *op.cit.*, p. 201 - who went on to rule till B.C. 324 when Candragupta Maurya ascended to the throne of Magadha - cf. Chattopadhyaya, S., *Bimbisāra to Aśoka*, pp.57 ff.
32. *Māgadhaṁ ca rājānaṁ Bahasatimitaṁ pāde vaṁdāpayat*
33. *JBORS.*, IV, p. 504; Konow, S., *op.cit.*, I, p. 29; *IHQ.*, V, p. 597.
34. Majumdar, R.C., (ed.), *op.cit.*, p. 214
35. Allan, J., *CCAI*, pp. XCVii-XCViii
36. Mittal, A.C., *op.cit.*, p. 270
37. Raychaudhuri, R.C., *op.cit.*, p. 332
38. *JNSI.*, XXVI, p.5
39. Sircar, D.C., *Selected Inscriptions*....I, p. 90; also cf. *MASI.*, I, pp. 10-15; *IHQ.*, (1929), pp. 601 f.
40. *ASWI.*, V, p. 65; Raychaudhuri, H.C., *op.cit.*, p. 357 note-1, pp. 367-368.
41. see *sufra*. pp. 196-197
42. Besides this cave, there are also other caves excavated during the age of Khāravela. Though there are no inscriptions in most of the caves, their contemporaneity has not been doubted - see *supra*. pp. 197-198.
43. Mitra, D., *Udayagiri and Khaṇḍagiri*, p. 14. also cf. Rapson, E.J., (ed.), *op.cit.*, p. 580

CHAPTER IV

Jaina Community

Jainism was not a monastic religion but a missionary one, i.e., religion intended not for the ascetics [both *sādhu* (monk) and *Sādhvī* (nun)] only, but for the lay community consisting of *Samaṇovāsaga* (the layman) and *Samaṇosiyā* (the laywoman)[1]. The followers of Jainism were genrally known as *Śrāvakas*[2] (hearers). The *Uvāsaga-dasāo*, the seventh *Aṅga* of the Jaina canonical texts, contains legends relating to ten *Śrāvakas*, many of whom were merchants, who by means of asceticism died as real Jaina saints, and then were reborn as gods in the heavens of the pious[3]. Besides the general appellation, one characteristic of the Jaina religion is its constituent division of the *Śrāvaka* (hearers) or lay disciples and *yatis* or monks[4]. A *Tīrthaṅka* or *Tīrthaṅkara*, He, who is an epithet of the supreme being and god of gods, omniscient, aware of the present, past and future, essence of the spirit, subduer of passion, proclaims the safety of the sacred religion of the *Jinas*[5]; known as the founder of *Tīrtha, Saṁgha* or the order which consists of *Sādhu* (monk), *Sādhvī* (nun), and *Śrāvaka* (lay-brother) *Śrāvikā* (lay-sister)[6].

Without entering into further elaboration on these particular terms we may concentrate our attention on the role of Mahāvīra in the formation of the Jaina organisation. As we have already seen, Mahāvīra had propounded his religion amongst the followers of Pārśvanātha, of course, with some innovation particularly on the philosophical plain[7].

In the process of organising his community Mahāvīra had to face certain minor chąllanges. During the early days when Mahāvīra was the head of the Jaina community there occurred an anti-community activity. The close association of Gośāla the head of the Ājīvikas[8] with Mahāvīra seemed to have sown the seeds of dissension in the Jaina order. As observed by P. Jash "Gośāla spent first six years of his carrier as a wanderer together with Mahāvīra, the twenty-fourth *Tīrthaṅkara* of the Jainas; but he parted company with the latter on account of doctrinal differences"[9]. After a six-year association, protesting against Mahāvīra's teachings Gośāla separated himself and claimed to be the head of the Ājīvikas, as a *Jina*, and lived naked like the Jainas[10].

On the contrary, A.L. Basham holds that Mahāvīra was a disciple or adherant of Gośāla[11]. Whatever might be the fact it is true that Gośāla was the head of the Ājīvika sect[12], and after his death, though their strength weakened considerably, they could have drawn the sympathy of some of the *Nirgranthas* within the Jaina community. On this score it has been suggested that the sympathy, in turn, might have manifested itself during the time of Bhadrabāhu, when the schism in the Jaina community took a positive turn[13].

Another minor challenge was thrown by a noble man called Jamāli, who according to the Śvetāmbara tradition[14] was the son-in-law of Mahāvīra[15]. Jamāli, who had embraced the religion of Mahāvīra, organised an opposition against the latter when Mahāvīra was in his fourteenth year of monkhood, and eventually left the community[16]. After that he persisted in his heretical opinions until his death. Two years after this event, i.e., when Mahāvīra was in his sixteenth year of monkhood, Tisagutta, venerable ascetic of the Jaina community made an attack against some of the views pertaining to philosophy, of the doctrine of Mahāvīra[17].

During the period of the spiritual leadership of Prabhava (Prabhava became the head of the community after Jambū Svāmī in 463 B.C.)[18]

two new sects viz., *Osavāla Jaina* and *Śrīmāla Jaina* arose in the Jaina community[19].

Before the final division of the Jaina *Saṁgha*, five more schisms have been traced out by scholars, which were also of similar nature as described above, and could not divide the Jaina order, but ultimately had to merge with the main order[20].

All these above-mentioned revolts within the Jaina community were, however, of minor nature and could not succeed to divide the Jaina *Saṁgha*. A much more severe blow struck the Jaina *Saṁgha* during the period of the pontiff Bhadrabāhu[21], and in the reign of Candragupta Maurya.

According to the Digambara traditions, Bhadrabāhu had predicted a terrible famine in the country of Magadha to last for a period of twelve years[22]. Keeping this in view Bhadrabāhu migrated to the Karṇāṭa country (present day state of Karnataka) along-with his followers. The remaining members of the community passed their days under the leadership of Sthūlabhadra, a disciple of Sambhūtivijaya; the latter being the senior contemporary of Bhadrabāhu.

The monks who stayed in Magadha met at Ujjaini subsequently while the famine was still continuing, and decided to wear a piece of cloth (*ardhaphālaka*) mainly as a token of concession to their infirmities. However, after the famine ended these monks remained stuck to their decision and continued with clothing. These *ardhaphālakas*, are considered as the forerunners of the Śvetāmbara sect of the Jainas[23]. In this context it has been observed that "thus one element of division was established amongst the Jaina, that of difference in practice, and it only remained, in order to make the division permanent, that they should have a differing sacred literature"[24]. There seemed to have been a difference of practices right from the days of Mahāvīra when he discarded his robe after thirteen months of his renunciation[25], and this practice eventually took its own course and ultimately led to the separation of the Jaina *Saṁgha*.

Besides the practice of wearing clothings, another development also occurred on the plane of canonical compilations. During the days of famine a general council had to be convened at Pāṭliputra under the leadership of Sthūlabhadra. In this council eleven *Aṅgas* were collected and the missing twelfth *Aṅga*, which contains the fourteen *Pūrvas* was renewed with the help of Sthūlabhadra[26]. On the other hand, when Bhadrabāhu returned to Magadha at the end of the famine he neither approved the practice of wearing clothing, nor did accept the work of the council.

Commenting on the so-called schisms in the Jaina *Saṁgha* before the eventual break up, it is held that it was "concerned quite subordinate points and were overcome in the pale of the order itself. The new formations which developed to remain are nearly exclusively concerned with formalities"[27]. Though there were already visible signs of disintegration, the final division of the Jaina order into Śvetāmbara, and Digambara took place in A.D. 79 or A.D. 82[29].

According to the Digambara tradition in the beginning, the Jaina monks did not wear any clothing, but following the Magadha famine the monks started wearing a single piece of cloth to avoid nudity while begging for alms[30].

For the final division, the Digambaras further held that once the *ardhaphālaka* monks were invited by Candralekhā, queen of the king Lokapāla of Valabhīpura. Finding these monks neither fully clothed or fully naked the king was displeased, and whereupon the queen asked them to be fully clothed. Then the *ardhaphālakas* began to put on white clothings and hence came to be called as *Śvetapaṭas* or Śvetāmbaras[31].

The Digambara tradition is supported by the following facts: (i) Mahāvīra is recorded to have said to Gautama "I have propounded the religion having faith in nudity"[32]. (ii) The famine of Magadha is referred to in several Jaina texts[33]. The connecting incident thereto relating to the migration of Bhadrabāhu to Karnataka has been attested to in an inscription at Śrāvaṇabelagolā belonging to the close of the sixth century A.D.[34] (iii) At the time of Alexander's invasion the Digambara Jaina monks were in significant number around the city of Takṣaśilā to attract the attention of the Greeks, practising endurance and commanding great reverence among the people[35]. (iv) Two Jaina temples[36] belonging to the early Christian era have been discovered at Mathura. It seems that these temples belong to the Digambaras, for the images enshrined in them are nude.

Like the Digambaras, the Śvetāmbaras also had their own traditions relating to the final schism of the Jaina Church. According to them Śivabhūti, a resident of Rathavīrapura caused to divide the Jaina order into two sects after 609 years of the death of Mahāvīra[37]. Following the division the monks used to remain nude while the nuns clothed[38]. The sect which was founded by Śivabhūti was called '*Boḍiya*'[39].

Like the Digambaras, the Śvetāmbaras also trace the beginning of the schism to the time of Candragupta. In a legend[40] it is stated that the Digambara Jainas could be seen in Ujjaini up to the time of Candragupta. But, one incident, in which the queen was horrified at the sight of 'sky-clad' Jaina and had a miscarriage, led to their transformation into Śvetāmbaras. Following this incident the king issued an order to the effect that the Jaina priests should be properly clothed whenever they visited the city of Ujjaini.

In the face of such contradictory accounts relating to the split in the Jaina order, a careful scrutiny is necessary to arrive at a reasonable conclusion. The canonical literature of the Jainas nowhere clearly draws any demarcating line for sectarian partition. The *Ācārańga sūtra*[41] testifies to the act of begging cloths (*Vatthesanā*) both for monks and nuns. The *Uttarādhyana sūtra*[42] states that the monks became worried about their old and torn-off garments. Further, in the same text[43] a monk is ordained not to complain about his cloths for, "at one time he will have no cloths, at another he will have some" .... The *Sūtrakṛtāṅga*[44] says that a monk "who washes and adorns his cloths, is far from being a naked monk". The *Sthāṇaṅga*[45] prescribes the use of garments under specific conditions. In this connection it may be pointed out that according to *Ācāraṅga sūtra*[46] and *Kalpa sūtra*[47], Mahāvīra did not discard his robe for a year and a month after his departure from home, and after that he walked about naked, and accepted the alms in the hollow of his hand. It is further recorded that even when Mahāvīra used his robe, it was only in the winter season[48].

Thus it is apparent that during the early days of Jaina history no specific rule was laid down in the sphere of clothings. As it has been observed, "the question of clothings was treated liberally; and this duplicity might be called the germ of the later schism of the order into the "naked" (*digambara, āśāmbara, dig-vāsas*), and the "whites" (*Śvetāmbara, Śveta-paṭa, Sitāmbara*, etc.)"[49]. The idea of complete detachment from worldly possessions was gradually gaining ground, and it distinctly manifested in its highest symbol which was life in the nude. Simultaneously two different schools adhering to two different interpretations of the core of Jainism were prevalent. It is to be noted that the rules concerning meditation, penance, residence and fasting did not seem to have been different in these two sects. The differences are primarily revealed more to practice than to moral philosophy. The alienation between the Śvetāmbaras and Digambaras was due to a more uncompromising conception of monkdom on the part of the latter which crystallizes around the idea of the ideal monk[50].

Though the Aśokan inscriptions speak of the *Nirgranthas* or the Jainas we have no specific evidence relating to their division. The earliest known epigraphical evidence that refers to the offering of cloths to the Jaina monks is the Hāthīgumphā record of king Khāravela. In line fourteen of the inscription it is recorded that in the thirteenth year of his reign, on the Kumārī hill (Udayagiri), he offered white cloths to the Jaina monks[51]. Further, an epigraphic record of Mṛgeśvaravarman of the Kadamba dynasty (5th century A.D.) attests to a distinct division of the monks on the issue of using clothing, where the king is said to have divided a grant equally for the use of the *Śvetapaṭas*, the *Nirgranthas* and the *Jina* shrine[52]. The idea of offering cloths to the monks itself tends us to believe that Śvetāmbara form of Jainism was prevalent at that time.

Both Śvetāmbaras and Digambaras were further divided into various sub-sects. The Śvetāmbaras are subdivided into three principal divisions viz., *Pujeṇa* (the followers of this sub-sect are thorough worshippers), *Duṇḍhiā* or *Bistolā* (this sub-sect, though recognises the images of *Tīrthaṅkaras*, does not indulge in worship with formal rites), and *Terapanthī* (this sub-sect neither believes nor worship the *Tīrthaṅkara* images)[53].

The Digambaras were also sub-divided into various sub-sects. Among them five are important viz., *Biṣapanthī* (always worship to a certain extent), *Terapanthī* (originated about in the 17th century, though acknowledges the images, does not believe in their worship), *Samaiyāpanthī* (originated in the 15th century, a non-idolatrous sect, but believe in the worship of sacred books), *Gumānpanthī* (flourished in the 18th century), and *Totāpanthī*[54].

Further, in the Digambara Jaina community, there arose a number of *saṁghas*[55]. *Mūla saṁgha* with its subjects, viz., (a) *Sinha saṁgha, (b) Nandi saṁgha*, (c) *Sena Saṁgha; Drāviḍa saṁgha; Yāpanīya saṁgha; Kāṣṭhā saṁgha* and *Māthura saṁgha*.

The monastic establishment on the Udayagiri and Khaṇḍagiri belonging to the period of Khāravela was inhabited by the Jaina ascetics belonging to the *Yāpanīya* sect. This is recorded in line fourteen of the Hāthīgumphā record of Khāravela[56]. On this score some other scholars incline to think that the Jaina monks referred to in the record perhaps belonged to the *Yāpana-saṁgha*[57].

Besides the two main sub-sects, Śvetāmbara and Digambara, the *Yāpanīya* existed there as a different sub-sect. As we have noted, though it bears some resemblances with that of the Digambara sub-sect, it was entirely different from both the Digambara and Śvetāmbara sub-sects.

Regarding the origin of Yāpanīya the *Darśanasāra* of Devasena[58] refers to a tradition which assigns its origin to Śrīkalasa, a Śvetāmbara monk, who had started this sect at Kalyana in V.S. 205 (A.D.145). This account shows that within sixty-six or sixty-nine (the final schism occurred in the year A.D. 79 or A.D. 82[59]) years of the main spilt of the Jaina community, this sect arose. According to another account, a certain queen of the king of Karahāṭaka was said to have asked the *Yāpanīya* monks to give up the use of cloths, which resulted in the latters' adoption of nudity while retaining the rest of the practices of the Śvetāmbaras[60]. Thus they lived naked and worshipped naked images, ate food by their palms, adorned with *Mayūrapicchī*; and believed that women could also attain *mokṣa* during their present life[61]. The *Yāpanīyas* are also recorded to have enjoyed royal patronage by the Kadambas, and more particularly Mṛgeśvaravarman (A.D. 475 A.D. 490)[62]. However, in course of time, they seemed to have been merged with other powerful sects[63].

After the division of the Jaina community both the sects developed their heirarchial orders in the organization of their respective communities. Within the Śvetāmbara sect there were *Gaṇas* (the school), *Kula* (the line), *Śākhā* (the branch), *Gumma, Phaḍḍaya*.

A *Gaṇa*, also came to be called as *gaccha*, consists of monks strictly observing the rules of conduct (*samācārī*) peculiar to that group only[64]. In this context a reference may be made to Mahāvīra, who had a cadre of eleven *Gaṇadharas*[65] (chief disciples), and each of them had several disciples under them. These *Gaṇadharas* are : Indrabhūti, Agnibhūti, Vāyubhūti (all brothers), Vyakta, Sudharman, Maṇḍita, Moriyaputra, Akampita, Acalabhrātā, Metārya, and Prabhāsa[66]. In this connection, it is interesting to note that all the *Gaṇadharas* of Mahāvīra were of Brahmin origin[67], which incidentally suggests the popularity of the cult of Mahāvīra among the Brahmanical society.

The *Gaṇa* is formed by many *Kulas* (the line), at the head of which are *ācāryas*[68]. The Jaina monks were further classified into various *śākhās* (the branch), which consisted of group of monks, sometimes belonging to one *Kula*, and educating themselves under their specified teachers[69]. The monks were further grouped in the form of various *Gummas* or followers of various *upādhyāyas*, who had been appointed by the *ācārya* of a *Gaṇa*[70]. This *Gumma* was further sub-divided into a number of *Phaḍḍayas* under a *Gaṇāvacchedaka*[71].

After the *nirvāṇa* of Mahāvīra a number of schools were established in the Śvetāmbara order, originating from different Jaina teachers who eventually assumed the role of heads of their respective schools which followed distinct religious practices.

The Digambara sect had also its own sub-divisions. It was especially after the Gupta period that there arose a number of sub-divisions owing to the popular influence of the monks. Besides, with the common division such as *Gaṇas*, the Digambaras introduced some independent nomenclatures for their divisions and sub-divisions. These are : *Saṅghas, Senagaṇa, Balātkāragaṇa* (having a number of *śākhās*, such as : *Balātkāragaṇa-kārañjā- śākhā, Balātkāragaṇa-lātura- śākhā, Balātkāragaṇa-Delhi-Jaipur- śākhā, Balātkāragaṇa-Nagaura- śākhā, Balātkāragaṇa-Aṭera- śākhā, Balātkāragaṇa-Iḍara- śākhā, Balatkāragaṇa -Bhānapura- śākhā, Balātkāragaṇa-surat- śākhā, Balātkārgaṇa-Jerahāṭ- śākhā); Kāṣṭhā-saṁgha* (having further sub-groups such as : *Mathura Gaccha* of *Kāṣṭhā-saṁgha, Lāḍa-bagaḍa-punnāṭa-gaccha* of *Kāṣṭhā- saṁha, Bāgaḍagaccha* of *Kāṣṭa- saṁgha,*

Nandī-taṭa-gaccha of *Kāṣṭhāsaṁgha); Mūla saṁgha, Nandī saṁgha, Pamatasama saṁgha, Punnāga- vṛkṣa-mula saṁgha, Śrī Saṁgha, Simha saṁgha, Ārya saṁgha, Deva saṁgha, Drāviḍa* or *Dramila Saṁgha, Iṅganeśvara saṁgha, Kāñchi saṁgha*, and *Kolattur saṁgha*[72].

In the Udayagiri and Khaṇḍagiri (Orissa) Jaina establishment, the inscription of Udyotakeśarī in the Navamuni cave (Khaṇḍagiri) refers to the *Ārya saṁgha* sub-division of the Digambara sect. This record inscribed on the inner side of the architrave of the verandah throws light on the facts regarding the Jaina monks bearing affinity with the *Āryasaṁgha*. The inscription[73] records the activities of the Jaina *śramaṇa* Śubhacandra who was a disciple of Kulacandra, the illustrious *ācārya* of the *Deśigaṇa* belonging to the *Grahakula* of the illustrious *Āryasaṁgha*. This event is recorded in the eighteenth regnal year of Udyotakeśarī. Another short inscription in the same cave also refers to both Kulacandra and Śubhacandra, the latter being the disciple of the former[74].

Though the above inscriptions do not mention the locality of the Jaina monk Śubhacandra, it is certain that he was present in the twin-hills during the eighteenth regnal year of the king Udyotakeśarī, and carried out his activities over there, for which he was honoured by the king. This evidence further proves the concentration of the Jaina followers in the region, who predominantly belonged to the *Deśigaṇa* fraction of the *Ārya saṁgha* belonging to the Digambara sect.

In this connection it is to be recalled that the four *śākhās* of the *Godāsa Gaṇa*[75], viz., (a) *Tāmraliptikā*, (b) *Koṭivarṣīyā*, (c) *Puṇḍravardhanīyā* and (d) *Dāsīkharabhatikā*[76] are nothing but those named after the regions and the towns. These places are primarily within the geographical jurisdiction of Bengal and parts of Orissa. The post-canonical texts mention the name of some countries like Iāṭa, Karṇāṭa, Drāviḍa, Gauḍa, Vidarbha, Mālava, Mahārāṣṭra, etc.[77], and also refer to the peculiar habits of the people and the state of

Jaina monaschism. The *Vyavahāra bhāṣya*[78] refers to the tradition of a certain king Toṣalika (Toṣali was a great centre of the Jainas) who guarded an image of the *Jina*. The same country was sometimes hit by torrential rains which damaged the crops, and hence the monks had to eat palm-fruits to maintain themselves[79]. In fact, there are many accounts and descriptions in the texts as well as in the *bhāṣyas* on the regional peculiarities of the Jaina monks. Even in the case of the administration of different Jaina Churches different lists of officials are referred to and it is, of course, difficult to explain the exact nature of their jobs[80].

In the preceding chapter[81] we observed that the message of the *Nirgrantha* religion was possibly carried to Orissa by the Jaina monks of southern Bengal. It is not unlikely that these monks belonged either to *Tāmraliptikā* or *Koṭivarṣīyā śākhā*. But the popularity of Jainism in Kaliṅga during the days of the Nandas shows that even before the birth of these *śākhās* and *gaṇas* the Jaina religion had a considerable following in Orissa.

References

1. Schubring, W., *The Doctrine of the Jainas*, p. 284
2. Shah, C.J., *Jainism in North India*, p. 2
3. Hoernle, R.A.F., *Uvāsaga-Dasāo*, i, pp. 1-44
4. Jacobi, H., *Kalpa sūtra*, intro., p. 4
5. *Syādvādyabhayadasārvāḥ sarvajñāḥ sarvadarśikevalinau* / *Devādhidevabodhidapuruṣottamavītarāgāptāḥ* // *Abhidhānacintāmaṇi*, Devādhidevakāṇḍa, verse -25
6. cf. Stevenson, S., *Heart of Jainism*, pp. 65-68; Nahar, P.C., and Ghosh, K.C., *An Epitome of Jainism*, intro. p. 2. The *Sādhus* (or muni) were the chief followers of Mahāvīra, organised under eleven Chief disciples, '*Gaṇadhara*' - (see infra. p.161), were world renouncers and were ordained not to hold property and quit their dwelling except during the time of begging. The women followers who renounced the world to join the order of Mahāvīra were known as *Sādhvīs* or nuns. A *śrāvaka* or lay-brother is a

house-holder supposed to keep his rule in a modified form by providing alms to the professed monk community. These laymen constituted the third order of Mahāvīra's community, while the fourth and last order consisted of laywomen.

7. see *supra*. pp. 67-68
8. cf. *ERE.*, I, pp. 259 ff. Gosāla belonged to the *Mañkhali*, picture exhibitor, or Maskarin class of religious mendicants - cf. Basham, A. L., History and Doctrines of the Ājīvikas, pp. 36, 78, 79 - Before advocating his theory of *niyativāda* or fatalism and starting to practise austerity and nudity - *Bhagavatī sūtra*, pp. 369 ff; *Ṭhāṇaṅga*, p. 233b; *Aupapātika sūtra*, 41, p. 196 - Gosāla joined the order of Mahāvīra in the latters second year as a monk, and both of them were said to have propagated the same religion for a period of six-years - *Bhagavatī sūtra* XV, I
9. *JJ.*, XVII, april, 1983, no. 4, p. 135
10. cf. *Aupapātika sūtra*, 41, p. 196; *Dialogue of Buddha,* II, pp. 227-229
11. Basham, A.L., *op.cit.*, pp. 256-263
12. for the Ājīvika sect see - *ERE.*, I, pp. 259-268; Barua, B.M., *The Ājīvikas*, and *Pre-Buddhist Indian Philosophy*, pp. 297-318; Law, B.C., *Historical Gleanings*, p. 37; Basham, A.L., *History and Doctrines of the Ājīvikas;* Sen, A.C., *Schools and Sects in Jaina Literature*, pp. 4-13; Jash, P., *An Obsolate Heretical Sect: Early History and Distribution in Eastern India*, *JJ.*, XIX, January, 1985, no. 3 pp. 75-83
13. *ERE.*, I, pp. 267-268
14. *Ācāraṅga sūtra.*, II, 15, 15; *Kalpa sūtra*, 109; also cf. Stevenson, S., *op.cit.*, p. 29
15. The Digambara works deny the fact of even Mahāvīra's marriage - *Padma Purāṇa*, 20, 67; *Harivaṁśa Purāṇa*, 60, 214
16. Stevenson, S., *op.cit.*, pp. 72-73; Rapson, E.J., (ed.), *CHI.*, I, p. 145; also cf. Sen, A.C., *op.cit.*, p. 44
17. Rapson, E.J., (ed.), *op.cit.*, p. 145
18. Nahar, P.C., and Ghosh, K.C., *An Epitome of Jainism*, p. 659
19. Stevenson, S., *op.cit.*, p. 69

20. Deo, S.B., *History of Jaina Mohachism*, pp. 79-80; Sen, A.C., *op.cit.*, pp. 44-45
21. Bhadrabāhu is the celebrated author of the *Kalpa sūtra*, where the tradition of the four *Jinas* viz., Ṛṣbhanātha, Ariṣṭanemi, Pārśvanātha and Mahāvīra have been cherished showing the early stages of the development of Jainism. According to Jaina traditions, Bhadrabāhu was the contemporary of Candragupta Maurya (324-300 B.C.). But in the genealogy of the Jaina pontiffs he has been placed in B.C. 365. This discrepancy has been rectified in favour of the former theory - cf., Sastri, K.C., *Jaina Sāhitya Kā Itihāsa* (Hindi), pp. 356-369
22. For the Magadha famine and the migration of Bhadrabāhu see - Charpentier, J., *The Uttarādhyayana sūtra*, intro. pp. 13-18; Stevenson, S., *op.cit.*, pp. 10-11, 70-72; Smith, V.A., *Early History of India*, p. 154; Rapson, E.J., (ed.), *op.cit.*, pp. 147-148; Nahar, P.C., and Ghosh, K.C., *op.cit.*, intro. pp. 8-10; Sharma, S.R., *Jainism and Karnataka Culture*, pp. 4-6; Deo, S.B., *op.cit.*, p. 81
23. *JA.*, VIII, no. i, p. 35; *Darśanasāra*, p. 60
24. Stevenson, S., *op.cit.*, p. 71
25. *infra*, p. 156
26. cf. Farquhar, J.N., *An Outline of the Religious of India*, p. 75; Stevenson, S., *op.cit.*, p. 72
27. Schubring, W., *op.cit.*, pp. 60-61
28. *Darśanasāra*, p. 7
29. Muni Ratnaprabhavijaya, *Śramaṇa Bhagavān Mahāvīra*, IV, Nihñava-vāda, p. 269; also cf. Nahar, P.C., and Ghosh, K.C., *op.cit.*, intro. pp. 8-10
30. see *supra*, p. 151
31. JA., XI, no. ii, pp. 6-7; *Bṛhatkathākoṣa*, 131
32. '*Mae acelaṭe dhamme paṇṇatte*' - *Sthāṇaṅga*, p. 460b
33. *supra*. p. 150
34. *EC.*, II, p.71, trans. pp. 1-2; also cf. *EC.*, II, intro. pp. 36-40; *IA.*, III, pp. 153-158
35. Rapon, E.., (ed.), *op.cit.*, pp. 321-322

36. Smith, V.A., *Jaina Stupa and other Antiquities of Mathura*, intro. p. 7
37. *Āvaśyakacūrṇī*, II, Vs. 145 ff., *Vṛtti*, pp. 418-426
38. for the story relating to Śivabhūti see - Jain, U.K., *Jaina Sects and Schools*, pp. 40-41; Muni Ratnaprabhavijaya, *op.cit.*, p. 272; Stevenson, S., *op.cit.*, p. 79
39. Deo, S.B., *op.cit.*, p. 80
40. *ASI.*, X, p. 55
41. *SBE.*, XXII, pt. I, pp. 157-165
42. *SBE.*, XLV, pt. II, p. 11
43. *Ibid.*, p. 11
44. *Ibid.*, p. 296
45. *Sthāṇaṅga,* II, 171, p. 137
46. *SBE.*, XXII, pt. I, p. 79
47. *Ibid.*, pp. 259-260
48. *Ibid.*, p. 79
49. Schubring, W., *op.cit.*, p. 50
50. *Ibid.*, p. 61
51. *EI.*, XX, pp. 88-89; also see *supra*, pp. 107-108
52. *IA.*, VII, p. 37
53. Nahar, P.C., and ghosh, K.C., *op.cit.*, p. 653. The first sub-sect is of the original stock, the second originated about the year 1580 A.D., while the third flourished in the year A.D. 1762 - *Ibid*
54. *Ibid.*, pp. 653-654
55. Schubring, W., *op.cit.*, p. 61; Nahar, P.C., and Ghosh K.C., *op.cit.*, p. 654
56. see *supra.*, pp. 107-110
57. *IHQ.*, XIV, p. 481, note 203
58. *Kallāṇe varaṇayare, duṇṇisae pañcauttare jāde, Jāvaṇiyasaṁghabhāvo*, sirikalasādo hu sevaḍado
59. *supra*. pp. 152-155

60. *BUJ.*, I, pt. vi, pp. 224-231
61. Jain, U.K., *op.cit.*, p. 133
62. *IA.*, VI, pp. 22-27; VII, pp. 33-35
63. cf. Deo, S.B., *op.cit.*, p. 555; Jain, U.K., *op.cit.*, pp. 133-136
64. *Aupapāṭikasūtra*, p. 74; *Oghāniryukti*, V. 691
65. In the *Utt. Sū.*, XXVII, 1, line-1, the *Gaṇadharas* are referred to as '*Gaṇahare*', denoting leader of a *Gaṇa* (group) under a *Tīrthaṅkara*. On the other hand, when there is no *Tīrthaṅkara* a *Gaṇadhara* is regarded as a man of superhuman capability - *Ibid.*, p. 322, note-1
66. for further details see *SBE.*, XXII, pt. I, pp. 286-287 also cf. Nahar, P.C., and Ghosh, K.C., *op.cit.*, pp. 649-650
67. *Ibid.*
68. *Aupapāṭika,* comm. p. 81
69. cf. *SBE.*, XXII, pt. I, pp. 288-289 and note-2 in page 288
70. *Aupapāṭika, sūtra*, p. 86
71. *Ibid.*
72. for details see Jain, U.K., *op.cit.*, pp. 83-132
73. *Oṁ śrīmadudyotakeśarīdevasya pravarddhamāne vijayarājye saṁvat 18 / Śrī āryyasaṁgha prativaddha grahakula vinirggatadeśīgaṇa ācāryyaṁ Śrīkulacandra bhaṭṭārakasya śiṣya su (śubhacandra) sya* // *IO.*, IV, no. 38, p. 243; also cf. *EI.*, XIII, p. 166
74. *IO.*, IV, p. 242
75. founded by Goḍāsa, disciple of Bhadrabāhu
76. *Kalpa sūtra, SBE.*, XXII, pt. I, pp. 288-294
77. *Bṛhatkalpabhāṣya*, III, p. 913
78. *Vyavahārabhāṣya*, 6, 115 ff.
79. *Bṛhatkalpabhāṣya*, II, 1060 ff.
80. The *Bṛhatkalpabhāṣya* Saṁgha Church hierarchy. The candidature depends more on account of his conduct and learning than on account of his life. The list runs like :

(a) *Ācārya - upādhyāya - bhikṣu - sthavira - kṣullaka* (II, 1447; III, 2407)

(b) *Ācārya-abhiṣeka-bhikṣu-kṣullaka- sthavira* (IV, 4336)

81. see *supra*. pp. 87-91

CHAPTER V

Jaina Monasticism

The term 'monasticism' is derived from the Greek word *'monachos'* (living alone). As the etymology denotes only one of the elements of monasticism it is remarked that "The term monasticism does, however, indicate what later became a socially and historically highly significant feature i.e., living alone in the sense of being unmarried or celibate, though this feature is not directly related to its etymology. Monasticism within these traditions - Brahmin, Hindu, Buddhist, and Jaina - do indeed live alone or in groupings set off from rest of their societies, analogously to Jewish, Christian, and Islamic monastics"[1].

Elsewhere, it is stated that the term is primarily reserved for the form of religious life led by those who, having alienated themselves entirely from the world, live in solitude; as, in fact, the etymology of the words such as 'monk', 'monastery', etc. clearly indicates[2].

In defining the term monasticism it is further explained that "monasticism is a term covering religious institutions, rituals and belief systems whose agents, members and participants attempt to practise religious works that are above and beyond those required by the religious teachings of their society or of exceptional individual religious and spiritual leaders in their society, i.e., those who have interpreted radically the tenents that apply to all believers or to the whole society"[3].

As one of the oldest monastically organised religion Jainism played an important and significant role in the history of monasticism itself.

It lays down various rules and regulations, doctrines and tenets to maintain and uphold its monastic activities in various stages of spiritual life. Monasticism in Jainism denotes the collective life of the monks (later on the nuns were also admitted) residing in an organised way at a fixed place under a supreme spiritual authority for personal liberation.

Our attempt to study the Jaina monastic order may well begin with a preview of the origin and early historical development of the monastic order in general in India. The earliest reference to trace monastic life in India are found in the *Ṛg-veda* where the terms such as '*munis*'[4] and '*yatis*'[5] occur. The *Aitareya Brāhmaṇa*[6], while showing a contempt for '*sanyāsa*' informs that the ascetics were putting on antelope-skin, grew beard, practised asceticism and discarded the desire for worldly life. *The Baudhāyana Dharmasūtra*[7] prescribes five vows, viz., (i) abstention from injuring living beings, (ii) truthfulness, (iii) abstention from appropriating the property of others, (iv) continence, and (v) liberality; which had to be observed by the Brahmanic ascetics.

It is generally believed that the 'Brahmanic asceticism' was the model out of which the Jaina and Buddhist monastic orders have sprung up, borrowing from it their various practices of ascetic life[8]. It is interesting to point out that Brahmanism, Buddhism and Jainism contain more or less common fundamental rules of ascetic morality, and it is, of course, very difficult to determine the exact magnitude of mutual exchange or borrowing of rules that took place between these three monachisms. For instance, of the five great vows taken by the Jaina monks except the fifth one, i.e., *aparigraha*, the rest are the same as those of the *Brāhmaṇa* ascetics[9]. Further the followers of early Jainism (pre Mahāvīra period) had been observing only the four great-vows '*cāujjāma dharma*'[10], and it is only later that the fifth vow was added.

Thus it seems that the first four great vows of the *Sanyāsins* belong to universal asceticism, and in further details there occurred differences[11]. If there would have been a borrowing, it is commented, "it was not so much of particular regulations as of the ideal of the ascetics"[12].

The term '*āśrama*' is not met with in the *Saṁhitās* or *Brāhmaṇas*[13], though there is an obscure reference to the four *āśramas* in the *Aitareya Brāhmaṇa*[14]. The reference in the above text generates considerable doubt in the light of the fact that there was not yet any clear difference between the third and the fourth *āśramas* in the *Chāndogya Upaniṣad*[15] which contains a much clear reference to the *āśramas*. Thus it is observed, "In the oldest *Upaniṣads*, there is evidence of only the first two or three *āśramas*, viz., that of a student, that of a householder, and that of a *yati* or *muni*. According to the *Chāndogya Upaniṣad*, a man reaches the summun bonum, even in the stage of a householder"[16].

Disagreeing with the theory that the Brahmanic asceticism was the model of Jaina and Buddhist monastic orders, some scholars have suggested that the ideal of the ascetics came down to the Jainas and the Buddhists from the previously existing heretical ascetic orders, and not from that of the *Brāhmaṇas*[17]. In this context it is further observed that following the decline of the Brahmanic values towards the close of the later Vedic period, there was a fruitful communion between some sections within the Vedic circle with that of the existing wandering group of ascetics (*munis*) in that period[18]. The Brahmanic ascetics did not seem to have regarded their fellow ascetics belonging to the heretical group as their equal. This is corroborated by the fact that as a rule a *Brāhmaṇa* passed through four, a nobleman three, a citizen two, and a *Śūdra* one of the *āśramas*[19].

Thus, it appears that the Jaina monastic order was closely related with that of the other heretical systems. In this context it may be underlined that whereas in Brahmanism the four-*āśrama* theory was a later day's conception, in Jainism liberation being achieved through the four-great-vows (during the pre-Mahāvīra period); which were also followed by the Brahmanic ascetics in a later period, was already prevalent during the age of Pārśvanātha, the twenty-third *Tīrthaṅkara*. At the same time it is possible that there might have been some interactions and borrowings, but that could easily be a two-way traffic.

It is thus obvious that the history of Indian monachism has a clear beginning. It can reasonably be suggested that the community of the wandering almsmen[20] were the forerunners of the later day monastic organisation. In any case between the Jaina and Buddhist monastic systems, it appears that the latter adopted with modification the existing tradition which was current in the Jaina system. This becomes clear when Gautama Buddha exhorts his followers to "Go along in accordance with what has been enjoined, having realized .... the supreme Goal of *Brahmacarya*, for the sake of which family men go forth from home into homelessness"[21].

The desire for spiritual realization formed the nucleus of the monastic movement. Remaining away from the society in seclusion, the renouncers strived for the ultimate quest. In the earlier period the system was called *Sanyāsa*, i.e., leaving ones' home, his belongings and embracing homelessness. When these renouncers live collectively following certain code of conducts and disciplines and with the purpose of self- realization; various terms, such as *Parivrājaka, Bhikṣu* and *Śramaṇa* came to be used for an ascetic. All these terms describe the mode of ascetic life which is referred to as '*Agārasma anagāriyam pabajjati*'[22] meaning entering the houseless state from that of the household. The aim of these ascetics was to seek release from the cycle of *Karma* through the practice of monastic life. In the *Uttarādhyayana sūtra*[23] eight kinds of *Karma* has been explained in which the soul having been bounded turns round and round in the cycle of births. This conception seems to have been entertained in Jainism particularly while it is found that the true implication of the term *Brahman* and the Vedic rituals were of no use. As a result, in the beginning the system was completely devoid of any sort of image worship.

The Jaina texts extol the reasons for renunciation. It is stated that people renounced the world whenever they became tired of this empirical life (*Samsāra-bhayodvignā*). The *Ṭhāṇaṅga*[24] provides the following reasons for renunciation : (i) *Chandā*, i.e., out of free will; (ii) *roṣa*, i.e. out of anger; (iii) *parijuṇṇā*, i.e., out of poverty; (iv) *Suviṇā*, i.e., by dream; (v) *paḍissulā*, i.e. for a vow; (vi) *sāraṇitā*, i.e., due to sudden remembrance of previous birth; (vii) *Rogīṇitā*, i.e., for illness; (viii) *aṇādhitā*, i.e., due to humiliation from some body; (ix) *devasannatti*, i.e., due to the direction of a god; and (x) *vacchānubandhita*, i.e., for one's son who had become monk. Elsewhere[25] the text also gives us examples of one (*tuyāvaitta*), becoming monk to avoid troubles, of one taken by conversion (*puyāvaittā*), of one pair of friends by mutual agreement (*saṅgārapavvajja*) and of one induced by instruction (*akkhātapavvajjā*). Some become monk to maintain themselves (*ihaloga*), or to get good food, or to get rid of debts (*moyāvaitta*), etc.

In this connection it is also to be noted that there are two categories of *Vyutsarga* (complete renunciation) - (i) *dravyavyutsarga* (renunciation of physical objects), and (ii) *bhavavyutsarga* (renunciation of mental states). It is further stated that the first category is of four kinds, viz., renunciation of *gaṇa* (society); of body; of articles; and drink. The second is subdivided into three kinds, viz., renunciation of four passions, of four forms of life and of eight *Karma-prakṛtis*[26].

Interesting descriptions relating to the initiation ceremony of the Jaina monks are found in the *Bhagavatī sūtra*. In an interesting manner the author depicts the initiation ceremony of prince jamāli. When Jamāli came out of the palace at Kṣattriya Kuṇḍagrāma, a long picturesque procession arranged by his father followed him up to the Bahusālaka *caitya* where Mahāvīra was to initiate him, at the request of the parents. Jamāli was also addressed and encouraged by his mother : "son, self control should be practised, passion should be conquered, exertion should be made". Jamāli then pulled out five handfuls of tuft of his hair, came to Mahāvīra and was initiated by him along with his five hundred followers. He read eleven *aṅgas* and practised penances and various sorts of meditations. Similar account of initiation is also described about Udayana, the king of Sindhu-Sauvīra in the north-western frontier provinces[28]. Layman like Ṛṣabhadatta[29] and Sudarśana[30] and the wanderer Skandaka[31] were also initiated after the simple ceremony of pulling out five handfuls of tufts of hair. Women named Devānandā[32] and Jayanti[33] also took to the state of homelessness after initiation from Mahāvīra. These rules and regulations are often practised everywhere in the Jaina monastic order for initiating a person into the fold of monasticism.

The Jaina community consists of the monastic order and the lay followers. The five great vows (*pañca-mahāvratas*)[34], viz., *Ahiṁsā, Sunṛta, Asteya, Brahmacarya* and *Aparigraha* constitute the basis of Jaina monastic conducts. All these vows are apparently the logical consequences of the theory of *Karma* which is the basic fabric of the Jaina religion[35]. As noted earlier[36] the animistic ideas of Jainism led the Jaina followers to lay emphasis on the doctrine of *ahiṁsā* which was further accompanied with self-torture to a great extent. The practice of self-torture with uncomplaining endurance for a period of twelve years had been necessary for the release of the soul. This practice had been observed by the Jainas in the early stage of their history before the rise of the Jaina monasteries in different parts of India. In this connection it may be noted that it is not easy to distinguish and pin-point the transitional phase between the philosophical endeavour and that of the monastic organizations. At the same time it may be observed that the later organisations must have been an outcome of the process of gradual evolution.

Gradually when the Jaina monastic order was firmly established, numerous rules, conducts and conventions were developed for its upkeepment. In this context it must be remembered that though the Jainas like other heretical schools prescribed a life of disinterestedness towards the world, the Jaina monks and nuns were not certainly homeless. Although they were not maintaining a family life they had the *saṁghas* of brothers and sisters leading a monastic life at different places, and hence were not a wandering community[37].

To enter the monastic order, as mentioned earlier, a Jaina monk had to take the five great vows. According to the first vow-*Ahiṁsā*, a monk is prohibited to kill any living being, whether subtle or gross, movable or immovable; and further restrained not to use harsh words or hurt anybody[38]. The second vow-*Sunṛta*, ordains a monk to speak truth always and to dissociate oneself with any word of untruthfulness[39]. The third vow-*Asteya*, prohibits a monk to take possession of anything which do not belong to him[40]. The fourth vow-*Brahmacarya*, asks a monk to renounce all kinds of sexual pleasures both physically and mentally[41]. According to the fifth vow-*Aparigraha*, a Jaina monk is required to renounce all attachments, whether little or much, small or great, living or lifeless[42]. In this context it may be noted that according to the *Uttarādhyayana-sūtra* the prince Ariṣṭanemi, son of the mighty king Samudravijaya of Sauryapura[43], plucked his hair with his hand and took to a life of mendicant[44].

While comparing the five great vows followed by the Jaina monks of Mahāvīra's time and onwards instead of four preached by Pārśvanātha (c. 250 years earlier), it may be noted that the fifth vow of celibacy (*Brahmacarya*) insisted on by Mahāvīra was implied in the fourth vow (*Aparigraha*) of Pārśvanātha. The *Uttarādhyayana sūtra*[45] thus explains in the words of Gautama to Keśi - "The first saints were simple but slow of understanding, those between the too simple and wise; hence there are two forms of the law. The first could with difficulty observe them, but those between them easily understood and observed them". Jacobi rightly observes that "as the vow of chastity is not explicitly mentioned among Pārśva's four vows, but was understood to be implicitly enjoined by them, it follows that only such men as were of an upright disposition and quick understanding would not go astray by observing four vows literally, i.e., by not abstaining from sexual intercourse, as it was not expressly forbidden. The argumentation in the text presupposes a decay of the morals of the monastic order to have occurred between Pārśva and Mahāvīra and this is possible only on the assumption of a sufficient interval of time having elapsed between the last two *Tīrthaṅkaras*"[46]. It shows clearly that Mahāvīra presented the vows of the Jaina monastic order in an amplified form of what Pārśvanātha implied in his four vows.

It is also to be noted in this connection that Mahāvīra also lay emphasis on nudity. While Pārśva allowed the use of two garments to his disciples, Mahāvīra proclaimed - "I have laid down the duty of nudity"[47]. The duty of '*pratikramaṇa*' is also ascribed to Mahāvīra who made an obligatory rule on all his disciples to confess and condemn all transgrations[48]. It is not unlikely that Mahāvīra might have borrowed these rigid rules from the *Acelakas* or *Nirgranthas*, the followers of Gośāla.

After taking the five great vows, a Jaina monk is further to be guided by the following qualities, such as : he should have compassion; be forebearing; be abstained, chaste and control[49]. Apart from these a number of other restrictions to be followed by a Jaina monk[50] are also mentioned. Perhaps the most important injunction for a Jaina monk was that a Jaina monk would live on alms through begging and not by buying[51]; and his few needs would be met only from begging; and besides this he should have nothing to call his own[52].

Since a Jaina monastic was not entitled to wordly life, he was supposed to stay outside separating himself from the society. In the early period there was no recommendation of a permanent habitat. They were forbidden to reside in places which were specially built for them, for it might arouse their passion for possession[53]. In the

Jaina *sūtras*[54] it is recorded that in dwelling places meant for the Jaina monk, it was difficult to secure and safeguard his senses from increased lust and passions. The *Pravacanasāra*[55] also opposes the permanent habitation of monks at one place for a longer period. For the abode of the Jaina monks it is recommended that he should stay on cremation grounds, in deserted houses, at the root of a tree, and in homes built by others for own use with perfect solitude[56]. It was only by doing so a monk would be able to acquire a high standard of self-control and avoid quarrels, passions and anger[57]. Elsewhere it is stated that a secluded abode should be used by a Jaina monk which was not often visited by women[58]. Thus, a similarity is seen with the Buddhist monks, who were also ordained to stay in forest, at the root of the tree, on a hill side, in a mountain cave, in the open air, on a heap of straw and under other shelters[59]. Further, a monk being resolved to live with other monks should be upright and free from desires, give up former connections which were longing for joy and would call at unknown homes for alms[60]. A monk is further ordained neither to build a home, nor to cause a building for him since the building activities hurt the living beings[61].

Thus in the early period the Jaina monks were forbidden to abode any permanent residence. Normally a monk stayed for one day in a village and for five days in a town[62]. The four months of rain retreat are interpreted by the commentator of *Mūlācāra* variously, as noted by some scholars[63]. However, with the pass of time the need for a permanent abode increased especially for the four-month period of the rainy season[64], when the monks could not go out for their daily begging of alms. Thus, the wanderers were forced to reckon with the monsoon conditions, which incidentally created an annual break in their wandering life. As a result they had to retreat during this period. The rule for such condition occurs in the canonical regulations of different sects : the Jainas call it *pajjusaṇa*; the Buddhists, *vassa*; and the Brahmins, *dhruvaśīla*[65].

Mahāvīra stayed the first rainy season in Aṣṭhikagrāma; three rainy seasons in Campā and Pṛṣṭicampā; twelve rainy seasons in Vaiśāli and Vaṇijagrāma; fourteen rainy seasons in Rājgṛha and Nālandā; six rainy seasons at Mithilā; two rainy season in Bhadrikā; one rainy season in Ālabhikā; one rainy season in Paṇitabhūmi; one rainy season in Śrāvasti, and the last one in the town of Pāpā in king Hastipāla's office[66]. These place names suggest that Mahāvīra traversed all over eastern India and also some parts of the upper Gangetic regions.

Jaina monks were forbidden to tour in the rainy season, because a stationary mode of life was necessary for not inflicting injury to vegetarian beings which grew up immensely in this season[67]. However, they were allowed to tour even during calamities for the following five reasons[68], viz., (i) in order to learn a particular text that was known only to an *ācārya* who had been undertaking a fast unto death; (ii) in order to prevent one's going wayward in a dangerous surrounding; (iii) for the spread of the faith; (iv) in case of the death of an *ācārya* or an *Upādhyāya*; and (v) to wait upon the *ācārya* and the *Upādhyāya* if they had been putting up in a place where there was no rain.

Following the foregoing discussions it apparently becomes clear that the Jaina monastic organization was the outcome of a later period while Jainism had spread in different parts of India. Further, with the spread of Jainism it became necessary to organise their community through monastic establishments. One such earliest monastic establishment was the twin-hills of the Udayagiri and Khaṇḍagiri in Orissa.

Before dealing with the monastic establishments in Udayagiri and Khaṇḍagiri, a reference must be made to the earliest *leṇas* as well as *vihāras* which are generally regarded as the precursors of the cave shrines. It has been wrongly observed that the monks of the Hinayāna faith of Buddhism appear to have been the first cave-settlers in the second century B.C.[69] In this context it may be pointed out that the cave-dwellings in the Barābar and Nāgārjunī hills, a little more than twenty-five km to the north of Gaya in Bihar, dedicated by Aśoka Maurya and his grandson Daśaratha to the monks of the Ājīvika sect, are the earliest specimen of the rock-cut cave architecture in India[70]. Dutt[71] further gives a graphic account about the residential-caves as follows : A residential-cave, except in the most primitive examples, had normally two parts (i) a 'living room' behind a narrow porch or verandah, and (ii) narrow dormitory cells which opened only into the living room. In *leṇas* as well as *vihāras*, the monk cells were designed for sleeping only; and the living room into which they opened, was designed for the inmates to meet together. The living room was a square rock-cut chamber with a ledge running along three sides, leaving the front open. Each oldest cell having one fixed rock-bed or two but never more than three; and in most instances there is a rock-pillow at one end. The bed occupies almost whole of the floor-space. The cells are semi-dark inside and rarely has a window. The doorways having a pair of wooden planks. Among the amenities provided are a niche in the longer side of the bed to keep cloths in, a niche in the wall for a lamp and a rod to hang cloths on. It seems that only in a later period the architecture of these cells was improved, the doorways were provided with some ornamental work on the outside, of which faint traces remain at the examples at Nasik and Ajanta.

The above accounts relating to the early cave monasteries seem to conform to some of the examples at Udayagiri and Khaṇḍagiri. The small cells having less architectural designs may be ranked with the early Buddhist cave-dwellings[72].

On the other hand, in the Udayagiri and Khaṇḍagiri cave, some considerable improvement relating to architectural patterns may be detected in the larger cells. They have open courtyard in front, pillared-verandahs, pilasters flanking the doorways and stone-benched-verandahs[73]. In this context, it is to be noted that in the Buddhist hermit-cells[74] these features also appear afterwards.

Gradually with the increase in the monastic population a lot of changes were incorporated in the monastic settlements. During the pre-Kuṣāṇa age a monastery was found to be a compact excavation designed to serve the living needs of a single *saṁgha* or one congregational unit. The arrangements in a monastery were as follows: hall of assembly, store-rooms, kitchen, scullery, refectory, steward's room, bath, room and court of cells[75]. The examples bearing such features are clearly noticed in the remains of Taxilā, in the Gāndhāra region (presentday north-west Pakistan) covering three, city-state known as Bhir Mound, Sircap and Sirsuk; and those found in the Sāñci region (in the modern Raisen district of Madhya Pradesh). These were the example patterns on which the *Leṇa*-type monasteries of the pre-Christian era used to be built[76].

Befitting to their religious system the Jainas built up their residences as well as sanctuaries at the twin hills in Orissa. Architectural similarities with the Buddhist *Vihāra* are noticeable, but difference at the same time exists in order to maintain their doctrinal peculiarities.

References

1. *Enc. Br.*, 15th ed., pp. 335-336
2. *ERE.*, VIII, p. 787
3. *Enc. Br.*, 15th ed., p. 336
4. *Ṛg-veda*, X, 136.2.4
5. *Ibid.*, VIII, 3.9
6. *Aitareya Brāhmaṇa*, VII, 13
7. *SBE.*, XIV, p. 729
8. *SBE.*, XXII, pt. I, intro. p. XXiv; Buhler, J.G., *Indian Sect of the Jainas*, p. 15; *ERE.*, VIII, p. 804; Rapson, E.J., ed. *CHI*, I, pp. 134-135
9. *ERE.*, VIII, p. 804
10. see *supra*. pp. 67-68
11. Pande, G.C., *Studies in the Origin of Buddhism*, pp. 321- 322

12. *Ibid.*, p. 322
13. Kane, P.V., *History of the Dharmaśāstras*, II, Pt. I, p. 418
14. *Ibid.*, p. 418
15. *Chāndogya Upaniṣad*, II, 23.1
16. *Poona Orientalist*, III, no. 4, p. 15
17. Dutta, S.K., *Early Buddhist Monachism*, pp. 51 ff.
18. Pande, G.C., *op.cit.*, p. 326
19. Max Muller, F., *Lectures on the Origin and Growth of Religion*, p. 343
20. Dutt, S., *Buddhist Monks and Monasteris of India*, p.24
21. *Mahāvagga*, 1, 11, 1
22. *Dīgha Nikāya*, I, 60.240; III, 55
23. *Utt. Sū.*, trans., Lalwani, K.C., XXXIII
24. *Ṭhāṇaṅga*, p. 473b
25. *Ibid.*, p. 128b and 276ab
26. *Bhagavatī sūtra*, 25, 7, 803
27. *Ibid.*, 9,33,385
28. *Ibid.*, 6,13,491
29. *Ibid.*, 9,13, 382
30. *Ibid.*, 11,11,432
31. *Ibid.*, 2,1,92
32. *Ibid.*, 9,33,382
33. *Ibid.*, 12,2,443
34. *SBE.*, XXII, pt. I, intro. p. XXiii
35. *ERE.*, VII, pp. 469-470
36. see *supra*. p. 65
37. Bhagat, M.G., *Ancient Indian Asceticism*, p. 13
38. *SBE.*, XXII, pt. I, pp. 202-204
39. *Ibid.*, pp. 204-205
40. *Ibid.*, pp. 205-207

41. *Ibid.*, pp. 207-208
42. *Ibid.*, pp. 208-210
43. *Utt. Sū.*, XXII, 3, 4, trans. Lalwani, K.C.
44. *Ibid.*, XXII, 24
45. *Utt. Sū.*, 23, 26-27, SBE., XLv, pt. II, pp. 122-123
46. *SBE.*, XLv, pt. II, pp. 122-123
47. '*nae acelate dhamme paṇṇatte*' - *Ṭhāṇaṅga*, p. 460b
48. '*cāujjāmao pañcamahāvvaiyam*' - *Bhagavatī sūtra*, p.99a ff.
49. *Utt. Sū.*, XXI, 13
50. *Ibid.*, XXI, 14-22
51. *Ibid.*, XXXV, 15
52. *Ibid.*, II, 28
53. *Mūlācāra*, 10.58
54. *Utt. Sū.*, trans. Lalwani, K.C., XXXV, 5
55. *Pravacanasāra*, p. 286, verse-13
56. *Utt. Sū.*, XXXV, 6; *Mūlācāra*, 9.21, 22
57. *Sūtrakṛtāṅga*, I. r. 1. 1
58. *Utt. Sū.*, XVI, 1
59. *SBB.*, XX, p. 204
60. *Utt. Sū.*, XV, 1
61. *Ibid.*, XXXV, 8, 9
62. '*gāmeyarādivāsī ṇayare pañcāhavāsiṇo dhīrā*' - *Mūlācāra*, 9, 19
63. Deo, S.B., *op.cit.*, p. 340
64. In the '*pratyākhyānī*' the sin lasts only for a period of four months, while it is confessed and given up at 'comasi' (sankt. *caturmāsī*) - Stevenson, S., *The Heart of Jainism*, p. 123. The accumulation of *Karma* would be worse if one does not confess till the quarterly *caturmāsī* - *Ibid.*, p. 166
65. cf. Dutt, S., *op.cit.*, p. 53
66. *Kalpa sūtra*, 122
67. Deo, S.B., *op.cit.*, p. 157

68. *Ibid.*, p. 157
69. Dutt, S., *op.cit.*, pp. 148-149
70. for details see *infra*. pp.207-208
71. Dutt, S., *op.cit.*, p. 150
72. see *infra*. p. 201
73. see *infra*. pp.203ff.
74. Dutt, S., *op.cit.*, p. 151
75. see plan of Pippala monastery in Taxila in Dutt, S., *op.cit.*, p. 212
76. cf. Dutt, S., *Ibid.*, pp. 211-214. *The Buddhist monuments of Taxila were earlier assigned to the Kuṣāṇa time* by Marshall, J., - *ASI, AR*, (1923-1924), pp. 61-62

SBJ	:	Sacred Book of the Jainas
SGAMI	:	Studies in the Geography of Ancient and Medieval India
SI	:	Selected Inscriptions Bearing on Indian History and Civilization
SII	:	South Indian Inscriptions
TP	:	Tūlasi Prajñā
Utt. Su.	:	Uttarādhyayana Sūtra
UUHO	:	Utkal University History of Orissa

CHAPTER VI

Jaina Art

The art in its three broad classifications, viz., architecture, sculpture and painting when carried out and expressed with some salient features of the Jaina religion is known as Jaina art. The Jaina followers have dedicated, like other religious communities various monuments both rock-cut and structural, in honour of the objects of worship and to the Jaina monks. These architectural objects were decorated with images of the *Tīrthaṅkaras* or sometimes with beautiful paintings on the walls. The twenty-four *Tīrthaṅkaras* are often shown with their respective *Śāsanadevīs* described in the Jaina pantheon. While exercising their art activities, the patronisers had designed the arrangements in a manner so as to conform to the Jaina architectural and iconographic canons. Besides, some secular relief panels are also carved in some important caves. Before coming to the point of our review it is necessary to enumerate a brief history of these caves and their bearings especially icons and paintings.

I

Architecture

The followers of the Jaina religion have dedicated a number of rock-out caves in the twin-hills of Udayagiri and Khaṇḍagiri (Lat. 20° 16′ N; Long 85° 47′ E). These hills are situated at a distance of six km to the west of Bhubaneswar, the capital of Orissa. The exact number of excavated caves cannot be ascertained at present as the site indicates the remnants of a number of caves which had been completely destroyed. It has been reported that the site was honey-combed and found to have altogether sixty-six caves[1], - forty-four in Udayagiri, nineteen in Khaṇḍagiri, and three in Nilagiri - an adjunct to the twin-hills. However, at present only thirty-three (eighteen in Udayagiri and fifteen in Khaṇḍagiri) caves are seen[2]. Not only in the history of the Jaina art but also in the history of Indian rock-cut architecture as a whole, these sites occupy a unique position.

Some of these caves bear definite proof to suggest their antiquity to the period of Khāravela and to the immediately succeeding period. At the same time some belong to a later date.

Dating

The precise dating of these monuments has been a matter of controversy. According to one view at least some of the caves might be dated as early as the fourth or fifth centuries B.C.[3]. According to another view most of the caves at Udayagiri and Khaṇḍagiri were excavated roughly from the fourth century B.C. to first century B.C.[4]. The same authority has suggested second century A.D. to be the latest phase of rock-cut activities in these hills, in which period Buddhism rose in Orissa and which, in turn, must have caused the end of the activities of the Jaina followers[5]. Elsewhere it is held that from the age of Aśoka Maurya the Jaina monks had been living in these hills, and that some of the caves must have been existed during that period[6]. Yet another view is that all the excavations in these hills were carried out within the one hundred and fifty years previous to the Christian era, though a short revival saw the addition of a few more caves in the Khaṇḍagiri in the medieval period[7].

In this connection it may be observed that since the Cedi king Khāravela had caused to engrave his inscription in the Udayagiri hill, that place, in all probability, was already a celebrated Jaina centre. This would, in turn, suggest that at least some of these caves were prior to the time of Khāravela[8]. As suggested by Mitra, "an earlier origin of the Jaina establishment on the hills is not entirely ruled out. It is also not unlikely that the Kaliṅga-*Jina* removed by the Nanda king and recovered by Khāravela had its original enshrinement on the hills and was reinstalled here by Khāravela"[9]

Circumstantial evidences place a number of caves to the age of Khāravela and to the period of his successors. The caves such as Hāthīgumphā, Mañcapurī and Svargapurīgumphā (the former being the lower storey and the later, upper), Bāgha-gumphā, Sarpa-gumphā, Jambeśvara-gumphā and Paṇaṣa-gumphā (all in Udayagiri); Ananta-gumphā, Tatowa-gumphā No. 1 and No. 2 (all in Khaṇḍagiri) bear inscriptions. These inscriptions are of Brāhmī character resembling that of the Hāthīgumphā record. Besides these inscribed caves, another cave at Khaṇḍagiri-Lalāṭendukeśarī-gumphā, also bears the inscription of the Somavaṁśī king Udyotakeśarī belonging to the eleventh century A.D.

Thus in a broader sense these inscribed early caves seem to belong to the period of Khāravela. At the same time it needs to be underlined that some of these inscribed caves were excavated in the period following that of Khāravela, since the donors are recorded to have been his successors[10]. The caves bearing no inscriptions cannot definitely be placed to a late period either. In this context some scholars have suggested that the caves without inscriptions might be treated as those donated by Khāravela himself[10]. From the point of stylistical consideration some of these caves might belong to a period that preceds that of Khāravela, and some other to the period of Khāravela, and yet some other to the succeeding period of Khāravela. In general it may be suggested that the rock-cut activities in these hills had been carried out during the period of the first century B.C. to first century A.D.[12]

As regards the chronology of the caves scholars have proposed divergent views. A group of art historians suggest that of the whole series, the natural cavern, Hāthīgumphā, was the oldest excavation[13]. Other scholars have suggested that the simpler and plainer caves preceded those caves which bear elaborate carvings[14]. A directly contradictory suggestion[15] to the above view that the small and simple caves were the production of a later period when the royal Patronage had been withdrawn, has also been suggested. According to this view "the richness of the carvings and the size of the structures depended probably more upon the liberality of the donor than upon development of style and taste ...."[16]. In regard to the sculptured examples it is contended that both the Bāgha and Sarpa *gumphās* are the oldest[17]

Donors

The royal donors mentioned in the inscription are : the Cedi king Khāravela, his unnamed chief queen, Vakradeva (a successor of Khāravela), and Vaḍukha (a royal prince).

In line fourteen of the Hāthīgumphā inscription, Khāravela is recorded to have donated caves to the Jaina monks on the *Kumārī-parvata*[18] (Udayagiri hill). Thus it seems probable that Khāravela must have donated a number of caves in the Udayagiri hill. Keeping in view his strong affiliations towards Jainism it may be stressed that under his patronage quite a good number of caves had been excavated.

A two-line inscription on the facade of the Svargapurī–cave (the upper storey of the Mañcapurī-cave) is found inscribed on the space between the second and third doorways. In this inscription[19] the chief-Queen *agamahiṣi*, is recorded to have donoted caves to the Jaina monks. Further, an inscription found on the verandah of the Mañcapurī-cave records that this portion of the cave was excavated by another king named Vakradeva[20] who styled himself as *Ārya, mahārāja* and *mahāmeghavāhana*. This Vakradeva appears to have been a successor of Khāravela for, generally rock-cut excavations start from the top[21] (the upper storey - Svargapuni-cave - is recorded to have been excavated by the chief-queen of Khāravela). Another inscription[22] inscribed on the right wall of the same Mañcapurī-cave bears the name of prince Vaḍukha, who had caused to donate that part of the cave. This prince appears to have been the son of Khāravela.

Besides these royal donors, some other people are also recorded to have excavated caves in the twin-hills. Short inscriptions in different caves bear such names. Thus in the Bāgha-*gumphā* inscription occurs the name of Bhuti[23]; in the Sarpa-*gumphā* inscription the names of Kamma, Halakhina and Culakmma[24]; in the Paṇaṣa- *gumphā* inscription the name of Culakmma[25]; and names of Mahamada, Bariya and Nakiya[26] in the Jambeśvana-*gumphā*. All these donors do not bear any title and they may have been either government officials or merchants or common people.

In regard to the religious affiliation of the caves at Udayagiri and Khaṇḍagiri, scholars have traced both the Jaina and Buddhist influence in them. The Buddhist symbols such as, *Bo*-tree, Buddhist-*Triśūla*, Votive-*stūpa*, railings and *svastika* marks are seen on some of the caves[27]. However, the remains and monuments in these twin-hills do not seem to support the above contention. On this point remarks by the competent art authorities should be underlined. Hence it is said that the *stūpas, svastikas*, barred-railings, railed-trees, wheels, the goddess *Śrī*, the *triśūlas* (open or pointed) are as common to Jainism as to other religions[28]. Further, it is observed that though the older excavations in these hills exhibit no characteristics peculiar to Jainism, no slightest trace of Buddhism is to be found; and the symbols are common artistic devices for all creeds in ancient India[29]. Elsewhere, it is maintained that these rock-cut cells "resolves itself into a collection of chambers, not Buddhist, but attributed to the opposing belief of the Jainas, as in their treatment there are certain features implying a connexion with the latter creed[30].

In this context, referring to various symbols[31] depicted on some caves, which are regarded by the Jainas as of good omen; and the architecture which only attest to the rigours of Jaina ascetic life, it is held that "there is no early relief which can definitely be regarded as indisputably illustrating Jaina religious mythology"[32].

There is no doubt that these caves were the handiwork of the Jaina followers. The Jaina king Khāravela, his chief queen, his successor Vakradeva and the prince Vaḍukha are recorded to have donated caves in this twin-hills. Besides, the various symbols, the inscriptions clearly refers to the Jaina affiliations of these caves.

In regard to the ground plan this group of caves stands quite apart. These caves excavated irregularly at different heights, were possibly without any canonical plan. The excavators seemed to have made use of natural cavern (at least in one example i.e., Hāthīgumphā, Udayagiri), and cleaves for the purpose. This method was adopted, perhaps owing to the very nature of the rock, which is coarse-grained sandstone of a varied texture, mostly soft, porous and incohering.

Among cave-excavations the following consist of a single cell: Chhoṭa-Hāthī-*gumphā*, Paṇaṣa-*gumphā*, Jambeśvara-*gumphā*, Bāgha-*gumphā*, Sarpa-*gumphā*, Hāthī-*gumphā*, Dhānaghara-*gumphā*, Haridās-*gumphā*, Jagannātha-*gumphā*, Roṣei-*gumphā* (all in Udayagiri); Tatwa-*gumpha* No. 1 and No. 2, Ananta-*gumphā*, Tentuli-*gumphā*, Dhyānaghara-*gumphā*, Bārabhujī- *gumphā*, Triśūla-*gumphā*, Ekādaśī-*gumphā*, and cave No. 15 (all in Khaṇḍagiri).

Apart from the single-cell caves, the following caves consist of two or more cells: Bājāghara-*gumphā* (two cells), Jayavijaya-*gumphā* (two cells), Gaṇeśa-*gumphā* (two cells), Pātālapurī-*gumphā* (four cells : two at the back and one each on either sides), all in Udayagiri; Navamuni-*gumphā* (originally consisted of two cells, but later on converted to a sanctuary), Lalāṭendukeśarī-cave (originally consisted of two cells, severely damaged now), cave No. 12 (originally consisted of two cells, only the remnant is seen now), cave No. 13 (originally consisted of two cells, and at present the remnant is seen), all in Khaṇḍagiri.

The most important excavations in these hills are the double-storeyed caves. These are Rāṇī-*gumphā*, Mañcapurī-*gumphā*, Alakāpurī-*gumphā* and Ṭhākurāṇī-*gumphā* (all in Udayagiri); Khaṇḍagiri-*gumphā* (in Khaṇḍagiri).

In the last group of caves one interesting architectural feature is noteworthy. As for example both in the case of Rāṇī-*gumphā* and Mañcapurī-*gumphā* the upper storey does not rise perpendicularly on and above the ground floor. The upper storey receds a few feet back into the rock creating an open terrace in front of its verandah. The upper storey of Rāṇī-*gumphā* is approached by a staircase and that of Mañcapurī-*gumphā* by a ramp. The above arrangement seem to have been adopted mainly due to the natural formation of the rock. In this connection it is further remarked that ".... it was adopted in consequence of the Buddhist *vihāras* of that age being, when of more than one storey in height, of a pyramidal form, each storey being consequently less in diameter than the one below it"[34].

In some of the important examples another peculiar architectural feature i.e., provision of an open court-yard, is seen. Thus Rāṇī-*gumphā* and Mañcapurī-*gumphā* (Udayagiri) are preceded by a open court-yard being formed after the levelling of the ground. Such a provision is singularly significant in asmuch as it is left uncovered unlike the contemporary rock-cut architectural monument in western India. This practice seems to have been effected owing to the rough nature of the rock. At the same time, behind such arrangement, a possibility of a certain view point of the architect cannot be ruled out. Hence it is observed that "Unfortunately few Indian palaces, or other buildings having open courtyards, have been built of such dimensions as to enable the spectator to receive in its entirety a view of any one side of the interior facade from any point within the court ...."[35]

In this group of caves the verandahs containing stone benches mark another peculiar characteristic. This arrangement is found in the following : Rāṇī-*gumphā*, Bājāghara-*gumphā*, Alakāpurī-*gumphā*, Jayavijaya-*gumphā*, Ṭhākurāṇī-*gumphā*, Pātālapurī-*gumphā*, Mañcapurī-*gumphā*, Gaṇeśa-*gumphā*, Jambeśvara-*gumphā*, Dhānaghara-*gumphā*, Haridās-*gumphā* and Jagannātha-*gumphā*, (all in Udayagiri), Tatwa No. 1 and no. 2, Tentuli-*gumphā*, and cave No. 13 (in ruins) all in Khaṇḍagiri. The benches provided in these caves measuere about one foot to one foot and six inches in height, run round the three sides of the verandah. This arrangement evidently had been for the purpose of seating and resting. In this example the artist perhaps went one step further, and as a result in one example, i.e., the Triśūla cave (Khaṇḍagiri) the inside is benched. Further, the walls of the verandah in some examples contain niches. Thus both the sidewalls of the verandah of the Tatwa cave No. 1 contain niches each having one, while two niches are found at the end of the verandah in the triśūla-*gumphā*. These were perhaps for the purpose of keeping personal articles of the monks. This practice, further seems to be a departure from the general practice of carving niches on the interior walls in other parts of Indian rock-cut architecture.

The entrance to the cave in this example at Udayagiri and Khaṇḍagiri is of very small dimension. Some of the doorways are simple, while in others the doorways are elaboratly done and flanked by side pilasters. In some of the examples at Udayagiri (Chhoṭa Hāthī-*gumphā*, Gaṇeśa-*gumphā*, Bāgha-*gumphā* and Haridāsa-*gumphā*) there are inward sloping jambs.

The interior of the caves in the twin-hills is originally austerely plain. In some of the examples such as Ananta-*gumphā*, Navamuni-*gumphā*, Triśūla-*gumphā*, cave No. 10 and Lalāṭendukeśarī-*gumphā*, all in Khaṇḍagiri and Gaṇeśa-*gumphā* in Udayagiri relief sculptures of Jaina *Tīrthaṅkaras* and in some, *Śāsanadevīs* were added later[36]. However, in elaborate examples the facade of the caves alongwith the brackets that support the ceiling of the verandah are embellished with relief panels and sculpture respectively. Further, unlike the contemporary examples in western India, the interior of these caves are adequately lighted. This had been effected both by the direct opening of the caves into the verandahs, and by the profusion of door-opening.

The interior of the caves are generally oblong in plan which is in contrast to the western Indian examples. However, in some caves, viz., Jagannātha-*gumphā* and Dhānaghara-*gumphā* (both in Udayagiri); Ananta-*gumphā*, in Khaṇḍagiri the ceiling is of sufficient height to admit a man standing.

Further, although the ceiling is generally flat still in some of the examples it is of a convex shape. The latter examples are found in caves, viz., Alakāpurī-*gumphā*, the lower storey of the Ṭhākurāṇī-gumphā, Pātālapurī-*gumphā*, Mañcapurī-*gumphā* and Haridāsa-*gumphā* (all in Udayagiri); Tatwa No. 2, Ananta-*gumphā* and Bārabhujī-*gumphā* all are in Khaṇḍagiri.

In carrying out the task, the Orissan rock-cutters seem to have copied some of the techniques and patterns of the existing structural houses. On this point some of the prominent features may be noted. In the examples such as : Chhoṭa Hāthī-*gumphā*, Gaṇeśa-*gumphā*, Bāgha-*gumphā* and Haridāsa-*gumphā*, all in Udayagiri; the doorway jambs slightly incline inwards, and demonstrate further a comparatively wide base of the doorway than the top. This arrangement was followed in structural buildings to counter the outward thrust. In this connection the arched-like ceiling in some examples noted earlier[36] may also be pointed out which is a technique adhered to in the thatched-house constructions. Further, in the caves preceded with pillared verandah[37], the pillars are surmounted with brackets and architraves which in turn support the roof of the verandah mark another borrowing from the existing structural houses. In the above examples, like the thatch house the roof of the verandah is comparatively lower than that of the roof of the cell.

At the same time, however, this group of caves also demonstrates a different and independent line of development. Thus, unlike the western Indian examples where the central hall of the monastery was surrounded with cells on three sides, in this example the cells are directly made open either to the outer air or into the verandahs. In this context, the examples in the Barābar and Nāgārjunī hills in the district of Gaya, Bihar is noteworthy. These caves are the earliest examples of the cave architecture in India dedicated to the monks of the Ājīvika sect. Of all these caves the Sudāmā cave bearing the inscription of Aśoka[38] dated in his twelfth regnal year seem to be the earliest. In the Nāgārjunī hill nearly one km to the north of the Barābar hill, there are three caves, each bearing the inscription of Daśarath, the grandson of Aśoka[39]. All these caves are exact translations in stone of the contemporary wood and thatched structures[40]. These eastern Indian examples might have influenced the rock-cut activities at Udayagiri and Khaṇḍagiri.

All the excavations in these twin hills were meant for the habitation of the Jaina monks. None of them had been designed as a shrine or a temple. Indeed the absence of a shrine is a striking feature in this group of excavations. It is in contrast to the contemporary western Indian Buddhist rock-cut architecture, where the *Caitya* was an indispensable part for a complete monastic establishment. In explaining the absence of the *caitya* hall in the eastern part of India, and for that matter in Orissa, and simultaneously its existence in the western part of India it has been suggested that "on the one side of India they always had, and continued to use, wooden halls for this purpose, while on the other side, having no such structures, they at once adopted the idea of carving them in the rock ...."[41]. This means that the Jaina followers in the eastern part of India made use of wooden halls as their *caitya* shrines. It is difficult to accept the above contention in the light of the fact that while some of the prominent features of the caves at Udayagiri and Khaṇḍagiri are derived from wooden structures already in vogue, the excavators failed to copy the wooden halls for the purpose of *caitya* shrine. Elsewhere, it is further held that "the nature of their religion did not require large assembly halls like the chaityas of the Buddhists"[42]. Closely following the above line of argument, it is observed that "apparently, there was no need in the ceremonial observances of the Jainas"[43]. The above contentions bear some credence only when it is noticed that the twin hills of Udayagiri and Khaṇḍagiri are honycombed with *Vihāras* being of smaller proportions comparatively. But, on the other hand some interesting references in the Hāthīgumphā inscription are noteworthy in this connection. A passage in lines fifteen and sixteen[44] has been interpreted to mean that Khāravela caused to build at the cost of 75,00,000 (paṇas) a magnificent religious edifice which was provided with a beryl chamber (hall) with quadrangular floor and painted ceiling[45]. Further, the above authority has suggested that the roofed quadrangle has a colonnade of pillars apart from the beryl chamber[46]. Others have held that king Khāravela caused to construct subterranean chambers and caves containing a *caitya* temple and remarked that ".... the *caitya* here was a structural building, probably standing on the summit of Khaṇḍagiri hill, and that it has consequently been destroyed ...."[47]

The edifice might have been built in the vicinity of the caves in the Udayagiri. Here it may be noted that an excavation[48] immediately above the Hāthīgumphā has yielded the lower portion of a large apsidal structure which is believed to have been a place of worship[49]. In this context, it is further remarked that "the plan of the entire complex is so similar to the Buddhist caitya-*gṛhas* with their apse, nave and side-aisles that it is very likely that the circular wall formed the sanctum of the apse and the oblong chamber the hall or nave"[50]; belonging to the age of Khāravela[51].

To understand the various types of caves in the twin-hills some specimen examples may be noted and explained. In this context the following remark is noteworthy: "The architectural treatment of the Rāṇī-*gumphā* is characteristic of the Orissan style of rock architecture as a whole and provides the key to the entire movement"[52].

The Rāṇī-*gumphā* (See Plate) is a double-storeyed excavation, each floor consisting of a central wing and two abutting wings, arrangd on the three sides of an open courtyard measuring 49′ × 24′. The upper storey rests on the ground floor receding some feet back into the rock. The resulting terrace in front of the upper verandah is supplied with a flight of steps in the side. Both the storeys are provided with a narrow pillared[53] verandah, and the doorways in the rear wall are flanked by pilasters which are further connected with almost semi-circular arches (in the western Indian example it is of horse-shoe-shape). The lower main verandah measuring 43′ opens into three cells. In the central cell there are three doorways, while the lateral cells have two doorways each. The main verandah of the upper storey is 43′ in length, which further opens into four cells having two doorways in each cell. Besides the main wing; the provision of two side wings of cells, and two small guard rooms in the ground floor make the cave one of the most distinguished examples.

The general arrangement of this cave indicate some special purpose which was attached to it. In this connection it is commented that while most of the cells in this cave "were for the accommodation of the monks, there are several supplementary chambers and recesses evidently devised for special purposes connected with the ritual ..."[54] Citing the friezes on the wall of the upper storey and the open courtyard along with its overlooking terrace, the same authority further rightly observed that ".... this arrangement of courtyard and terraces forming the Rāṇī-*gumphā* constituted an open air theatre in which the scenes depicted in the sculptured frieze around it were brought to life by being performed on festivals as a kind of passion play[55]"

Like the Rāṇī-*gumphā*, the Mañacapurī-*gumphā* is also a double-storeyed excavation. The lower storey of this cave, known as Mañcapurī, was excavated by *mahārāja* Vakradeva and prince vaḍukha[56], while the upper storey, known as Svargapurī was excavated by the chief queen of Khāravela[57]. It is probable that the upper storey was an earlier excavation than the lower one. Both the storeys are preceded by a pillared verandah. In the upper storey there are three chambers, each of which is entered by a single doorway. The roof of the verandah of the upper storey has fallen. The lower storey which is comparatively bigger than the upper one, has five chambers, each entered by one doorway. Besides, there are two side rooms on the two sides of the verandah. There is a stone bench running along the back and the two sides of the verandah. The doorways are flanked by pilasters bearing cruciform capitals and superimposed by winged lions, which, in turn, support the archading containing relief panels.

One of the interesting features of this cave is the arrangement of the railing friezes in front of the rock between the two storeys, but mostly obliterated. The railing consists of square upright posts (*thaba*) with three double-convex crossbars (*sūcī),* which is further surmounted by the architrave rounded on the top. This arrangement resembles the railings that surround the *stūpas* at Sāñcī, Bhārhut and Bodhgayā belonging to the Suṅga period.

The Gaṇeśa-*gumphā*, situated on the highest peak of the Udayagiri, consists of two low-roofed cells preceded by a benched verandah in front measuring thirty feet in length and six feet in breadth and seven feet in height. The inner excavation measures seven feet and six inches in depth and thirty feet in length. The verandah in this cave is approached by a flight of steps, which is flanked by two elephants seemingly serving as guardians. The verandah was originally supported by five pillars and two side pilasters, but at present only three pillars are existent. The two cells of this cave are entered by four doorways, two in each cell. The shafts of the pillars which form the facade of the cave are square below and above, but octagonal in the middle (this type of pillars are common in the twin-hills). The pillars are provided with brackets which bear figures in relief, and in turn support the overhanging caves. The door-openings are flanked by pilasters with capitals consisting of a pair of addorsed animals such as Bull, Horse, Lion, and Deer, seated upon the corbelled abacus and the stepped base. In one example, i.e., on the front face of the left pilaster is carved in high relief a standing guard, clad in *dhoti* and scarf and wearing a turban. The arches being supported by the pilasters are filled with flowers and creepers issuing from the mouth of *makaras*, with *nandipada* or *śrīvatsa* in the top centre. From the one springing of the arch-band to another there runs horizontal railing consisting of two crossbars, octagonal upright posts being placed at regular intervals, and the superimposing coping stone.

The Bāgha-*gumphā* ("Tiger-cave") -(See Plate)- in the Udayagiri is a small cave but typical of a series of caves on this twin-hills (to this type also belongs the Sarpa-*gumphā* in the same hill). In this example the facade of the cell has been conceived and executed in the form of an expanded jaws of a Tiger, and so was it named. The antichamber which consists of a cell, measures nearly eight feet in width, six feet in depth and three and a half feet in hight; assumes a false appearance of the gapping mouth of a Tiger, while the doorway like that of the gullet. The door-jambs slope inwards and are flanked by pilasters on pot bases and superimposed by winged creatures as capitals. It may be noted that this cave was excavated by the town judge Subhuti or Bhuti[58], who definitely did not belong to the royal household. The exact implications of this cave along with that of the Sarpa-*gumphā*, however, cannot be ascertained.

The Ananta-*gumphā* on the Khaṇḍagiri, a single-storeyed and single cell cave, is one of the few important excavations on the hill. In front of the cave there is an open courtyard formed by the levelling of the high ledge to the north. The cave is preceded by a verandah measuring twenty-six feet in length and seven feet in breadth. There were originally four doorways[59] in the rear end of the verandah opening into the antechamber which measures twenty-four feet in length and seven feet in breadth. The ceiling of the cell is curved at its rear end. The doorways are flanked with persepolitan-like pilasters which bear some interesting features. The pedestal of the pilaster is formed by overlapping slabs which support a vase, out of which the shaft of the pilaster rises. However, all the pilasters are not provided with this kind of base. The shaft is rectangular at the bottom and at the top (except the example with a lotus capital), and octagonal at the centre. The shaft is surmounted with a spreading abacus in sections (in one example there is a full-blown lotus as abacus); which, in turn, supports an animal capital formed by pairs of reclining animals (in some cases there are winged animals). These pilasters, in turn, support archadings which are decorated with both human and animal figures and floral designs. Each arch is adorned with two three- headed snakes arising out of the middle of it. On top of the archading runs a long railing; a portion of which consists of three cross-bars, upright-posts and an architrave, while another portion is broken at regular intervals with battlemented pyramids. This kind of arrangement is a new feature in this group of caves, which was also noticed in the art of Bharhut in central India.

Following are the Caves at Udayagiri

Cave - 1. Rāṇī-*gumphā*

Cave - 2. Bājāghara-*gumphā*

Cave - 3. Chhoṭa-Hāthī-*gumphā*

Cave - 4. Alakāpurī-*gumphā*

Cave - 5. Jaya-Vijaya-*gumphā*

Cave - 6. Paṇaṣa-*gumphā*

Cave - 7. Ṭhākurāṇī-*gumphā*

Cave - 8. Pātālapurī-*gumphā*

Cave - 9. Mañcapurī-*gumphā*

Cave - 10. Gaṇeśa-*gumphā*
Cave - 11. Jambeśvara-*gumphā*
Cave - 12. Bāgha-*gumphā*
Cave - 13. Sarpa-*gumphā*
Cave - 14. Hāthī-*gumphā*
Cave - 15 Dhānaghara-*gumphā*
Cave - 16. Haridāsa-*gumphā*
Cave - 17. Jagannātha-*gumphā*
Cave - 18. Roṣei-*gumphā*

Following are the Caves at Khaṇḍagiri

Cave - 1. Tatowa-*gumphā* No. 1
Cave - 2. Tatowa-*gumphā* No. 2
Cave - 3. Ananta-*gumphā*
Cave - 4. Tentuli-*gumphā*
Cave - 5. Khaṇḍagiri-*gumphā*
Cave - 6. Dhyānaghara-*gumphā*
Cave - 7. Navamuni-*gumphā*
Cave - 8. Bārabhujī-*gumphā*
Cave - 9. Triśūla-*gumphā* (otherwise called Sātabakharā or Mahāvīra *gumphā*)
Cave - 10. (unnamed)
Cave - 11. Lalāṭendukeśarī-*gumphā*
Cave - 12. Ekādaśī-*gumphā*
Cave - 13.
Cave - 14. names are not known
Cave - 15.

The caves in both the hills mentioned above can be classified into following groups :

Table A (Udayagiri)

Sl. No.	Classification	cave no.
1	Rock shelter (Natural cavern)	14
2	Single cave without appendage	3, 6, 12, 13
3	Single cave with narrow pillar less verandah	18
4	Single cave with benched pillared-verandah	11, 15, 16, 17
5	Multiple-cell cave with benched-pillared-verandah	2, 5, 8, 10
6	Double-storeyed cave with pillared-benched-verandah	4, 7
7	Double-storeyed cave with pillared-benched-verandah and open courtyard	1, 9

Table B (Khaṇḍagiri)

1	Single cave without appendage	3
2	Multiple cave with pillared verandah	7
3	Double-storeyed cave	4, 11
4	Single cave with pillared verandah and open-courtyard	1, 8, 9
5	Single cave with pillard verandah	5, 6
6	Single cave with benched-verandah	2

Sculpture

In the field of Indian fine arts, the Jaina iconography and sculpture occupy a distinguished place. Among the various kinds of Jaina sculpture, the images of twenty-four *Tīrthaṅkaras*, needless to point out, occupy a unique position. All these *Tīrthaṅkaras* have been provided with their respective cognisance, *yakṣa* and *yakṣiṇī* figures[1]. Among all the accessory figures, the *yakṣa* and his female counterpart *yakṣiṇī*, also called *Śāsanadevatās* or attendant spirits are most important. The history of the *yakṣa* and *yakṣiṇī* figures in Indian art is rather instructive. As Coomaraswamy observes: "Behind the pale of Aryan orthodoxy and its tendency to abstract symbolism there lay an extensive and deep-rooted system of popular beliefs and cults and a decided tendency to anthropomorphic representation. These popular beliefs implied an iconography, such we actually find at Bhārhut of *Yakṣas* and *Nāgas*, *Devatās* and *Vṛkṣakas*, the Earth and Mother-goddesses and divinities of fertility, fairies and goblins and human heroes".[2] While dealing with the origin and early history of the *yakṣa* and the *yakṣī* Benjamin Rowland also draws attention to the point that "Among the Dravidian gods were innumerable place spirits, tutelary deities, and powers of nature conceived as personal beings. First the *yakshas* .... they were tree-spirits who were also worshipped as guardians of the mineral treasures hid in the earth and associated with the idea of wealth and abundance. The female conterpart of the *yaksha* was the *yakshi*, a sort of Indian dryad the spirit of the fertility of the tree"[3]. A *yakṣa*[4] is a devotee of the *Tīrthaṅkaras*. It is from the Gupta period that these *Śāsanadevatās* began to accompany the *Jina* icons. However, their affiliation with the *Jina* images was neither systematised nor found universally. On the other hand, we have the sole example of, Ambikā, the *yakṣiṇi* of Nemināthа, the twenty-second *Tīrthaṅkara* belonging to the Kuṣāṇa period[5]. It is only from the 8th century A.D., that all the twenty-four *yakṣas* and *yakṣiṇīs* were introduced in the Jaina iconography[6]. Simultaneously, in the same period, the nine planets (*navagrahas*)[7] started appearing on the two sides of a *Tīrthaṅkara* image.

In the iconographic representation of the *Tīrthaṅkaras*, the Jainas also incorporated various divine or semi-divine accessory figures who are generally depicted surrounding the main image. These figures are those of *Gaṇadharas*[8], *Gandharvas*[9], *Vidyādharas* and *Vidyādharīs*[10].

Besides the *Tīrthaṅkara* images along with their accompanying figures, various divinities found their way into the Jaina iconography. These deities are *Śruta-devī*[11] or Sarasvatī, the sixteen *Vidyādevīs*[12] or the goddesses of learning, and the goddess *Śrī*[13] or Laksmī.

The ten *Dikpālas*[14], guardians of the quarters, are an important group of divinities in the Jaina pantheon. These *Dikpālas* are always subservient to *Tīrthaṅkaras*, who were served and cared for by the *Dikpālas*. Towards the end of the eleventh century A.D. the figures of the mothers of all the *Tīrthaṅkaras*, each with a child on her lap also appeared in the Jaina pantheon. One particular form of sculpture, i.e., the artistic *āyagapaṭṭas*[15] belonging to the Suṅga-Kuṣāṇa period, mainly from Kaṅkāli Ṭilā in Mathura enriched the Jaina sculptural heritage was perhaps the sole creation of the Jainas.

The Jainas have a remarkable representation in art which may be regarded as a substitute for the Hindu Trinity, popularly known as *Caumukhī* and has a further name of '*Sarvatobhadra-pratimā*'[16]. Four important *Tīrthaṅkaras* are represented in this form of art on four sides with their characteristic symbols[17]. Another peculiar characteristic of the Jaina art particularly of south India - the free standing pillars known as *mānastambhas*[18] in front of the Jaina temples is noteworthy.

Among the secular representations the statues of *ācāryas*[19], donors and patrons belonging to the early medieval period are important.

In introducing various accessory deities into their pantheon, the Jainas seem to have copied it from the Brahmanical divinities. Thus it is observed that "In the hierarchy of the Jaina deities, especially in its broder outlines, many of the subsidiary members of the pantheon were direct copies of the Brahmanical Hindu divinities"[20]. Further, it is to be pointed out that though occasional reorientations were effected in early and medieval Jaina art, the names and iconographic features of most of the subsidiary divinities are similar to those of their Brahmanical counterparts.

The characteristic features of a *Jina* image have been referred to in various early medieval works. Thus, according to *Bṛhatsaṁhitā*[21] "the god of the *Arhats* (the Jainas; i.e., any of the 24 *Tīrthaṅkaras*) should be shown nude, young and beautiful in appearance, with a tranquil expression and arms reaching down to the knees; his breast should have the (auspicious) *Śrīvatsa* mark"[22].

The *Pratiṣṭāpāda*[23] states that a *Tīrthaṅkara* image should be depicted as a youth, and not as an old man or as a boy; and should bear the *Śrīvatsa* mark on the chest and should not bear nails or hair. The image should be made either of good metal or stone and should display the virtues of an ascetic. The *Pratiṣṭhā-sārodhāra*[24] speaks that a *Tīrthaṅkara* image should have a calm and serene face. The *Pratiṣṭhāsārasaṅgraha*[25] narrates that the icon of a *Tīrthaṅkara* should be young, nude and bear in chest a *Śrīvatsa* mark. His height should be 108 *aṅgulas*. The figure should not bear hair in the arm-pit or on any other part of his body and also no line for the moustache.

The *Vivekavilāsa*[26] speaks that a *Tīrthaṅkara* image should be depicted bearing *Śrīvatsa* on the chest and *uṣṇīṣa* on the head, arms reaching down to the knee and crowned by a double umbrella. The *Rūpamaṇḍana*[27] (one of the most important iconographic texts) gives an exhaustive account on the iconographic features of a *Jina* image.

Apart from the subsidiary figures, which have been discussed earlier, one of the most important characteristics of a *Jina* icon is its *lāñchanās*, which are manifested in the presence of the following eight *pratihāryas*[28] :

1. *Divyataru* or Aśoka or the particular tree under which the Enlightenment was attained;
2. A throne-seat;
3. Trilinear umbrella and a lion seat;
4. *Aura* of a beautiful radiance;
5. *Divya-dhvani*;
6. Showers of celestial blossoms;
7. Two *cowries*; and
8. Hevenly music[29].

A *Tīrthaṅkara* is always depicted with his cognisance or *cinha*, by which he is recognised. Other symbols of a *Jina* icon are mirror, urn, cane-seat (shaped like an hourglass), two small fish, flower garland and the book[30].

Apart from the characteristic features of the *Jina* image, the *Rūpamaṇḍana*[31] also describes seven *Śāsana-devatās* with their colour, *Vāhana* and other attributes. With some minor variations the *Aparājitapṛcchā* also describes the above seven *Śāsanadevatās*[32] respectively.

In our present problem of investigation relating to Orissa, the discussions are centred round the relief panels on the facade of the caves at Udayagiri and Khaṇḍagiri. A good number of round sculptures of Jaina *Tīrthaṅkaras* alongwith the other deities of the Jaina pantheon, discovered from different parts of Orissa are further discussed. All these apart, the more important sculptural representation on the walls of some of the caves at Udayagiri and Khaṇḍagiri belonging to the early medieval period, are discussed. In this connection it may be pointed out that though the other forms of Jaina sculptural art are not available so far, the possibilities of their availability cannot be doubted.

The facade of a good number of caves at Udayagiri and Khaṇḍagiri are decorated with sculptural panels in relief, which stylistically resemble the carvings on the railings and gateways (*toraṇas*) of Bhārhut and Sāñcī. Both religious and secular themes are depicted following broadly the primitive practice. Human figures both male and female; animal figures such as, elephant, horse, deer, monkey and geese; and that of plant life have been found depicted. Besides, a good number of scenes depicting both indoor and outdoor life are represented. They include storeyed structures, a cave doorway, seats, stools, jars, plates, ropes, umbrellas, musical instruments, straight swords, oblong shields, bows with arrows etc.

The carvings on the caves in general are simultaneously rude and vigorous. The quality of stiffness is very much there, though a conscious attempt is to overcome the qualities of immobility and stiffness is clearly discernible. In some of the important examples the artist seems to be at least partially successful in handling the problems of perspective, plasticity, naturalistic modelling and composition of both the forms and background. As observed by a critic, "The workmanship of the carvings is by no means uniform, but, taken as a whole, the execution displays a decided advance on the work of Bhārhut (second century B.C.)[33]. The Bhārhut reliefs are represented on the stone railings and gateways of *stūpas* "most likely dates from about 150 B.C., in the Śuṅga period"[34]. The carvings here are best complimented by Fergusson. According to him, "Some animals, such as elephants, deer, and monkeys, are better represented there than in any sculpture known in any part of the world; so too are some trees, and the architectural details are cut with an elegance and precision that are very admirable. The human figures, too, though very different from our standard of beauty and grace, are truthful to nature, and, where grouped together, combine to express the action intended with singular felicity. For an honest purpose-like pre-Raphaelite kind of art, there is probably nothing much better to be found elsewhere".[35]

In the present context, the study of Jaina religion through its sculptural representations in the caves of Udayagiri and Khaṇḍagiri, should be taken into consideration. The depiction of various symbols, if studied carefully, would throw considerable light in the proposed field of investigation. The following symbols pertaining to the Jaina creed are carved on the Udayagiri and Khaṇḍagiri caves : *Śrīvatsa*[36], *Svastika*[37], *Nandipada*[38], tree within railing[39], trilinear umbrella[40], snake[41], elephant, lion, bull, lotus[42] and *Śrī*[43]. In those early days, when image worship was not in vogue, these symbols are significant for the study of a religion in particular. Coomaraswamy observes on the importance of the symbols: "many of which have remained in use to the present day, lies in the fact that they represent a definite early Indian style amounting to an explicit inconography"[44]. Of course, it is true that in the early days of Indian history and religion these symbols were very much popular among and common to almost all the religious creeds. But keeping in view the architectural activities of the Jaina followers in the Udayagiri and Khaṇḍagiri caves[45], the symbols depicted therein may well be attributed to that of the Jaina creed.

The following caves bear the various kinds of Jaina symbols :

Udayagiri Caves

Rāṇī-*gumphā* (Lower storey)

In the right wing, the central arch over the doorway is crowned with a *śrīvatsa*, while that of the side arch with a *nandipada*. The arches, on the doorways of the two guard-rooms (excavated at the angles where the left and right wings meet that of the main), bear the *nandipada* as finial.

Upper storey

In the main wing, on the triangular portions above the arches, symbols of *śrīvatsa, nandipada*, lotus and snake are carved.

Alakāpurī-*gumphā*

In the upper cell, near the top of the right pilaster, an elephant is depicted entwined by a snake.

Jayavijaya-*gumphā*

On the space between the arches over the two doorways (this cave is a two-celled monastery each having a single doorway), there is the depiction of a sacred tree within a railing worshipped by a couple on either side. Besides, there is an umbrella depicted over the tree alongwith two banners by its sides.

Mañcapurī-*gumphā* (Lower storey)

In this cave all the four semi-circular arches over the four doorways are crowned either by *śrīvatsa* or *nandipada*.

Gaṇeśa-gumphā

In this cave (a two-celled one, each having two doorways) all the four arches above the doorways endowed with symbols of either *nandipada* or *śrīvatsa* in the top centre.

Bāgha-*gumphā*

To the right-hand side of the doorway arch, on the wall there is a triangle-headed symbol within a railing at the beginning of the inscription and at the end, a *svastika* symbol.

Khaṇḍagiri Caves

Tatwa-*gumphā* (no. 2)

All the three doorways of this single-cell cave have an arch over it, and are crowned by the symbol of *nandipada*.

Ananta-*gumphā*

In this cave all the arches over the four doorways are either crowned by a *nandipada* or a *śrīvatsa*.

On the third tympanum there is the depiction of *Śrī* or Lakṣmī (Plate - II) in a Lotus-lake. She is shown with stalks of full-blown lotuses entwining around her arms. She is being bathed by two standing elephants on lotuses on her sides pouring water over her from two pitchers. In this context the following observation is noteworthy : "The pediment sculptures of the Ananta include a standing *Māyā Devī* with elephants. In Buddhist art this would represent the Nativity of Buddha, in Hindu art *Gaja-Laksmī*, but what it represents, unless perhaps the Nativity of Mahāvīra, we do not know; it is one of many motifs, such as the *triratna*, and the *caitya*-tree, which are elsewhere Buddhist, but here employed in Jaina art"[46].

On the fourth tympanum there is depicted a tree within a railing under an umbrella (See Plate) . This sacred tree is worshipped by a woman offering a lotus on the left. On the right, a man is standing with folded hands. To the further left and rifht of the women and man two dwarfish figures are seen bringing a tray of offerings and spouted jars respectively.

On the top of all the four arches two three-headed serpents are depicted having their hoods raised and issuing out from the ton centre of the arches.

Further, in the interior, on the back wall of the cell there is carved a *nandipada* on a stepped pedestal the latter being flanked on either side by a set of three symbols : a triangle-headed symbol and a *śrīvatsa* both again on two stepped pedestals, and a *svastika*.

Besides all these recognised symbols on the outer wall of the Mañcapurī cave in the Udayagiri there is a significant relief (See - Plate) . On the space between the second and the third doorways, over the railing which is carved on the springing of the arches there was perhaps an object of worship but obliterated completely. On the right there are four standing figures with folded hands, and on the left an elephant, suggesting probably that the devotees came by that elephant. The second figure from the right is wearing a crown. His scarf is distinct from that of the other figures. This distinction suggests that he was perhaps a royal figure. All the figures depicted are wearing *dhotis*, scarfs and heavy *Kuṇḍalas*. Above the figures are seen the symbol of sun and two flying *gandharvas* carrying musical instruments. On the extreme left corner a flying *vidyādhara* is carved hastening towards the worshipping object with a tray of flowers held in his left hand. The relief composition clearly suggests a religious object being worshipped with great veneration by the king and other royal members. It has been suggested that the subject of the relief "is no doubt the worship of some Jaina religious symbol"[47]. The royal figure among the worshipping figures of the relief is possibly the great Cedi king *Kaliṅgādhipati* Khāravela, who recovered the Kaliṅga *Jina* from the king of Magadha.

While dealing with the identification of the king exhibited on the relief, the following are to be considered. In the right wing of the lower storey of the Rāṇī-*gumphā*, in the space between the second doorway-arch and that of the third from the right are depicted three human figures - one male and two females with folded hands in an attitude of devotion. All of them seated on a bench flanked by women holding a tray and a vase on the left and right side respectively. An umbrella is visible over the male figure apparently suggesting that he is the king.

In the same cave, in the main wing, in the same position, and in the third relief panel from the right is depicted a royal personage under an umbrella, seated on an animal and also accompanied by his attendants. Further, in the fifth, sixth, seventh and eight relief panels there are also the depiction of a king along with his followers. The king in these panels is shown with an umbrella over him.

In the ninth panel there is the carving of the scene of reception that was accorded to the king. The king is depicted standing on the right and an umbrella is held over him by an attendant. Two of his men are holding swords over their shoulders. To the left there are six figures, four women and two men wearing turbans. Amongst the women, three are carrying pitchers on their heads, while the kneeling fourth women is kneeling down and is shown offering the contents of her pitcher.

It is interesting to note in this connection that the entire series of panels depicted on this wing of the Rāṇī-*gumphā*, barring the first two panels, has a royal figure. The king in the relief panels may well be taken as Khāravela. In this context it may be pointed that since Khāravela had led successful campaigns against Magadha to recover the *Jina* of Kaliṅga he was depicted for perpetuity for his act in stone relief panels.

A king with his queen are also depicted on the fifth compartment in a long frieze that occupy the space in between the arches of the main wing of the upper storey of the Rāṇī-*gumphā*. The king is seated on the extreme left, with his right hand held against his chest. On the right of the panel the queen is shown sitting with five of her attendants. All the attendants are seen engaged in their duties. This scene is apparently a dancing one for in the centre of the frieze three women are depicted dancing while three others sitting on the ground playing different musical instruments. Judging by its architecture and various relief panels, it may be suggested that the cave was excavated during the age of Khāravela, and the royal figure in the relief panels may well be that of Khāravela.

In course of our analysis it is to be further noted, as Coomaraswamy[48] has observed that in the Rāṇī and Gaṇeśa *gumphā*, the "scenes, which include the hunting of a winged deer, fighting scenes, the carrying off a woman, etc., have not been identified, but may be presumed to be taken from Jaina legends and to have an edifying value equivalent to that of the Buddhist *Jātakas*".

From the close of the age of Khāravela to the end of the Gupta period very few sculptural remains pertaining to Jainism have been found from Orissa. On the contrary, from the post-Gupta period onwards, and throughout the early medieval period a good number of Jaina sculptures have been found from different parts of Orissa. These stone sculptures are caved in the round, and may be taken as a veritable treasure house for the study of the Jaina creed, art and iconography. Besides these stone sculptures, some bronze Jaina icons have also been found from different parts of Orissa.

The village Podasingi[49] situated in the district of Keonjhar has yielded a number of Jaina images. The earliest inscribed image of a Jaina *Tīrthaṅkara* (Ṛṣabhanātha) in Orissa is found from this village, and the image is depicted as seated on a lotus pedestal in *dhyānamudrā*[50]. A bull, the cognisance of Ṛṣabhanātha, is shown below the image. In front of the bull there is depicted a lamp and two kneeling figures with folding hands, identified with Bharata and Bāhubali[51]. The image of Ṛṣabhanātha shows a well-proportioned physique with half-closed eyes, curly hair, *uṣṇīṣa*, and elongated earlobes. Behind the head there is a round halo, *prabhā-maṇḍala*[52], and above the head on either side two flying *Gandharvas* holding garlands are carved.

From the same place another image of Ṛṣabhanātha has also been found. It is shown in the posture of *yoga* known as *Kāyotsarga*[53] (dedication of the body) on a lotus pedestal supported by two lions. The bull is carved below the pedestal. The image is flanked by *Gaṇadharas* on either side. The image exhibits half-closed eyes, elongated ears, and a *jaṭā* as head-dress with some locks falling on the shoulders. The head is further crowned by an umbrella. Behind the head there is the round halo. Two flying *Gandharvas* holding garlands are carved on either side of the round halo. Near the umbrella is seen a musical instrument being played on by a pair of hands. Scholars have assigned the above two figures to the eighth century A.D. on stylistical grounds and held that these figures exhibit features of the Gupta tradition[54].

An image of Pārśvanātha has been discovered from the village of Kosali situated in the district of Mayurbhanj. This image (See Plate) is depicted in *Kāyotsarga* pose on a lotus which is placed on a serpant. The lotus-pedestal is flanked by two figures on either side. On to his left there is a kneeling figure with folding hands; while on the right a seating figure is depicted holding an object. Close to these small figures are seen the figures of *yakṣa* to the right and *yakṣiṇī* to the left, both standing on lotuses and in *tribhaṅga* pose. The serpant is depicted on its coils behind the main figure and raises it seven-hoods over the head of the image. The head of the image wears a *jaṭā* in three tires, while the ears are elongated. Near the raised hood on either side on the top corners are carved two figures of *Vidyādharas*.

In the present Jagannātha temple at Baripada in the District of Mayurbhanj, the images of *Tīrthaṅkaras*, such as, Ṛṣabhanātha, Neminātha, Pārśvanātha, and Mahāvīra are found set against the wall of the inside gate. The black-granite-stone image of Pārśvanātha (See Plate) is depicted in *Padmāsana* with his palms, the right one on the left, placed on his soles. The chest of the image bears a prominents *rīvatsa* symbol. The ears are elongated and touch the shoulders. The image is crowned by a thirteen-hooded serpant.

The findings from Khiching in the district of Mayurbhanj include some interesting specimens. Among these the figures of Ṛṣabhanātha and Mahāvīra on one stele (See Plate) now preserved in the British Museum, London, is considered as a beautiful and iconographically important specimen. It belongs to the period circa ninth-tenth centuries A.D.[55] On the stele the image of Ṛṣabhanātha is depicted to the right and that of Pārśvanātha to the left. Both the images are in identical posture, i.e., *Kāyotsarga*, standing on a *padma-pīṭha* which contains five double-pettled lotuses - three full and two half. Below the *padma-pīṭha* and on the pedestal there are carved bull (the cognisance of Ṛṣabhanātha) and lion (the cognisance of Pārśvanātha) respectively on the right and left of the stele. On the pedestal are also visible some kneeling devotees with folded hands. Both the images are flanked by two *cauri*-bearers on either side standing on the *Padmapīṭha*. The figures are well proportioned and carved with delicacy. The eyes are half-closed and the ears are elongated. The image of Ṛṣabhanātha wears a tiered crown parted in the middle, while in case of Pārśvanātha the hair on the head is presented by snail-cell curls. Further, both the *Tīrthaṅkara* images are crowned by a quadrilinear umbrella over their heads. Behind the head of both the figures are carved a simple round halo, which carry at its edge two flying figures. Above these flying figures are further carved two small trilinear umbrellas on either side of the quadrilinear umbrella.

The village Charmpa situated near the present Bhadrakh Railway Station was an important centre for Jaina art and religion during the ninth and tenth centuries A.D.[56]. This place has yielded a number of Jaina *Tīrthaṅkara* images. Amongst the images that are at present housed in the Orissa State Museum at Bhubaneswar, the images of Ṛṣabhanātha (the first) Ajitanātha (the second) Śāntinātha (the sixteenth) and Mahāvīra (the last) are significant.

The image of Ṛṣabhanātha is depicted standing on a pedestal in *Kāyotsarga* posture. The image is flanked by Bharata and Bāhubali on either side. Below the pedestal is carved the *Vṛṣabha* - the cognisance of the first *Tīrthaṅkara*. The image wears a *jaṭā*, of which some of the looks fall on the shoulders. On the back slab there is carved the figures of eight planets, four on either side. At the top of the slab, behind the head of the image, are relieved two flying *Gandharvas* on either side.

Ajitanātha is depicted seated in *dhyānāsana* - meditative pose with his hands placed on the legs. His *Gaja* (elephant) is carved below the pedestal. This image wears a *jaṭā*-knot at the top of the head. The head is crowned by a trilinear umbrella and a *Kalpa-vṛkṣa*. The image is flanked on either side by figures of *Gaṇadharas* holding *cauris* in their right hands at the bottom, and flying *Gandharvas* with garlands in their hands at the top.

The image of Śāntinātha (See Plate) is shown seated in *dhyānāsana*. His cognisance *Mṛga* (deer) is carved below the pedestal. The *Tīrthaṅkara* wears a *jaṭā*-knot. Like the previous image, this one is also flanked on either side by figures of *Gaṇadharas* holding *cauris* in their right hands at the bottom, and that of flying *Gandharvas* holding garlands at the top.

The image of Mahāvira is depicted in *Kāyotsarga* posture. One of the interesting features ofthis image is that *Siṁha* (Lion), the cognisance of Mahāvīra is carved at each corner of the pedestal.Flanking the image on eithersidethereare the figures of *cauri*-bearers standing on lotus which are placedon the heads of the lions. The face of this *Tīrthannkara* image is mutilated badly.

Except the image of Ṛṣabhanātha, all the three images exhibit deep-cut-marks on their body. This cut-marks evidently indicate the rigours of the austerities through which a *Tīrthaṅkara* is supposed to pass in order to make himself fit and competent to attain the final knowledge.

The image of Pārśvanātha (See Plate) found from the village Pundal[57] in the district of Balasore is depicted in *Kāyotsarga* posture on a lotus pedestal. On the pedestal, stand on either side of the image, the *Gaṇadharas* holding *cauri* in their right hands; both of them depicted in *tribhaṅga* pose. Below the lotus pedestal is carved seven small figures holding certain objects. The eyes are half-closed and the ears are elongated. The image wears a *jaṭā*-knot. The image is crowned by a seven serpent's hoods, which is futher shown in the back of the figure on its coils. The trilinear umbrella is shown on top of the image just from the top of the figures of *Gaṇadharas*, the figures of eight planets, four on each side, are carved. All these eight planet figures are depicted in *dhyānāsana*. The ninth planet *ketu* does not find a place in the carvings. Above the figures of the planets arecarved figures of *Gandharvas*, two each in either side. Above them on the topcorners are carved the figures of flying *Vidyādharis* on either side. Two figures of Fairies are also carved on the topflanking the trilinear umbrella.

Amongst the findings from the Bhimapur village in the Balasore district, the image of Mahāvīra (See Plate) is noteworthy. This granite-stone image is depicted in *Kāyotsarga* posture on a pedestal. Below the pedestal may be recognised the figure of a lion - the cognisance of Mahāvīra, and other small figures in folding hands. The eyes of the image is shown half-closed. The head wears a *jaṭā*-knot, which, in turn, crowned by a trilinear umbrealla on top. Behind the head there is a semi-circular *prabhā*. Close to the right leg ofthe image is seen a kneeling devotee with folding hands. On the pedestal, colse to the image on both the sides arethe figures of two *Gaṇadharas* holding *cauris*in their right hands, carved in *tribhaṅga*pose. On both the sides of the image, just from above the *Gaṇadharas* are carved the miniature figures of all twenty-four *Tīrthaṅkara* figures are shown in *Kāyotsarga* posture. Flanking on either side of the trilinear umbrella on top of the head, are carved two flying figures with certain certain objects in their hands.

Amongst the findings of the Jhadeswarapur village[58] in the Cuttack district, the six feet image of Mahāvīra is significant. This image is depicted in *Kāyotsarga*posture on a pedestal. The elongated earlobs, half-closed eyes and above all the *jaṭā*-- knot on top of the head, which, in turn, crowned by a trilinear umbrella are all in tune to the aesthetic import of the image. The image is flanked by two *Gaṇadhara* figures on either side holding *cauris*. Just above the *Gaṇadhara* figures on either side holding cauris. Just above the *Gaṇadhara* figures, there is depicted the figures of eight planets, four on each side. Aobve the planet figures are carved two flying figures on either side. Two small figures are also seen, which are flanking the trilinear umbrella.

The region around the Prāchī Valley[59] has yielded a considerable number of Jaina images. One image of Ṛṣabhanā now housed inside the Swapaneśwara temple in the villageof Adasapur has been assigned to the seventh century A.D.[60]. This image is carved in *Kāyotsarga* posture on a lotus petal placed on the middle of a pedestal which is flanked bytwo lions. On the pedestal are also carved two other lotus petals on either side of the middle one. Belowthe feet of the figure is carved the bull, the cognisance of Ṛṣabhanātha, which is flankedbytwo figures of *Upāsikās* on either side on lotus petals with fly whisks on their heads. The image wears*Kuṇḍalas* in both of his ears and *jaṭā* on topof his head. Behind the head there is the *prabhā* carved exquisitely. The aesthetic qualities of this image are discernible in its divine grace and the anatomical perfections. On the either side of the image there carved the figures of allthe twenty-four *Tīrthaṅkaras*, twelve in each side in pairs. On top of the *Tīrthaṅkara* figures, flanking the main image are carved the figures of divine musicians holding musical instruments.

The region under the Jeypur sub-division in the southern most district of Koraput has yielded some *Tīrthaṅkara* images and other Jain relics. Among the finds six Ṛṣabhanātha images have been discovered from Kamta (two), Charamula (one), Bhairavasingapur (two) and Jamunda (one) villages, at present housed in the district museum at Jeypur[61] . The images from Kamta measure 98 × 50 cm and 75 × 45 cm, from Charamulā 81 × 40 cm are carved outof black-granite, while those from Bhairavasinghapr 56 × 36 cm and 51 × 33 cm, from Jamunda 58 × 34 cm are carved out of chlorite. All the images have been assigned to the post-Gupta period[62].

All the figures of Ṛṣbhanātha bear almost identical features, and depicted in *paryaṅkāsana* on a lion throne with their hands in *yoga-mudrā*. At the bottom of the seat is carved the bull, the cognisance of Ṛṣbhanātha, in three examples, while it is damaged in other three. Further, below the seatand above the pedestal few *Tīthaṅkara* images are carvedin *dhyānamudrā* in two examples. The images wear elongated ear-lobs and a *Jaṭāmukuṭa* some of the locks of which falling on the shoulders. In all the images the head is crowned by a trilinear umbrella, which, in turn, is surmounted by a drum player and a tree of perfect knowledge. Behind the head, in all images there is a round or egg-shaped halo with flying *Gandharvas* atthe edges with garlands. Flanking the images at the bottom there is *yakṣa* Gomukha sitting or standing tothe right, while to the left there are devotees with *Śāanadevā* Cakreśvarī sitting in the middle. In some images around the ha'o is carved figures of *makaras*, elephants, devoteesand musicians playing various musical instruments. The face along with the front side of the torso of all the images have been badly mutiliated. The *śrīvatsa* mark may be seen faintly in somes.

During the tenth and eleventh centuries A.D., the region of Udayagiri and Khaṇḍigiri became once again a flourishing centre of Jaina religion and art in Orrissa. In this age some of the caves of these hills were converted into sanctuaries with the carving of the *Tīrthaṅkara* images along with their *Śāanadevīs* on the inside walls of the caves. Here it may be pointed out that the cave excavations were of earlier period dating back to the centuries around the Christian era, while the carvings were added during the eleventh and twelfth centuries A.D. and even later.

Images of the Jaina pantheon are to be found in the following caves, although most of the images are now in a mutilated state : Gaṇeśa-*gumphā* (Udayagiri), Ananta-*Gumphā*, Navamuni-*gumphaā*, Bārabhujī-*gumphā*, Triśūla- *gumphā*, cave no. 10 (this cave is so far unnamed) and Lalāṭendukeśarī-*gumphā*, all in Khaṇḍagiri. Gaṇeśa-*gumphā* contains the image of a single *Tīrthaṅkara*, and a figure of Gaṇeśa; Ananta-*Gumphā*, a single *Tīrthaṅkara* image; Navamuni-*gumphā*, ten *Tīrthaṅkara* images, seven *Śāsanadevīs* and a figure of Gaṇeśs; Bārabhujī-*gumphā*, twenty-five *Tīrthaṅkara* images, (Pārśvanātha being represented twice), twenty-six *Śāsandevīs*; Triśūla-*gumphā*, twenty-four *Tīrthaṅkara* images, (Pārśvanātha being represented twice), twenty-six *Śāsanadevīs*; Triśūla-*gumphā*, twenty-four *Tīrthaṅkara* images; cave no. 10, two *Tīthaṅkara* images and one *Śāanadevī*; and Lalāṭendukeśarī-*gumphā*, image of eight *Tīrthaṅkaras*.

For the age of these above carvings scholars have tentatively assigned the period eighth to eleventh centuries A.D., but at the same time observed that "the caves containing medieval Jaina figures need not necessarily be as late as that, for we have in the Gaṇeśa- *gumphā*, one of the old caves, an instance of an image of Gaṇeśa having been carved out of the back wall of the cave at a much later date[63]". However, the inscriptions of the Somavaṁśī king Udyotakeśarī[64] bound in the Navamuni-*gumphā* and Latātendukeśarī- *gumphā* apparently suggest that the caves were converted into sanctuaries during the eleventh and twelfth centuries A.D. Apart from the epigraphical evidences, stylistical considerations of the sculptures in the cave also conform to the above fact.

The Ananta-*gumphā* (Khaṇḍagiri), a long cell cave, contains an unfinished *Tīrthaṅkara* image. On the back wall of the cave below the symbols of *śrīvatsa* and *svastika* which are carved to the right of a *nandipada* on a stepped pedestal, the Tīrthaṅkara image was carved.

The Navamuni-*gumphā*, originally a two dwelling- cell cave, converted into a sanctuary by excavating the floor to greather depth and by carving the figures of *Tīrthaṅkaras*. The partition-wall between the cells was also made to broken. On the back wall of what was originally the right cell, there are the images of seven *Tīrthaṅkaras* (See Plate) : Ṛṣabhanātha (the first), Ajitanātha (the second), Sambhavanātha (the third), Abhinandana (the fourth), Vāsupūjya (the twelfth) (See Plate) , Pārśvanāatha (the twenty-third) and Neminātha (the twenty-second) ion high relief. All these *Tīrthaṅkaras are carved in a row within niches rounded at the top, and seated in yog-mudra*[65] with the legs crosed. The treatment of their *jaṭās* is very much interesting. Neminātha, the sixth one from the left wears his spiral curls arranged in a top-knot. The first, fourth, fifth and seventh representation from the left wear tied *jaṭās* being folded on their heads. The second and third relieved images have their *jaṭās* arranged in the shape of a cone. All the *Tīrthaṅkara* images are crowned with a trilinear umbrella on top of their *jaṭās*, which are flanked by a pair of hads playing musical instrumets. One of the peculiar features of these images is the absence of the *Śrīvatsa* mark on their dhests. All *Tīrthaṅkara* images are flanked on either side by standing fly-whisk-bearers wearing Loin-cloth.

Below the row of these *Tīrthaṅkara*, are carved respectively in another row and in medium relief, their *Śāsanadevīs*-Cakreśvarī, Ajitabalā, Duritārī, Kālikā, Caṇḍī, Ambikā and Padmāvatī preceded by the figure of kGaṇeśa in the left. All these *Śāsanadevīs*-are relieved within niches rounded at the top. They are clad in *śāḍnīs* and short scarfs placed on their chests and left shoulders, and are bedecked in ornaments.

Besides these *Tīrthaṅkara* images and their *Śāsanadevīs*, on the right-hand wall of the cave are carved two unde figures of Ṛṣabhanātha and Pārśvanātha in moserate relief, but without their *Śāsanadevīs*. Both the images are depicted in *yogāsana* posture on a lotus and flanked by figures of fly-whisk-bearers. The unfinished image of Ṛṣabhanātha has his cognisance, bul below his seat and around *prabhā* behind his head. Pāśvanātha sated under a seven-hooded snake and weare his *jaṭā*. Flanking the hoods are two flying figures holding a garland, Below the lotus-seat of the image there is carveda*ghaṭa* which is flanked by a *ṇāga*-figure.

Further, on the left wall there is the compatatively small figure of Candrapreabha, the eighth *Tīrthaṅkata*. Canraprabha is seated on a lotus and has has cognisance *śaśī (moon) below.*

In this cave the importance of Pārśvanātha is easily discernible since he is represented twice and is made distinguished by his serpent hoods.

Adjacent to Navamuni-*gumphā* is the Bārabhujī-*gumphā*, a veritable treasure house of Jaina sculptures. This *gumphā* is a long chamber, the height of which was increased by digging out the floor. The dividing walls werealso removed to convert it into a long sanctuary and subsequently the carvings occurred in the walls of cave and verandah.

All the three sides of the antechamber are relieved with twenty-four seated *Tīrthaṅkaras*, and one standing image of Pārśvanātha at the beginning of the back wall. All the twenty-four *Tīrthaṅkara* images are depicted in *yogāsana* on doubled petalled lotuses supported on lions, and crowned by trilinear umbreallas. Below the lotus-seats are carved their distinctive cognisances, which do not always tally with the traditional prescriptions. All the images except that of Pārśvanātha show halo behind their heads. Like in the previous cave here also the *śrīvatsa* mark is absent. All the*Tīrthaṅkaras* areflanked by standing attendants holding fly-whisks. The trilinear umbrella is flanked on either side on top corner of each compartment by flying figures holding garlands. In between them on top are seen musical instruments played by hands.

Below the twenty-four *Tīrthaṅkaras*, their respective *Śāsanadevīs* are carvedin a row. Except Nirvāṇī, the *Śāsanadevī* of Śāntinātha, he sixteenth*Tīrthaṅkata* and Naradatta, the *Śāsanadevī* of Muninātha, the twentieth *Tīrthaṅkata* all other *Śāsanadeyīs* are depicted in *ardhaparyaṅkāsana*[66]. *Śāsanadevī* Nirvāṇī is shown seated cross legged, while Naradattaas lying. Twenty of the *Śāsanadevīs* are shown seated on seats, while the fourth, sixteenth, twenty-second and twenty-third are represented on lotuses, and below the lotus there are depected their animalmounds. All the *Śāsanadevīs* wear śāḍhīs, and are richly ornamented with necklaces, ear ornaments, girdles and bangles. Besides, Naradatta and Padmāvatī, the latter is the *Śāsanadevī* of Pārśvanātha, who are crowned by a capopy of snake, all other *Śāsanadevīs* bear haloes behind their heads.

The standing image of Pārśvanātha carved in the beginning ofthe back wall is larger in sixe than the rest represented in groups. However, this time Pārśvanātha is not providedwith his *Śāsanadevī*. This image is depicted in *Kāyotsarga* pose on adoubled-petalled ltus, topped a serpent. On the top flanking the head are flying figures holding garlands, and inbetween these figures there are carved musical instruments being played by hands. A three-hooded *nāga* is shown seated with folding hands on either side of the image, while a fly-whisk-bearer depicted standing one above the other.

Two twelve-armed figures of *Śāsanadevīs* are carved on the left and rith walls of the verandah, and hence the name Bārabhujī-*gumphā*. On the left wall there is the figure of Cakreśvarī, the *Śāsanadevī* of Ṛṣabhanātha seated on a double-petalled lotus. She isdepicted wearing *śāḍī*,ornamented profusely and crowned by a *mukuṭa*. One of her right hands is in *varadāmudrā*[67], while the second and third hold a sword and a disc respectively. One of her left hands is held against her chest, while three other hold a shield, a bell and a dise. The other attrubutes are notintact. Below her lotus- pedestal there is the figure of a devotee with a water-pot and further below a figure of *Garuḍa*. Above the head of this *Śāsanadevī* there is carved her *Jina* Ṛṣabhanātha with his cognisance, bull below.

Ajitabalā, the *Śāsanadevī* of Ajitanātha is shown seated with her bull below, in the same pose as that of Cakreśvarī, under her *Jina* who is depicted with his cognisance *Gaja* (elephant). A few attributes are recognised such as banner, *aṅkuśa*, dise in the right hands; and water-pot, twig and dise in the hands.

Adjacent to Bārabhujī-*gumphā*, there is excavated the Triśūla-*gumphā* which was converted to a sanctuary in the same manner as that of the former. This cave contains on the threesides of the antechamber the images of twenty-four *Tīrthaṅkaras* in relier[68]. The carving is crude and has been assigned to the period not earlier than the fifteenth century A.D.[69]

Amongst all the *Tīrthaṅkaras*, eight, viz.,Ṛṣabhanāanātha, Ajitanātha, Śītalanātha, Śreyāṁśanātha, Vāsupūjya, Vimalanātha, Pārśvanātha and Mahāvīra; the first, second, tenth, eleventh, twelfth, thirteenth, twenty-third and twenty-fourth *Tīrthaṅkara* respectively are depicted in *Kāyotsarga* posture. The height of these standing images is larger than those of their seated counterparts. Ṛṣabhanātha is the largest figure in the whole group.

All the remaining images of *Tīrthaṅkaras* are depictedseatedin *yoga mudrā* on lotuses resting on a pedestal being supported by lions. All of them are provided with fly-whisk-bearers.

In the entire group of figures one peculiarity is seen in the arrangement. That is the figure of Pārśvanātha is placed in the centre under a seven-hooded canopy, This is unusual since Pārśvanātha, instead of being shown befor Mahāvīra, is depicted in the centre of the group.

Further, the base of the fifteenth *Tīrthaṅkara* is blocked by a masonry structure. On this are placed three chlorite images of Ṛṣabhanātha. All the images stand on a double-petalled lotus in *Kāyotsarga* pòsture and withoutany garment . Below the lotus there are the depiction of bulls, the cognisance of the *Tīrthaṅkara. The images are flanked by standing fly- whisk--bearers wearing* dhotisand decked in ornaments. On topthere are flying figures with garlands, and musical instruments played by hands. The back slab of the figures, except that of the smallest one is relieved by the figures of eight plantes four on each side of the image. The larges among these figures bears a trefoil arch behind its head. The *śrīvatsa* symbol is absent in all the figures. On stylistical ground these three images have been assigned to the eleventh-twelfth century A.D.[70]

Three relief figures (See Plate) two of Ṛṣabhanādha and one of the Āmrā, the *śāsanadevī of Neminātha are carved on the back wall of cave no. 10 (the cave is now destroyed). The figures of Ṛṣabhanātha are dipicted in Kāyotsarga* pose on a double-petalled lotus, below is a bull. The pedestal is supported by a pair of lions. Each of the figures is flanked by *cauri*-bearers on the pedestal, while there are eight *grahas* on the two sides of the figure. On the top near the head, are two fly-whisk-bearers. The figure to the left is topped by a trilinear umbrella over its head. In the other example the central trilinear umbrella is further flanked by two trilinear umbrellas. Both the figures wear *jaṭā- mukuṭas*. The figure of Āmrā, which is partly mutilated, stands in a tribhaṅga pose under a mangotree, on the top of which is here *Jina*.

Near cave no. 10 is the Lalāṭendukeśari- *gumphā*, also damaged. On the back and left walls of the left cell (originally it consisted of two cells with a benched-verandah in front) are carved two figures of Ṛṣabhanātha and three of Pārśvanātha, while on the right cell there are two figures of Pārśvanātha and one of Ṛṣabhanātha. All the figures are dipicted in *Kāyostsarga* pose.

In the Udayagiri caves, the Gaṇeśa-*gumphā* has a rather crude representation of a *Tīthaṅkara* image seated in *yoga-mudrā*. On stylistic grounds it may belong to a late period in comparison with those in the Khaṇḍagiri caves.

Besides the stone sculptures, a good number of bronze images pertaining to the Jaina creed have been found from Orissa. One icon of Ṛṣabhanātha found from Kakatpur in district Puri now preserved in the Indian Museum, Calcutta, is interesting. The icon is in *Kāyotsarga* pose on a lotus pedestal, below which is the bull. The head wears a *jaṭā-mukuṭa*, some of the lock of which falling over the shoulders.

Of the bronze icons, that have come to light so far from Orissa, those from Achutrajpur near Banapur (now preserved in the Orissa State Museum, Bhubaneswar) in the district of Puri are most striking. These icons are datable to the eighth and ninth centuries A.D.[57] No two images are alike, for which scholars have doubted their local casting[58]. The icon Āmrā is sitting elegantly in the *Lalitāsana* posture on a *padma-pīṭha*. She holds a twig with a bunch of mangoes on her right palm, while the left fore-arm supports the back of a child seted on her left thigh. Her right leg is pendant, close to which there is a seated small figure. Behind the figure is the back-rest. The lintel and jambs of the back-rest shows beaded edge. The back-rest is superimposed by a oval *Prabhā* which is topped by three diminishing umbrellas.

The icon of Ṛṣabhanātha is seated in *Saṁparyaṅkāsana*. With half-closed eyes concentrating on the tip of the nose, oval face, elongated ear-lobs, full lower lip, expanding chest, the icon fully conforms to the *yoga-mudrā*.

The icon of Candraprabha displays the aesthetic quality with roundish face, elongated ear-lobs, short neck, broad shoulders and expanding chest. The icon is standing in the *kāyotsaga* pose on a lotus, which rests on a high pedestal. The fingers of the long, hanging arms are gently touching the lowest part of the thigh.

The icon of Vāsupūjya is represented with his *yakṣa*, Kumāra and *yakṣiṇī*, Caṇḍī. In the composition the *yakṣa* and *yakṣiṇī* are given importance. The *Tīrthaṅkara* is seated cross-legged with palms rested on the soles. The *yakṣa* and *yakṣiṇk* of the *Tīrthaṅkara* are seated side by side in the *mahārājalilā* posture on an oblong hollow pedestal. Both of them are wearing anklets, a waist band, bangles, armlets, ear-ṣtuds, a neckless, an *upavīta* and a *mukua*. Below the pedestal are seen seven male figures which along with one in between the seated *yakṣa* and *yakṣiṇī* probably stand for the eight *grahas*.

Another icon of a *Trthaṅkara*, is seated cross-legged in *padmāsana* on a lotus pedestal and flanked by two male attendants. The palms rest on the toes (the right one is one the left). The hair is arranged in tiny curls, and the *uṣṇīṣa* is rendered by two super-imposed rows of pellets. The plastic quality is highlighted by the disciplined body with high shoulders, expanded chest, narrow waist, placid face with half-closed eyes and elongated ear-lobs. The back-rest of the throne is elaborately ornamented with beaded lines and a row of flowers between the mouldings. The ends of the lintel are decorated with lotuses above which are peched *makaras*. Behind the head of the icon is a roundish halo with moulded border. In the absence of any cognisance or symbol it is not possible to identify the icon.

References

1. Fergusson. J., *A History of Indian and Eastern Architecture*, II 10 - 19 in Udayagiri and 12 in Khaṇḍagiri; Marshall, J.H., in *CHI* (ed.) Rapson, E.J., I, p. 579 - altogether 35 caves. *BODG*. (Puri), follows the numbers in the map after p. 284, referred to by Fergusson, J.; *BDGP*., p. 251-44 in Udayagiri, 19 in Khaṇḍagiri and 3 in Nilagiri. This is also referred to by Shah, C.J., *Jainism in North India*, p. 151; Shastri, K.A.N., (ed.), *A Comprehensive History of India*, II, p. 721 - refers to a little over 35 excavations; Brown, P., *Indian Architecture*, p. 35 - refers to 325 excavations; Mitra, D., *Udayagiri and Khaṇḍagiri*, mentions 33 excavations.
2. see *infra*. pp.
3. Ganguly, M.M., *Orissa and Her Remains*, p. 32
4. *BODG*. (Puri), p. 303
5. *Ibid*.
6. *BDGP*., p. 24
7. Brown, P., *op. cit*., p. 35. Here it is to be noted that the same scholar has wrongly assigned B.C. 160 to the *Hāthīgumphī* Inscription.
8. also cf., Mitra, D., *et al*., *Orissa Review* (Monument special) p. 15
9. Mitra, D., *Udayagiri and Khaṇḍagiri*, p. 5
10. see *infra*. p. 97
11. *JISOA* ., XV, (1947), p. 45
12. Elsewere (see *supra*. pp 112ff) it has been shown that after the downfall of the Cedi rule in Orissa, Jainism receded to the background. Keeping this in view the span of time, i.e., first

century B.C. to first century A.D., for these rock-cut caves does seem probable.

13. Fergusson, J. and Burgess. J., *The Cave Temples of India*, p. 66; Fergusson. J., *Illustrations of the Rock-cut Temples of India*, p. 11; Marshall, J.H., *op.cit.,d p. 579*
14. Chakravorty, M.M., *NRDCUK.*, p. 5
15. *ASI.*, *AR.*, (1902-1903), p. 41
16. *Ibid*
17. Fergusson, J., and Burgess, J., *op.cit.*, p. 68
18. see *supra*. p. 107
19. see *supra*. pp. 111-112
20. *ASI., AR.,d (1902-1903), p., 41; Majumdar, R.C. and Pusalkar, A.D. (eds.), The Age of Imperial Unity*, p. 212. Others read the name of the king as Kudepasiri - *El.*, XIII, p. 160; Kudepa-*IHQ.*, XIV, p. 160.
21. Mitra, D., *et al., Jaina Art and Architecture*, I, (ed.), Ghosh, A., p. 76. On the other hand this Mañcapurī cave is presumed to have been excavated earlier than the upper storey and it has been suggested that the king Vakradeva was the father of Khāravela-Majumdar, R.C. and Pusalkar, A.D., (eds.), *op. cit.*, p. 212
22. *EI.*, XIII, p. 160
23. *EI.*, XIII, pt. II, no. 7; Barua, B.M., *OBI.*, pp.99- 100
24. Barua, B.M., *op.cit.*, pp. 81-82; Mitra, R.L. *Antiquities of Orissa*, II, p.30
25. Barua, B.M., *op. cit.*, pp. 86 ff; Mitra R.L., *op.cit.*, p.30
26. *EI.*, XIII, pl. II, no. 8; Barua, B.M., *op.cit.*, pp. 105-106
27. Ganguly, M.M., *op.cit.*,pp. 40, 50, 57
28. Fergusson, J., *History of Indian and Eastern Architecture*, II, p. 11; Chakravarty, M.M., *op.cit.*, p. 5; Smith, V., *A History of Fine Art in India and Ceylon*, p. 84; Commaraswamy, A.K., *History of Indian and Indonesian Art*, p. 37
29. *ASI.*, *AR.*, (1902-1903), p. 40

30. Brown, P., *op.cit.*, p. 34
31. On the Jayavijaya-*gumphā* (Udayagiri) and Ananta- *Gumphā* (Khaṇḍagiri) there is tree in relief. On the back wall of Ananta-*gumphā* also appears a *nandipada* on a pedestal flanked on either side by a set of three gymbols such as, a triangle-headed on (*bhadrāsana* ? or *Sthāpana* ?), *Srīvatsa and svastika.*)
32. Mitra, D., *Udayagiri and Khaṇḍagiri*, p. 16
33. Fergusson, J., and Burgess, J., *op.cit.*, p. 78
34. *ASI.*, XIII, p. 91
35. for a detail discussion see *infra* pp. 252ff
36. see the above paragraph.
37. see table in - A.
38. Sircar, D.C., *SI.*, I, pp. 75-76
39. *Ibid.*, pp. 77-78
40. for details see - Fergusson, J., *History of Indian and Eastern Architecture*, I, pp. 130-133; Coomaraswamy, A.K., *History of Indian and Indonesian Art,* p. 18; Borwn, P., *op.cit.*, pp. 12-13; Rowland, B., *The Art and Architecture of India*, pp. 64-65
41. Fergusson, J. and Burgess, J., *The Cave Temples of India*, p.92
42. Fergusson, J., *op.cit.*, II, p. 9
43. Rapson, J., (ed.), *op.cit.*, I, p. 579
44. '*Satasahasehi śilāhi śilāthambhāni ca (cetiyam) kārāpayati pātālika catare ca beduriya gabhe thaṁbhe patithāpayati panatariyā satasahasehi*'
45. *JISOA.*, XV, (1947), p. 47
46. *Ibid.*, p. 47
47. Fergusson, J., *Illustrations of the Rock-cut Temples of India*, p. 14
48. Mitra, D., in *Indian Archaeology (1958-1959), a Review*, (ed.), Ghosh a., pp. 38-40
49. Mitra, D., in *Jaina Art and Architecture*, I, p. 78
50. *Ibid.*, p. 78
51. *Ibid.*, p. 82

52. Brown, p. *op.cit.*, p. 36
53. The pillars of the lower storey have already disappeared, but in the case of the supper storey a few are preserved.
54. Brown, P., *op.cit.*, p. 36
55. *Ibid.*, p. 36
56. *supra.*, p. 197
57. *supra.*, pp. 196-197
58. *EI.*, XIII, p. 163
59. At present two doorways are visible, while another one is converted into a window.

II

1. *Rūpamāṇḍana*, pp. 98-99.
2. Commaraswamy, A.K., *History of Indian and Indonesian Art*, p. 46
3. Rowland, B., *The Art and Architecture of India*, p. 49
4. It is believed that Indra appointed one *yakṣa* and one *yakṣiṇī* to serve on each *Tīrthaṅkara* as attendants on the right and left sides of the image - cf. Gupta, R.S., *Iconography of the Hindus, Buddhists and Jainas,* p. 176.
5. Gupte, R.S., *op.cit.*, p. 175
6. Shah, U.P., *Studies in Jaina Art,* p. 19
7. A group of iconic representation numbering nine called as *navagrahas* in the Jaina cosmology. They are Sūrya the sun-god; *Candra*, the moon-god; *Maṅgala*, the planet Mars; *Budha*, the son of the moon; *Bṛhaspati*, the planet Jupitor; *Śukra*, the teacher of the demons; *Śani*, the saturn-god; *Rāhu* and *Ketu*, the snake-deity - Bhattacharya, B.C., *The Jaina Iconography*, pp. 117-121.
8. The *Gaṇadharas*, attendants to the Jaina *Tīrthaṅkaras* are shown invariably on either side of the main figure. They are always represented as holding *cauris*, and one of them might be shown with his hands clapsed in adoration.
9. The *Gandharvas* are divine musicians in Indian mythology.
10.

The *Vidyādharas* and *Vidyādharīs* are celestial beings who are always represented in flying posture holding garlands. This was probably a development in the Gupta period - cf. Shah, U.P., *op.cit.*, p.14

11. *Śruta-devī* meaning 'Goddess of śruti' seems to be at the head of the collective body of the sixteen *Vidyādevīs*.

12. The *Vidyādevīs* are sixteen in number namely, Rohiṇī, Prajñapti, Vajra-śṛṁkhalā, Vajrāṁkuśā, Apraticakrā or Jāmbunadā, Puruṣadattā, Kālī, Mahākālī, Gaurī, Gāndhārī, Mahājvālā or Jvālāmālinī, Mānavī, Vairoṭī, Vairoṭī, Acyutā, Mānasī and Mahāmānasī - see Bhattacharya, B.C., *op.cit.*, pp. 122-132

13. In Jainism the conception of *Śrī* is quite old. The goddess is mentioned in the *Kalpasūtra* as one of the objects of the dream of Devānandā in whose womb Mahāvīra was conceived - Sūtras, 3-4, (*SBE*), XXII, pt. I, p. 219; and that of Triśalā to which womb the embryo was transferred - *Sūtra*, 36 (*SBE*), *Ibid.*, pp. 232-233. This goddess *Śrī* is the same as the Sirimā *devatā* of Bhārhut railings and the *Śrī* of the vedic Śrī-sūkta - cf. Shah, U.P., *op.cit.*, *p.* 7

14. The ten *Dikpālas* are Indra, Agni, Yama, Nairta, Varuṇa, Vāyu, Kubera, Īśāna, Brahmā and Nāga - see Bhattacharya, B.C., *op.cit.*, *pp. 108-116.*

15. Among the most interesting sculptures are the *āyagapaṭṭas* or votive tablets which are usually square. They also bear inscriptions in Brahmi characters which can scarcely be later than the beginning of the Kuṣāṇa period. Some bear in the centre the representation of a seated *Jina* with shaven head of the type of the larger cult image of Pārśvanātha from Kaṅkāli Ṭilā. Other reliefs include representation of Harinegamesa a minor divinity connected with the nativity of Mahāvīra - For details, see Smith, V.A., *The Jaina Stupa and other Antiquities of Mathura*, pp. 13 ff.

16. *Vāstu-Śāstra*, II, see chapter on Jain and Buddhist Iconography, p. 12

17. The four-fold figures with Ṛṣabhanātha, Pārśvanātha, and two other *Jinas* are on each side found from Mathura belongs to the Kuṣāṇa period - Smith, V.A., *op. cit.*, pp. 46ff. These figures are based on the ancient Jaina tradition of *Samavasaraṇa*, Bhandarkar, D.R.,

in *IA*., XL, pp. 125-130, 153 ff. - a square or circular assembly hall believed to have been erected by gods for the sermons of the *Jinas*. In the centre of the hall is placed a *Jina* on one side with images of the same *Jina* placed on other three sides to make him visible to the whole audience.

18. *JA*., I, no. 3, p. 52. The *mānastambhas* (Pride pillars) are also known as *mānavakastambhas* are set up with images on top and at the base - cf. Shah, U.P., *op.cit.*, p. 23. These pride pillars stand on three tiers of pillars adorned with bells and flags, and surrounded by three walls. The images of the *Tīrthaṅkaras* are worshipped at the feet of the pillars accompanied by music and dansing. There are step-walls of precious stones with lotuses on the four sides - cf. Pereira, J., *Monolithic Jinas*, p. 55

19. The Jaina *ācāryas* or teachers are symbolically represented by *sthāpanas* or *sthāpanācāryas*. These are kept in front while a Jaina monk gives a discourse. Literally it denotes the installation of the figure or symbol of the *ācārya* when he was not personally present - see Shah, U.P., *op.cit.*, p. 113

20. Banerjea, J.N., *The Development of Hindu Iconography*, p. 561

21. *Ājānulambabāhuḥ śrīvatsāṅkaḥ praśāntamūrtiśca / Digvāsāstaruṇo rūpavāṁśca kāryorarhatāṁ devaḥ // Bṛhatsaṁhitā*, 58, 45

22. This translation is offered by Banerjea, J.N., *op.cit.*, p. 588

23. *Pratiṣṭhāpāda*, 151-152

24. *Pratiṣṭhāsārodhāra*, 1, 62

25. *Pratiṣṭhāsārasaṅgraha*, 4, 1, 2, 4

26. *Devasyordhvasya cārcā syājjānulaṁbibhujadvayā /*
Śrīvatsoṣṇiṣayuktaṁ dve chatrādiparivārite //
Vivekavilāsa, 1, 130

27. *Rūpamaṇḍana*, VI, 33-39

28. *Vāstu-śāstra*, II, chapter on Jain and Buddhist Iconography, p. 8

29. The heavenly music consists of five musical instruments called *pañcamahāśabdas*; *Śṛṅga* (the horn), *Tammata* (the drum), *Śaṅkha* (the counch-shell), *Bherī* (the trumpet), and *Jayaghaṭa* (the cymbal) - *ibid.*, p. 9

30. *Ibid.*, p. 9

31. Gomukha, the Yakṣa of Ṛṣabhanātha - *Rūpamaṇḍana*, VI, 17; Cakreśvarī, the Yakṣiṇī of Neminātha, *Ibid*., VI, 19; Pārśva (Popularly known as Dharaṇendra, the Yakṣa of Mahāvīra, *Ibid*., VI, 20; Padmāvatī, Yakṣiṇī of Pārśvanātha, *Ibid*., VI, 21; Mātaṅga, Yakṣa of Mahāvīra, *Ibid*., VI, 22; Siddhāyikā, Yakṣiṇī of Mahāvīra, *Ibid*., VI, 23

32. *Aparājitapṛcchā*, 221; 43, 15-16, 36, 55, 37, 56, 38

33. Mitra, D., *Udayagiri and Khaṇḍagiri*, p. 14

34. Coomaraswamy, A.K., *op.cit*., p. 31

35. Fergusson, J., *A History of Indian and Eastern Architecture*, p. 36

36. This symbol is one of the five distinguishing features of a Jaina figure - *Bṛhatsaṁhitā*, 58, 48; also see *supra*, p. 224. The symbol *Śrīvatsa* along with that of *Svastika* are among the *Aṣṭamaṅgalas* (the Eight auspicious objects) of the Jainas. They are *Svastika, Śrīvatsa, Nandyāvarta, Vardhamānaka, Bhadrāsana, Kalasa, Darpaṇa*, and *Matsya* - *Aupapātika sūtra*, sū. 31, pp. 68-69. A Jaina *Tīrthaṅkara* image in *dhyānamudrā* is distinguished the *Śrīvatsa* mark executed on his chest from that of the image of the Buddha in the same pose (The images of *Tīrthaṅkaras* and the Buddha depicted in *dhyānamudrā* are quite similar). But, in the *Tīrthaṅkara* images from south India, this mark is absent - cf. *Ancient India*, no. 6, January, 1954, pp. 44- 46.

37. This symbol signifies *svasti* (*śānti*). This is one of the "most widely distributed decorative, or more accurately speaking, symbolic motifs" - Coomaraswamy, A.K., *op.cit*., p. 13

38. It is the same as what is called *tri-ratna* - *jñāna, darśana* and *caritra*, the fundamentals of the Jaina religious practice - Shah, U.P., *op.cit*., p. 81

39. This is known as *Caitya-vṛkṣa*, the tree of enlightenment. The Jainas as well as the Buddhists adopted tree-worship in a different way. These were the trees under which their leaders obtained Enlightenment, and so represented and worshipped. for details see *Rūpamaṇḍana*, VI, pp. 98-99

40. According to the Digambara tradition, *Chatra* - the umbrella is the seventh *maṅgala* of the *Aṣṭamaṅgalas* - *Tiloyapaññati*, 4, 738, Vol. I, p. 236

41. *Phaṇī*, the snake is the cognisance of Pārśvanātha. Further according to Digambara tradition a palace of the king of snakes (*Nāgendra-bhavana*) is one of the sixteen dreams of Mahāvīra's mother - *Mahāpurāṇa (Ādipurāṇa)*, XII, 101- 119; *Harivaṁśa*, VIII, 58-74

42. The elephant, bull, lion, lotus and *Śrī* are auspicious for the Jainas, for these objects were seen in the fourteen dreams by both Devānandā to whose womb Mahāvīra descended - *Kalpasūtra, sūtra-3, 4, SBE.*, XXII, pt. I, p. 219; and Triśalā to whose womb he was transferred by Harinegamesin *-Ibid., sūtras* - 33, 34, 35, pp. 231-232; *sūtra* - 42, p. 236; *sūtra* - 36, pp. 232-233. For the interpretation of some of the fourteen dreams see - *JISOA.*, III, no. 2, pp. 125-144

43. see note above. The goddess *Śrī* is the same as the *Sirimā devatā* of Bhārhut railings, and the *Śīī of the Vedic Śrī-sūkta* - Saha, U.P., *op.cit.*, p. 7

44. Coomaraswamy, A.K., *op.cit.*, p. 45

45. for details see *supra*, pp. 192ff.

46. Coomaraswamy, A.K., *op.cit.*, p. 38

47. Mitra, D., *op.cit.*, p. 37

48. Coomaraswamy, A.K., *op.cit.*, p. 38. For the description of reliefs see Fergusson, J., *A History of Indian and Eastern Architecture*, II, pp. 14-15; Fergusson, J., and Burgess, J., *The Cave Temples of India*, pp. 80-85, 87-88; *BODG* (Puri), pp. 287-292

49. see *supra*, pp. 129-131

50. The images of *Tīrthaṅkaras* are shown only in two postures, i.e., *dyyāna-mudrā*, seated cross-legged in meditation; and *Kāyotsarga-pose* (for the *Kāyotsarga* pose see note no. 53 below). Both the *mudrās* are yogic, as Jninism believes in penance *(tapasyā)* - *śramyaṁtiti śramaṇaḥ tapasyaṁtītyartha/*

51. *OHRJ.*, X, no. 3 (1961), pp. 74 ff. Bharat and Bāhubalīare sons of Ṛṣabhā. For a detail account see Pereira, J., Monolithic Jinas, pp. 46-54

52. The *prabhā-maṇḍala* is otherwise called *Siras-cakra* (nimbus), the origin of which may be traced in "the disk of gold placed behing the alter to representthe sun"- Coomaraswamy, A.K., *op.cit.*,

p. 41. The First use of this nimbusin Indian iconography is not certainly known - *Ibid.*, p. 41, note 1

53. Besides Ṛṣabhanātha and Mahāvīra; all the other *Tīrthaṅjaras* had passedaway in the *kāyotsarga* posture - a posture, in which a man stands with his arms hanging stiff with his body. The other three *Tīrthaṅkaras* attained release when seated on the lotusthrone - Bhaṭṭacharya, B.C., *op. citd.*, p. 20
54. Ghosh, A., (ed.), *op,cit.*, I, p. 160
55. Shah, U.P., *op.cit.*, p. 26
56. see *supra*, p. 133
57. see *supra.*,p. 134
58. see *supra.*,p. 136
59. see *supra.*, pp. 138-140.
60. Roy, P.K., in *ISBJ.*, p. 42
61. These findings have been reported with photographs in *JOH.*, I, no. 1, pp. 20-21
62. *Ibid.*, p. 21
63. *ASI.*, *AR.*, 1902-1903, p. 41
64. see *supra.*, pp. 142-143
65. A sitting posture in which the palms of the hands in the from the lotus- buds should be laid upon one anbother beside the belly.
66. In this posture one leg hangs angularly, while the other remains folded . This posture is not common to the *Jina* images, but instances are found in case of the *Yakṣiṇī*figures.
67. This is theposture in which one sits at ease keepinbg his hands opening outwords, also known as *vīra mudrā*.
68. for a detailed account of the images seeGanguly, M.M., *Orissa and her remains*, pp. 50-55
69. Mitra, D., *Udayagiri and Khaṇḍagiri*, p. 65
70. Mitra, D., *op.cit.*, p. 67
71. Mitra, D., *Bronzes from Achutrajpur*, pp. 44-52
72. *Ibid.*, p. 44

SELECT BIBLIOGRAPHY

Primary Sources

I. Indigenous Literary Works:

A. Vedic and Classical Sanskrit Texts :

Abhidhānacintāmani of Hemacandra (comm.), H. Sastri, Varanasi, 1964

Aitareya Brāhamaṇa, (ed.), S. Samasrami, Asiatic Society of Bengal, Calcutta, 1962, Samvat

Arthaśāstra of Kautilya (ed.), R. Shamasastri, Mysore, 1909.

Aṣṭādhyāyī of Pāṇini, Two Volumes, (ed. and trans.), S.C. Vasu, reprint, Delhi, 1962

Atarva Veda, (ed.), R.S. Acharya, Bareli, 1969.

Bālamanorama on Siddhāntakaumudī of Bhaṭṭoji Dikṣita, Four Volumes, Delhi, 1967

Baudhāyana Dharmasūtra, (ed.), Srinivasacharya, Mysore, 1907

Brahma Purāṇa, (ed.), P. Tarakaratna, Calcutta, 1909

Brahmāṇḍa Purāṇa,(ed.), J.L. Shastri, Delhi, 1973

Brhadāraṇyaka Upaniṣad, (trans), Swami Madhavananda, Pub. Advaita Ashrama, Almora, 1952

Brhat Samhitā of Varāhamihira, (ed.), M.M.S. Dwivedi, Kasi, V. Samvat 1952

Kurma Purāna (ed.), A.S. Gupta, Varanasi, 1972

Mahābhārata, (ed.), ASB., 1836

Mahābhārata, (ed.) H. Sidhantavagish, Calcutta, 1930

Mahābhārata, (ed.), BORI., Poona, 1944, 1947, 1953, 1960

Mahābhārata, (ed.), Venkateswar Press, (no date)

Manusmṛti, (ed.), N.R.A. Kavyatirtha, Bombay, 1946

Matsya Purāṇa, (ed.), P. Tarkaratna, Calcutta, 1908

Padma Purāṅa, (ed.) P.Tarkaratna, Calcutta, 1912

Rāmāyaṇa, (trans), M.N. Dutta, Calcutta, 1892- 94

Raghuvaṁśa, (ed.and trans.), G.R. Nandargikar (3rd end.), Bombay, 1897

Ṛg Veda Samhitā, Vedic Research Institute, Poona, 1946

Skanda Purāṇa, (trans.), P. Tarkatirtha, Calcutta, 1039 B.S.

Vyākaraṇa Mahābhāṣya of Patañjali, Gurukula Jhajhar, 1931

B. *Jaina Texts :*

i. *Canonical :*

Ācāraṅga Sūtra, (trans.), H. Jacobi, *SBE.*, XXII, pt. I, reprint, Delhi, Varanasi, Patna, 1964

Antagaadasāo, (Comm.), Abhayadeva, Ahmedabad, 1932; (ed.), P.L. Vaidya, Poona, 1932

Aupapātika Sūtra, (ed.), Agamodaya Samiti, Bombay, 1916

ĀVaśyaka Sūtra of Sudharma, Agamodaya Samiti, Bombay, 1916-1917

Āvassaya (Āvaśyaka) Bhāsya, (Comm.), Haribhadra, Agamodaya Samiti, Bombay, 1916

Bhagavaī, (comm.), Abhayadeva, Abhayadeva, Agamodaya Samiti, Bombay, 1921

Bhagavatī Sūtra, (trans.), M. Weber, Berlin, 1886

Bṛhatkalpa bhāsya, (comm.), Malayagiri and Ksemakirti, Bhavanagar, 1933-1938

Daśavaikālika Sūtra, (trans.), K.C. Lalwani, Delhi, 1973

Kalpa Sūtra, (trans.), H. Jacobi, SBE., XXII, pt. I, reprint, Delhi, Varanasi, Patna, 1964

Nandi, (comm.), Malayagiri, Bombay, 1924

Nāyādhammakahāo, (comm.), Abhayadeva, Agamodaya Samiti, Bombay, 1919; (ed.), N.V. Vaidya, Poona, 1940

Oghāniryukti, (comm.), Dronacarya, Bombay, 1919

Samvāyaṅga, (comm.), Abhyayadeva, Ahmedabad, 1938

Sutrakṛtāṅga, (trans.), H. Jacobi, SBE., XLV,pt. II

Ṭhāṇaṅga, 3 parts, (comm.), Abhayadeva, Agamodaya Samiti, V.S. 1975

Uttarādhyayana Sūtra, (trans.), H. Jacobi, *SBE.*, XLV, pt. II; (trans.), K.C. Lalwani, Calcutta, 1977; (ed.), J. Charpentier, Uppasala, 1922

Uvāsagadasāo, (comm.), Abhayadeva, (ed.), P.L. Vaidya, Poona, 1930; (trans.), R. Hoernle, Calcutta, 1888

Vavahāra (Vyavahāra) bhāṣya, (comm.), Maḷagiri, Bhavnagar, 1926; (ed.), W. Schubring, Leipzig, 1918

ii. *Non-canonical:*

Abhidhāna Rājendrad of Vijaya Rajendra Suri, Vol. III, Ratlam, 1914

Aparijitapṛcchā of Bhuvanadeva, (ed.), P.A. Mankad, Baroda, 1950

Āvaśyaka Cūrṇi, (ed.), Jinadasa Gani, Ratlam, 1928

Bṛhatkathākoṣa of Harisene, (ed.), A.N. Upadhye, Bombay, 1943

Darsanasāra of Devasena, (ed.) N. Premi, Bombay, 1918

Haribhadrīya Vṛtti, (ed.) Agamodaya Samiti, Bombay

Harivaṁśa f Jinassena, (ed. and trans.), M.N. Dutta, Calcutta, 1897

Mahāpurāṇa of Jinasena and Gunabhadra, (ed.), P.L. Vaidya, Bombay, 1937

Mūlācāra of Vattakera, 2 parts, Manikkcandra Digambara Jaina Granthamala Samiti, Bombay, 1921, 1923

Pariśiṣṭaparvan, (ed.), H. Jacobi, Calcutta, 1932

Pārśvanāthacarita of Sri Bhavadeva Suri, (ed.), Pandit Hargovind Das and Pandit Bechar Das, Banaras, V.E., 2438

Prabandhacintāmaṇi, (trans.), Tawney, Calcutta, 1901

Pratiṣṭāsārasaṅgrahae of Vasunandi, Sholapur, 1925

Pratiṣṭāsārodhara of Āśādhara, (ed.), Pandit Manohar Sastri, Bombay, V.S. 1974

Pravacanasāra of Kunda Kundacārya, (ed.), A.N. Upadhye, (2nd ed.), Bombay, 1935

Rūpamaṇana of Sūtradhāra Maṇḍana, (ed.), B. Srivastava, Varanasi, 1964

Samarāṅgaṇa Sūtradhāra of Bhoja, Lucknow, 1965

Samayasāra, SBJ., Vol. VIII, Lucknow

Tiloyapaññati of Yativṛśabha, 2 Vols., (ed.), A.N. Upadhye and Hiralal Jaina, Sholapur, 1943, 1951

Triṣaṣṭiśalākāpuruṣacarita, (trans.), Johnson, *GOS*., Barada, 1930

C. *Buddhist text :*

Aṅgutara Nikāya, (ed.), R. Morris & E. Hardy, PTS., London, 1918

Ārya Mañjuśrīmūlakalpa, (ed.) T. Ganapati Sastri, Trivandum, 1925

Commentary on the Dhammapada, I, (ed.), H.C. Norman, *PTS*., 1906

Dīgha Nikāya, (ed.), J. Kashyap, Pali Publication Board, Bihar Govt., 1958

Jātakas, (ed.) Fausboll, 7 vols. London, 1877-1879; translated under the editorship of E.B. Cowell, 7 vols. Cambridge, 1895-1907

Mahāparinibbāna Suttānta, (trans.), T.W. Rhys Davids and C.A.F. Rhys Davids, *SBB.*, III, pt. II, London, 1951

Mahāvaṁśa, trans. W. Geiger, *PTS.*, London, 1912

Millindapñho, (ed.), R.D. Vadekar, Bombay, 1940

Samyutta-Nikāya of the Sutta-Piṭaka, pt. I, ed. M.L.Freer, *PTS.*, 1960

Sutta Nipāta, (ed.), D. Andersen & H. smith, London, 1913

Vinaya Piṭṭaka, (trans.) T.W. Rhys Davids & H. Oldenberg, *SBE.*, Oxford, 1881-1885

II. *Foreign Accounts :*

Buddhist Records of the Western Word, II, (trans.), S. Beal, London, 1905

Classical Accounts of India, R.C., Majumdar, Calcutta, 1960

McCrindle's Ancient India as described by Ptolemy, (ed.), S.N.M. Sastri, Calcutta, 1927

McCrindle's Ancient India s described by Megasthenes and Arrian, (ed.), R.C. Majumdar, 2nd ed. Calcutta, 1960

The Periplus of the Erythrean Sea, (trans.), W.H. Schoff, London, 1912

Pliny's Natural History, (ed.), W.H. Schoff Leipzig, 1892- 1902

Travels of Hiuen Tsang, (trans.), S. Beal, 4 vols. Calcutta, 1957-1958

Watter's on Yuan Chwangs Travels in INdia, II. (eds.), T.W. Rhys Davids & S.W. Bushell, London, 1905

III. *Archaeological Sources :*

i. *Epigraphs :*

Barua, B.M., *Old Brahmi Inscriptions in the Udayagiri and Khaṇagiri Caves*, Calcutta, 1929

Basak, R.G., *Aśokan Inscriptions*, Calcutta, 1959

Nahar, P.C., *Jaina Lekha Sangraha*, 3 vols. Calcutta, 1918, 1927, 1929

Rajaguru, S.N., *Inscriptions of Orissa*, vols. I-V Brahmapur, Bhubaneswar, 1958, 1960, 1961, 1966

Sen, A.C., *Aśoka's Edicts*, Calcutta, 1956

Sircar, D.C., *Selected Inscriptions bearing on Indian Epigraphy Delhi*, 1965, *Inscriptions of Aśoka*, third ed. New Delhi, 1975

Sewell, R. & Aiyanger, S.K., *Historical Inscriptions of South India*, Madras, 1932

Tripathi, S., (ed.), *Inscriptions of Orissa*, VI, Bhubaneswar, 1974

ii. *Monumental* :

Bachhofer, L., *Early Indian Sculpture*, 2 vols. Pairs 1929; first Indian reprint in one volume, New Delhi, 1974

Banerji, R.D., *Eastern Indian School of Medieval Sculpture*, Calcutta, 1933

Baruna, B.M., *Bārhut*, 3 vols. Calcutta, 1934

Chanda, R.P., *Medieval Indian Sculptures*, Indian, 1936

Cunningham, A., *The Bhilsā Topes or the Buddhist Monuments of Central India*, London, 1854, *The Stūpa of Bhārhut*, London 1879

Fergusson, J., *Illustrations of the Rock-cut Temples of India*, London, 1945, *A History of Indian and Eastern Architecture*, 2nd ed., London, 1910

Fergusson, J. and Burgess, J., *The Cave Temples of India*, Delhi, 1969

Marshall, J.H. & Foucher, A., *The Monuments of Sanchi*, 3 vols., Calcutta, 1940

Smith, V., *The Jaina Stūpa and other Antiquities of Mathura*, Allahabad, 1901, *History of Fine Art in India and Ceylon*, 2nd ed. Oxford, 1930

IV. *Secondary Works*

Acharya, P., *Studies in Orissan History, Archaeology and Archives*, Baripada, 1969, *Oiśāra Pratnatatva O Anyānya Pravandha*, (Oriya), 2 vols. Bhubaneswar, 1969

Agrawala, V.S., *Indian Art*, Varanasi, 1965 *Ancient Indian Folk Cults*, Varanasi, 1970, *Indian as known to Pāṇini*, Varanasi, 1963, *Heritage of Indian Art*, Delhi, 1964

Aiyanger, S.K., *Some Contributions of South India to Indian Culture*, Calcutta, 1923, *Ancient Indian and South Indian History and Culture*, 2 vols., Poona, 1941

Aiyanger, R., Rao, S., *Studies in South Indian Jainism*, Madras, 1922

Asher, F., *The Art of Eastern India*, Delhi, 1980

Bagchi, P.C., *Pre-Aryan and Pre-Dravidian Indian*, Calcutta, 1929, *Studies in Tantras*, Calcutta, 1939

Banerjee, J.N., *Development of Hindu Iconography*, Calcutta, 1956

Banerjee, P., *Early Indian Religions*, Delhi, 1972

Banerji, R.D., *History of Orissa*, I, Calcutta, 1930

Barth, A., *The Religons of India*, London, 1921

Barodia, U.D., *History and Literature of Jainism*, Bombay, 1951

Barua, B.M., *The Ājīvikas, pt. I, Calcutta, 1920, A History of Pre-Buddhistic Indian Philosophy*, Calcutta, 1921, *Studies in Buddhism*, ed. B.N. Chaudhury, Calcutta, 1974

Basak, R.G., *The History of North-Eastern India*, Calcutta, 1934

Basham, A.L., *History and Doctrines of the Ājīvikas*, London, 1951, *The Wonder that was India*, London, 1954, *Aspects of*

Ancient Indian Culture, Poona, 1966, (ed.), *A Cultural History of India*, Oxfored, 1975

Bhagat, M.G., *Ancient Indian Asceticism*, New Delhi, 1976

Bhandarkar, R.G., *The Early History of Deccan*, Calcutta, 1928

Bhandarkar, D.R., *Some Aspects of Ancient Indian Culture*, Madras, 1940

Bhattacharya, B.C., *Jaina Iconography*, Delhi, 1974

Bhattacharya, B.T., *The Indian Buddhist Iconogrpahy*, revised ed., Calcutta, 1968

Bhattacharys, N.N., *Jain Philosophy in Historical Outline*, Delhi, 1976

Bloomfield, M., *The Life and Stories of the Jain Savior Pārśvanātha*, Baltimore, 1919

Bose, N.K., *Canons os Orissan Architecture*, Calcutta, 1932

Brown, P., *Indian Architecture :* Buddhist, Hindu, Bombay, 1965

Bahler, J.G., *On the Indian Sect of the Jainas*, London, 1903

Chakraborty, H., *Asceticism in Ancient India in Brahmanical, Buddhists, Jaina and Ājīvika Socieites*, Calcutta, 1973

Chakraborty, K., *Society, Religion and Art of the Kuṣāṇa Indian*, 1981

Chakraborty, N.N., *Rājaśekhara O Kāvyamimāṁsā* (Bengali), Visva-Bharati, 1960

Chakladhar, H.C., *Aryanisation of Eastern India*, Calcutta, 1962

Chand, B., *Jainism in Indian History,* Varanasi, 1951, Lord Mahāvīra, Banaras, 1948

Chanda, R.P., *Indo-Aryan Races*, Reprint, Calcutta, 1969, *Bhañja Dynasty of Mayurbhanj and their Capital Khiching*, Mayurbhanj, 1929, *Beginnings of Art in Eastern India, MASI*, no. 30, *Medieval Indian Sculpture*, Varanasi, 1972

Chandra, M., *Indian Art,* Bombay, 1964

Chatterjee, A.K., *A Comprehensive History of Jainism*, Calcutta, 1978

Chattopadhyaya, K.P., *Ancient Indian Culture Contacts and Migrations*, Calcutta, 1965

Chattopadhyaya, S., *Early History of North India*, third revised ed., Delhi, 1976, *Some Early Dynasties of South India*, Delhi, 1974, *Racial Affinities of Early North- Indian Tribes*, New Delhi, 1973, *Social Life in Ancient India*, Calcutta, 1966, *Bimbisāra to Aśoka*, Calcutta, 1977

Chaudhury, G.C., *Political History of Northern India from Jaina Sources*, Amritsar, 1963

Chaudhury, S.B., *Ethnic Settlements in Ancient India*, Calcutta, 1955

Coomaraswamy, A.K., *History of Indian and Indonesian Art*, London, 1927, first Indian ed. New Delhi, 1972, *Yakṣas*, 2 pts, reprint, Delhi, 1971, *Elements of Buddhist Iconography*, reprint, Delhi, 1972

Crooke, W., *Religion and Folklore of Northern India*, London, 1925

Cunnigham, A., *The Ancient Geography of India*, Varanasi, 1963

Das, D.R., *The Early History of Kaliṅga*, Calcutta, 1977

Das, H.C., *Cultural Development in Orissa*, Calcutta, 1985

Das, M.N., *Yuge Yuge Utkaliya Dharma O Sabhyatā*, (Oriya), Balasore, 1952, *Glimpses of Kaliṅga History*, Calcutta, 1954 , (ed.), *Side Lights on the History and Culture of Orissa*, Cuttack, 1978

Dasgupta, K.K., *A Tribal History of Ancient India - Numismatical Approach*, Calcutta, 1974

Dasgupta, S.B., *Obscure Religious Cults*, Calcutta, 1969

Dasgupta, S.N., *A History of Indian Philosophy*, I, (Indian edition) Delhi, 1975

De, S.C., *Guide to Orissa Records*, 5 vols. Bhubaneswar, 1961-1965

De, S.K., *History of Sanskrit Literature*, I, Calcutta, 1947

De Bary, W.T., (Compiled), *Sources of Indian Tradition*, Delhi, 1972

Dehejia, V., *Early Buddhist Rock-cut Temples* ... London, 1972

Deo, S.B., *History of Jaina Monachism*, Poona, 1956

Desai, P.B., *Jainism in South India and Some Jaina Epigraphs*, Solapur, 1957

Desmukh, P.S., *The Origin and Development of Religion in Vedic Literature*, London, 1933

Dey, N.L., *The Geographical Dictionary of Ancient and Medieval India*, London, 1927

Dikshitkar, V.R.r., *The Puranic Index*, 3 vols., Madras, 1951-1955

Divakara, S.C., *Mahāśramaṇa Mahāvīra*, (Hindi), Mysore, 1968

Dutt, N., *Early Monastic Buddhism*, 2nd ed., Calcutta, 1971 , *Early History of the Spread of Buddhism* ... London, 1925

Dutt, N.K., *The Aryanisation of India*, 2nd ed., Calcutta, 1971

Dutt, S., *Early Buddhist Monachism*, Calcutta, 1924 , *Buddhist Monks and Monasteries of India*, London, 1962

Eliot, C., *Hinduism and Buddhism*, vols. I-III, London, 1921

Elwin, V., *Tribal Myths of Orissa*, Calcutta, 1954

Eschmann, A., Kulke, H., Tripathy, G.C., (eds.), *The Cult of Jagannātha and the Regional Tradition of Orissa*, New Delhi, 1978

Evans, P.E.E., *Theories of Primitive Religion*, Oxford, 1975

Fabri, C.L., *History of the Art of Orissa*, Orient Longman Ltd., 1974

Farquhar, J.N., *An Outline of the religious Literature of India*, Oxford, 1920

Fergusson, J., *The Tree and Serpant Worship*, London, 1868

Fishcher, K.F., *Caves and Temples of the Jainas*, Aliganj, 1956

Fick, R., *The Social Organisation in North-East India in Buddhist Time*, Calcutta, 1920

Foucher, A., *Beginnings of Buddhist Art in India*, London, 1908

Frazer, Sir J.G., *Worship of Nature*, London, 1926

Fuchs, S., *The Aboriginal Tribes of India*, London, 1973

Ganguly, M.M., *Orissa and Her Remains*, Calcutta, 1912

Ganguly, D.K., *Historical Geography and Dynastic History of Orissa*, Calcutta, 1975

Ghosh, A., (ed.), *Jaina Art and Architecture*, 3 vols., New Delhi, 1974, 1975

Ghosh, N.N., *Early History of India*, Allahabad, 1948

Goetz, H., *India (Art of the World)*, Bombay, 1959

Gonda, J., *Changes and Continuity in Indian Religion*, Hague, 1965

Gorden, D.H., *The Pre-historic Background of Indian Culture*, Bombay, 1958

Goswami, A., *Orissan Sculpture and Architecture*, Calcutta, 1956

Gupte, R.S., *Iconography of the Hindus, Buddhists and Jainas*, Bombay, 1972

Hiralal, H., *Ancient History of the Jaina Religion*, Jamnagar, 1902

Hodson, T.C., *The Primitive Culture of India*, London, 1922

Hopkins, E.W., *Origin and Evolution of Religion*, Varanasi, (no date) , *The Religions of India*, Boston, 1895

Institute of Oriental and Orissan Studies (Sponsored), *International Seminars on Buddhism and Jainism*, Cuttack, 1976

Jacobi, H., *Studies in Jainism*, Ahmedabad, 1946

James, E.O., *History of Religions*, New York, 1957 , *Comparative Religion ...*, London, 1961

Jain, C.L., *Jaina Bibliography*, Calcutta, 1945

Jain, H., and Upadhye, A.N., *Mahāvīra his Times and his Philosophy of Life*, Varanasi, 1944

Jain, J.C., *Bhārat Ke Prāchīn Jaina Tīrtha* (Hindi), Banaras, 1950 , *Life in Ancient India as Depicted in the Jaina Canons*, Bombay, 1947

Jain, J.P., *Jainism, the Oldest Living Religion*, Banaras, 1951 , *The Jaina Sources of the History of Ancient India*, Delhi, 1964

Jain, K.C., *Lord Mahāvīra and his Times*, Delhi : Varanasi : Patna, 1974 , *Jainism in Rajasthan*, Sholapur, 1963

Jain, K.P., *Bhagavān Mahāvīra our Mahātmā Buddha*, (Hindi), Surat, V.S. 2493

Jain, M.U.K., *Jaina Sects and Schools,* Delhi, 1975

Jaini, J.L., *Outline of Jainism*, Oxford, 1940

Jaini, M.C., *Life of Mahāvīra*, Allahabad, 1908

Jash, P., *History of Śaivism*, Calcutta, 1974 , *History and Evolution of Vaiṣṇavism in Eastern India*, Calcutta, 1982 , (ed.), *Religion and Society in Ancient India*, Calcutta, 1984 , *Some aspects of Jainism in Easter India*, New Delhi, 1989

Jash, P., *History of the Parivrājaka*, Delhi, 1991

Jayaswal, K.P., *History of India*, Lahore, 1933

Jayatilleke, K.N., *Early Buddhist Theory of Knowledge*, London, 1963

Kane, P.V., *History of Dharmaśāstra*, 5 vols. Poona, 1930-1953

Kapadia, H., *A History of the Canonical Literature of the Jainas*, Bombay, 1941

Keith, A.B., *Religion and Philosophy of the Veda and Upaniṣads*, 2 vols. Harvard Oriental Series - 31, 32 - 1925 , *A History of Sanskrit Literature*, Oxford, 1928

Krishna Rao, B.V., *A History of the Early Dynasties of the Andhradesa*, Madras, 1942

Kosambi, D.D., *An Introduction to the Study of Indian History*, Bombay, 1956 , *The Culture and Civilization of Ancient India in Historical Outline*, Delhi : Bombay, reprint, 1975

Kulke, H., Das, M.N., Das, G.N., & Behera, K.S., (eds.), *Orissa - A Comprehensive Bibliography of an Indian State*, Bhubaneswar/Heidleberg, 1978

Lang, A., *Myth, Ritual and Religion*, 2 vols.

Kramrisch, S., *Indian Sculpture*, Calcutta, 1933 , *Art of India through the Ages,* London, 1954

Lathe, A.B., *An Introduction to Jainism*, Bombay, 1905

Law, B.C., *Buddhist Studies,*, Calcutta, 1931 , *India as described in early texts of Buddhism and Jainism*, London, 1941 , *Mahāvīra : His Life and Teachings*, London, 1937 , *Tribes in Ancient India*, Poona, 1943

Lowie, R.H., *Primitive Religion*, London, 1960

Macdonell, A.A., *A History of Sanskrit Literature*, London, 1917, *Lectures on Comparative Religion*, Calcutta, 1925

Macdonell, A.A., & Keith, A.B., *Vedic Index and Names and Subjects*, I, Varanasi, 1958

Macnicol, N., *Indian Theism*, 2nd. edn., Delhi, 1968

Mackay, E.J.H., *The Indus Civilization*, London, 1935

Mahatab, H.K., *The History of Orissa*, (R.K. Mookherji endoment Lectures) Lucknow, 1947 , *The History of Orissa*, 2 vols. Cuttack, 1959, 1960, *Oḍiśā Itihāsa* (Oriya), I, Cuttack, 1964

Majumdar, B.C., *Orissa in the Making*, Calcutta, 1925

Majumdar, R.C., Pusalkar, A.D., Majumdar, A.K. (eds.), *History and Culture of the Indian People*, vols. I-V, Bhāratīya Vidyā-Bhavan, Bombay, 1965, 1968, 1970, 1964, 1966

Majumdar, R.C., *Corporate Life in Ancient India*, Calcutta, 1922 , *History of Bengal*, I, reprint, Patna, 1971

Marshall, J., *Mohenjodaro and the Indus Civilization*, 3 vols. London, 1931

Marshman, J.C., *The History of India*, III, London, 1867

McPherson, W., *Reports upon the Khonds of the Districts of Ganjam and Cuttack*, Madras, 1842

Max Muller, F., *Lectures on the Origin and Growth of Religion*, (delivered in 1878), Varanasi, 1964

Mehta, M.L., *Jaina Culture*, Varanasi, 1969

Mehta, R.N., *Pre-Buddhist India*, Bombay, 1939

Mehta, P.D., *Early Indian Religious Though*, London, 1956

Mirashi, V.V., *Studies in Indology*, 3 vols. Nagpur, 1960- 1962

Mishra, B., *Orissa Under the Bhauma Kings*, Calcutta, 1934 , *Dynasties of Medieval Orissa*, Calcutta, 1936 , *Ādivasī Samāja O Sanskruti*, (Oriya), Bhubaneswar, 1977

Mishra, K.C., *The Cult of Jagannātha*, Calcutta, 1971

Mitra, D., *Bhubaneswar*, New Delhi, 1961 , *Buddhist Monuments*, Calcutta, 1971 , *Udayagiri and Khaṇḍagiri*, New Delhi, 1975 , *Bronzes from Achutrajpur*, Orissa, Delhi, 1978

Mitra, R.L., *The Antiguities of Orissa*, 2 vols, Calcutta, 1875, 1880

Mittal, A.C., *An Early History of Orissa*, Varanasi, 1962

Mohanty, S., & Das, G., (eds.), *Laxīnārāyaṇa Granthāvalī*, (Oriya), Part, I, Cuttack, 1971

Mohapatra, K.N., *Śrī Khāravela*, (Priya), Bhubaneswar, 1961

Mohapatra, R.P., *Udayagiri and Khaṇḍagiri Caves*, New Delhi, 1981 , *Jaina Monuments of Orissa*, New Delhi, 1984

Mookherjee, R.K., *Chandragupta Maurya and his Times*, Delhi, 1966

Motilal, B.K., *The Central Philosophy of Jainism* (Anekāntavāda), Ahmedabad, 1981

Mukerjee, S., *Some Aspects of Social Life in Ancient India*, Allahbad, 1976

Mukherji, R.K., *A History of Indian Civilization*, I, Bombay, 1958 , *The Culture and Art of India*, London, 1959

Murthy, S.G., *Jaina Vestiges in Andhra*, Hyderabad, 1963

Nahar, P.C., and Ghosh, K.C. *An Epitome of Jainism*, Calcutta, 1917

Norbeck, E., *Religion in Primitive Society*, New York, 1961

Oldenburg, H., *Budda, His Life, His Order, His Doctrine,* reprint, Delhi, 1971 , *Ancient India, its Language and Religions*, Chicago, 1898

Oman, J.C., *Cults, Customs and Superstitions of India*, reprint, Delhi, 1971 , *The Mystics, Ascetics and Saints of India*, London, 1903

Oursel, P.M., *Ancient India and Indian Civilization*, London, 1934

Pande, G.C., *Studies in the Origins of Buddhism*, Allahbad, 1957

Panigrahi, K.C., *Archaeological remains at Bhubaneswar*, Calcutta, 1961 , *Chronology of the Bhaumakaras and the Somavaṁśīs of Orissa*, Madras, 1961 , *Itihāsa O Kimbadanti* (Oriya), Bhubaneswar, 1963 , *History of Orissa*, Cuttack, 1981

Pargiter, F.E., (ed.), *Purāṇa Text of the Dynasties of the Kāli Age*, Oxford, 1913 , *Ancient Indian Historical Tradition*, Delhi, 1962

Pereira, J., *Monolithic Jinas*, Delhi, 1977

Persler, H.N., *Primitive religions in India*, Madras, 1971

Piggot, S., *Prehistoric India*, London, 1961

Prabhu, P.H., *Hindu Social Organisation*, fourth ed. Bombay, 1963

Princep, J., *Essays on Indian Antiquities*, (ed.), Thomas, E., 2 vols, reprint, Delhi, 1971

Pratt, J.B., *India and its Faith*, 1916

Puri, B.N., *India in the time of Patañjali*, Bombay, 1957

Radhakrishnan, S., *History of Indian Philosophy*, 2 vols. London, 1923 , *Eastern Religions and Western Thought*, London, 1940

Radin, P., *Primitive religion, its Nature and Origin,* New York, 1957

Rajaguru, S.N., *History of the Gaṅgas*, 2 parts, Bhubaneswar, 1968, 1973

Rao, S.K.R., *Jainism in South India*, Madras, 1970

Rao, T.A.G., *Elements of Hindu Iconography*, 2 vols. 2nd. ed, Delhi, 1971

Rapson, E.J., (ed.), *The Cambridge History of India*, I, first India reprint, Delhi, 1955

Ray, H.C., *Dynastic History of Northern India*, I, Calcutta, 1931

Ray, N.R., *Maurya and Sunga Art*, Calcutta, 1965 , *Ideas and Image in Indian Art*, New Delhi, 1973

Raychaudhuri, H.C., *Studies in Indian Antiquities*, Calcutta, 1958 , *Political History of Ancient India*, Seventh ed. Calcutta, 1972

Raychaudhuri, P.C., *Jainism in Bihar*, Patna, 1956

Raw Linson, H.G., *India : A Short Cultural History*, ed. C.G. Seligman, London, 1937

Renou, L., *Religions of Ancient India*, Delhi, 1972

Rhys Davids, T.W., *Buddhist India*, 3rd ed. Calcutta, 1957 , *Early Buddhism*, Delhi, 1976

Risley, H., *The Peoples of India*, London, 1915

Rowland, B., *Art and Architecture of India*, Penguin Books, Third revised ed. 1970

Rowney, H.B., *The Wild Tribes of India*, reprint, Delhi, 1974 , *Orāon Religion and Customs*, Ranchi, 1928

Roy, S.C., *The Hill Bhūyāns of Orissa*, Ranchi, 1935 , *The Orāons of Chhotanagpur*, Ranchi, 1915

Ruben, W., *Studies in Ancient Indian Thought*, Calcutta, 1966

Sah, A.P., *Life in Medieval Orissa*, Varanasi, 1976

Sahu, N.K., (ed.), *A History of Orissa*, by Hunter, W.W., Stirling, A., & Beames, J., 2 vols. Calcutta, 1956 , *Buddhism in Orissa*, Cuttack, 1958 , *Utkal University History of Orissa*, I, Cuttack, 1964 , (ed.), *New Aspects of History of Orissa*, Sambalpur, 1971

Saletore, B.A., *Medieval Jainism*, Bombay, 1938

Sangave, V.A., *Jaina Community : A Social Survey*, Bombay, 1959

Saraswati, S.K., *A Survey of Indian Sculpture*, second revised ed. New Delhi, 1975

Sastri, K.A.N., *The Colas*, Madras, *Development of Religion in South India*, Bombay, 1963 , (ed.), *The Age of the Nandas and Mauryas*, 2nd. ed., Delhi, 1967 , *Cultural Contacts between Aryans and Dravidians*, Bombay, 1967

Schubring, W., *The Doctrines of the Jainas*, reprint, Delhi, 1962

Sen, A.C., *Schools and Sects in Jaina Literature*, Calcutta, 1931

Sen, A. , *Animal Motifs in Ancient Indian Art*, Calcutta, 1971

Sen, B.C., *Studies in the Buddhist Jātakas* : tradition and polity, Calcutta, 1974

Sen, K.M., *Hinduism*, Middlesex, 1961

Shah, C.J., *Jainism in North India*, Bombay, 1932

Shah, U.P., *Studies in Jaina Art*, Varanasi, 1955

Sharma, B.N., *Social and Cultural History of Northern India*, New Delhi, 1972

Sharma, H.D., *Contributions to the History of Brahmanical Asceticism*, Poona, 1939

Sharma, R.S., *Ancient India*, 2nd ed., New Delhi, 1980, (ed.), *Indian Society : Historical Probings*, New Delhi, 1974

Sharma, S.R., *Jainism and Karnataka culture*, Dharwar, 1940

Sircar, D.C., *The Successors of the Śātavāhanas*, calcutta, 1939 , *Studies in the Geography of Ancient and Medieval India*, Delhi, 1960 ,*Studies in the Religious Life of Ancient and Medieval India*, Delhi, 1971

Smith, V.A., *Early History of India*, Oxford, 1924

Sivaramamurti, C., *Indian Sculpture*, New Delhi, 1961 , (The) *Art of India*, New York, 1977

Sogani, K.C., *Ethical Doctrines in Jainism*, Sholapur, 1967

Sorenson, S., *An Index to Names in the Mahābhārata*, Delhi, 1963

Srivastava, V.C., *Sun Worship in ancient India*, Allahbad, 1972

Stevenson, S., *The Heart of Jainism*, (first Indian edition), New Delhi, 1970

Subuddhi, U.K., *Bhaumakaras of Orissa*, Delhi, 1977

Sukla, D.N., *Vāstu Śāstra*, Chandigarh, (no date)

Tambiah, C.J., *World Conqueror and World Renouncer*, Cambridge University, 1976

Thakur, U., *Some Aspects of Ancient Indian History and Culture*, New Delhi, 1974

Thapar, R., *Ancient Indian Social History*, Orient Longman, 1978

Tiele, C.P., *Outlines of the History of Religion*, London, 1892

Toynbee, A., *An Historians Approach to Religion*, Oxford, 1957

Rylor, E.B., *Religion in the Primitive Culture*, New York, 1958 , *Primitive Culture*, Murray, 1920

Upadhyaya, S.C., *Jaina Iconography Mainly in Śvetāmbaras*, Bombay, 1969

Varma, V.P., *Early Buddhism and its Origins*, New Delhi, 1973

Vasu, N.N., *The Archaeological Survey of Mayurbhanj*, I, Calcutta, 1911

Vats, M.S., *Excavations of Harappa*, Delhi, 1950

Vogel, J.P., *Indian Serpant-Lore or the Nāgas in Hindu Legend and Art*, London, 1926 , *Archaeological Museum At Mathura*, Delhi, 1971

Wagel, N., *Society at the Time of the Buddha*, Bombay, 1963

Warren, H., *Jainism*, 2nd. ed., Arrah, 1916

Weber, M., *The Religions of India*, New York, 1967

Wheeler, M., *The Indus Civilization*, Cambridge, 1953

Williams, J.G., (ed.), *Kalādarśana*, New Delhi, 1981

Williams, M., *Brahmanism, Hinduism*, 4th ed., London, 1891 , *A Sanskrit-English Dictionary*, Oxford, 1956 , *Religious Though and Life in Ancient India*, London, 1883

Winternitz, M., *A History of Indian Literature*, II, Calcutta, 1933 , *(The) Jainas in the History of Indian Literature*, (ed.), Jina Vijaya Muni, Ahmadabad, 1946

Workman, H.B., *The Evolution of Monastic Ideal ...*, London, 1927

Yazdani, G., (ed.), *Early History of the Deccan*, London, 1960

Zimmer, H., *Myths and Symbols in Indian Art and Civilization*, (ed.), Campbell, J., New York, 1962 , *The Art of Indian Asia*, 2 vols., (ed.), Campbell, J., Princeton, 1968

Williams, L.D. (ed.), *Buddhism*, [illegible] New Delhi, 1961.

